Inclusive Learning and Educational Equity

Volume 4

This book series reflects on the challenges of inclusive education as a strategy for improving educational equity, and includes in-depth analyses of disparities in education and the mechanisms by which they operate. It studies the development of educational processes and pedagogical interventions that respond to the tensions between education policies that promote competition and those designed to promote inclusion at individual, classroom, school, district, national, and international levels. Finally, it presents research and development activities in teacher education that respond to the challenges of preparing teachers for the changing demographic of schooling. Increasingly throughout the world, a broad concept of inclusive education has begun to emerge as a strategy for achieving basic education for all learners regardless of cultural, developmental or linguistic differences. Although considered an important aspect of a global human rights agenda supported by the multilateral Global Partnership for Education, basic education is a complex endeavour that is subject to the forces of globalization, and the exclusionary pressures associated with migration, mobility, language, ethnicity, disability, and intergenerational poverty. The reciprocal links between these factors and educational underachievement has led to an increasing interest in the development of inclusive education as a strategy for improving educational equity. By addressing these and related issues, this series contributes important advances in knowledge about the enactment of inclusive education. This series: Offers a critical perspective on current practice Stimulates and challenges further developments for the field Explores global disparities in educational provision and compares developments Provides a welcome addition to the literature on inclusive education.

More information about this series at http://www.springer.com/series/13450

Margarita Schiemer

Education for Children with Disabilities in Addis Ababa, Ethiopia

Developing a Sense of Belonging

Margarita Schiemer
Department of Education
University of Vienna
Vienna, Austria

This book is published with the support of the Austrian Science Fund (FWF): PUB 468-Z29.

 Der Wissenschaftsfonds.

Inclusive Learning and Educational Equity
ISBN 978-3-319-60767-2   ISBN 978-3-319-60768-9   (eBook)
DOI 10.1007/978-3-319-60768-9

Library of Congress Control Number: 2017943971

Printed on acid-free paper

This Springer imprint is published by Springer Nature
The registered company is Springer International Publishing AG
The registered company address is: Gewerbestrasse 11, 6330 Cham, Switzerland

To Andreas, Levin and Ilja

Preface

With this book I want to put a focus on the cultural aspects of inclusive education and its implications. For countries of the global South, inclusion and inclusive education need to be discussed on different grounds compared to Western countries. Aspects like *feeling like a family* and *developing a sense of belonging* may be more important in Ethiopia compared to other cultural environments. In the book I analyse these contexts. I look at how certain aspects influence inclusion, equity in education and the life of children with disabilities in Ethiopia. The Appendix provides details about the research process and the methods which were used.

The results of the study I am presenting were embedded in a study of a bigger project[1] initiated by the University of Vienna. This project focused on environmental factors that support or restrict activity and participation of school-aged children with disabilities in the field of education in different societal and cultural contexts. These different contexts had been given by including three capitals of different countries, namely, Vienna (Austria), Addis Ababa (Ethiopia) and Bangkok (Thailand), in the research design. The following discussion is based exclusively on the data from Ethiopia which was collected from 2010 until 2012.

Vienna, Austria   Margarita Schiemer

---

[1]CLASDISA, project no. P22178, financed by the Austrian Science Fund (FWF)

Acknowledgements

After having spent some years working on this study, the result can be presented. During these years, I have met a lot of people with lots of stories to tell, be it people related to the research or friends I made. I want to thank all those people who have accompanied me on this journey through very valuable experiences, because they made them so rich and meaningful.

Above all, I would like to thank all the participants of this research project, especially the children, parents and teachers who spared no effort to speak to us and endow us with a small insight into their personal concerns, hopes and dreams. I am also very grateful to all the other experts who shared a lot of their time to inform us about the current situation of people with disabilities in Ethiopia.

It is amazing how many people one can meet in such a short period of time. I am still overwhelmed by the cordiality and friendliness with which I was received in the schools and in Ethiopia in general. I will always remember the conversations with the children, not only the interviews but also the talks we had beyond. Seeing their ambitions and their energy and motivation was refreshing. Yet, I was also accompanied by other emotions throughout the field research. The interviews with parents often came with feelings of sadness and despair. In situations where mothers started crying during our interviews, it was especially hard for me. Conducting research in this field of study can be a journey through many emotional ups and downs. Fortunately, I always had people around me who supported me and who were there to discuss experiences that were difficult to handle alone. In this respect I want to give special mention to my family and my Ethiopian friends.

I want to say a special thank-you to my assistant, Yeshitla Mulat, who was a supporter and friend throughout the process of the field research and beyond. He dealt with all eventualities, problems and challenges in a very professional way, and it was enriching and fruitful for me to work with him in the field during these last few years. The colleagues from the Special Needs Department at the Addis Ababa University also supported me with all their effort. Lani Florian supported me during the revisions of the manuscript being published as a book. I want to especially thank her for giving me the opportunity and trust to work on such an important project.

My supervisor Univ. Prof. Dr. Gottfried Biewer was the one who employed me in 2009 and gave me the opportunity to participate in a big project that brought me ample possibilities to learn and grow. I want to say a special thanks to him for this and the appreciation he shows me continuously.

I also want to thank my colleagues from the Department of Education, Special Needs and Inclusive Education Research Unit, at the University of Vienna for listening to my experiences from the field. The working group on international and intercultural special needs education gave me important input during our profound discussions on my texts. Last but not least, the Viennese core team was refreshing and supportive as well as exhausting. I want to thank them for the experiences we had together, which included everything from despair up to excitement and happiness. I will never forget this time!

Contents

List of Figures

List of Network Views

List of Tables

Chapter 1
Introduction

Abstract The introduction presents the most important aspect of the book to the reader. It shortly describes the research and elaborates my experiences as a researcher in the field. Furthermore, it provides some insight into the capability approach. This leads to a discussion of the topic of poverty also in relation to the major outcomes of the research. Towards the end of this chapter, a short reference is made to the Ethiopian history concerning issues of disability and education. Last but not least, the objectives of the book are clarified.

> We have to examine the overall capability that any person has to lead the kind of life she has reason to want to lead, and this requires that attention be paid to her personal characteristics (including her disabilities, if any) as well as to her income and other resources, since both can influence her actual capabilities. (Sen 2004, 3)

Being able to go to school to be educated and to be granted the same opportunities as other children is one of the essential aspects in education. This again is closely related to the future life aspects of income and poverty and hence individual well-being and quality of life.

It is known that about nine out of ten children with disabilities are not schooled in countries of the global South (UNICEF 2013). This is a shocking fact, and it is important to react to this situation in order to create equal possibilities for everyone through equity in education. According to the United Nations Convention on the Rights of Persons with Disabilities (UNCRPD), and not only since this Convention was adopted, education is defined as a human right for everyone.

This book, however, does not explore the majority of children who are not schooled. Instead, the perspective is on those who are lucky enough to be able to attend school. Working from that angle has opened up the opportunity to look at the situation from within the school environment. This is only logical, as attending school is not a guarantee for receiving quality education.

Writing this book has given me the possibility to further develop the ideas and discussions which arose in the context of my research. Even though it was challenging, I have thoroughly enjoyed the experience. Speaking about experiences, the most interesting aspect of my work is without a doubt the challenge and adventure of opening my senses to a new culture, a new society and an unknown country and people.

© The Author(s) 2017
M. Schiemer, *Education for Children with Disabilities in Addis Ababa,
Ethiopia*, Inclusive Learning and Educational Equity 4,
DOI 10.1007/978-3-319-60768-9_1

The research involved 20 children with different disabilities who were attending different schools in the Ethiopian capital. During numerous interviews, they, their parents and their teachers told me about their experiences at school as well as about their hopes, dreams and fears. Listening to them was fascinating for me and made me thankful for their openness. But understanding their stories did not only come through listening. Being aware of my background, I knew I had to be careful concerning the bias I brought with me and the interpretations I would automatically make. I did not know very much about the culture, traditions and way of life of the interviewees. Therefore, it was indispensable to make a great effort to understand all of these aspects and become aware of the meaning and influence which these cultural, societal and traditional environments had on people with disabilities in their society and on their participation in social life. On the following pages, I am going to tell the story of how the children, parents and teachers who participated in my research dealt with challenges in their particular situations in the schools and communities in Addis Ababa, how some of them were able to "develop a sense of belonging" and what education meant for them. The aspect of "feeling like a family" plays a major role in this context. The aim of this book is to explore what all this means and how we can understand the situation of the children with disabilities in their educational environments. In addition, I am going to discuss the significance of inclusive education in relation to equity in education on the grounds of the capability approach (Sen 1979, 2009).

It may not have to be mentioned that conducting this research was one of the greatest opportunities I have had in my academic life so far. The results of this study are striking because of the new aspects which have been revealed.

Arriving in Addis Ababa for the first time in May 2009, it was exciting for me to dive into this new culture and country. Seeing the people, moving around in the city by public transport with all the traffic, smelling the smells and getting used to the thin air, as Addis Ababa lies on 2400 m altitude, were adventures in itself.

One can see lots of children in different kinds of school uniforms at the end of the day or in the morning going to school using public transport. Their uniforms have different colours depending on their school. This makes a colourful scene and, with all the children's voices, a very lively one.

Disability is present everywhere in the city. Lots of the people with disabilities are beggars – children, women and men. However, some schools accept children with disabilities, and hence disability is an issue for these school communities.

Talking to all my interviewees, listening to them sharing their hopes and dreams, seeing the children's motivation to be a good student and being able to help their parents, I became very close to them and emotionally involved in their lives. We know that education is no miracle cure against poverty, but it seemed that many of the participating parents and children were convinced otherwise. One thing that had me thinking the most after having concluded my research was the concern about the high expectations which the children and parents had as soon as the children started school. I became very worried about the future of these children and about whether they would be able to achieve their goals or whether they would lose hope again as soon as they failed to find a job or to finish their education.

However, reality also shows that education does in a considerable number of cases open up spaces and possibilities for leading a better life. This made me wonder about the right to education and, consequently, the question of equity. Looking at these issues from the angle of social justice, it is certainly the aspect of being granted equal opportunities in life and possibilities to participate in social life as a valued member. In other words, educational equity is a main pillar for creating equal chances for individuals to reach a certain quality of life. With Amartya Sen's capability approach in mind, it becomes clear that differences, or inequalities, exist naturally amongst human beings. These inequalities have to be addressed and given special attention when working towards social equity and equality of opportunities. Providing some insight into the capability approach will show clearly what I mean by that.

First of all, why is it called capability approach? Sen explains that "[t]he expression was picked to represent the alternative combinations of things a person is able to do or be – the various 'functionings' he or she can achieve" (Sen 1992/2009, 30). Further exploring the relevant literature, one can find statements like the following: "[Sen] pleaded for a metric of well-being which measured something falling between primary goods and utility [...] He called that something 'capability' [...]" (Cohen 2009, 17 f). Hence, the capability approach is about the well-being of people (or groups) which can be reached by being or doing the things which they are capable of.

The main reason for developing the capability approach was related to issues of poverty and development. It addresses the aspects of freedom and opportunities in a person's life and asks how this person can live a quality life and reach well-being. Consequently, the capability approach tries to identify value objects "and sees the evaluative space in terms of functionings and capabilities to function" (Sen 1993/2009, 32). One definition used by Sen for development is as the expansion of human freedoms (1999). In his book *Development as Freedom*, Sen speaks of freedom as the primary end and the principal means of development. The first is defined as having a constitutive role and the second as having an instrumental role (1999, 36).

> The constitutive role of freedom relates to the importance of substantive freedom in enriching human life. The substantive freedoms include elementary capabilities like being able to avoid such deprivations as starvation, undernourishment, escapable morbidity and premature mortality, as well as the freedoms that are associated with being literate and numerate, enjoying political participation and uncensored speech and so on. (Sen 1999, 36)

Accordingly, education can lead to certain freedoms of a person. In her recent critical article "Capabilitarianism", Robeyns (2016) offers an alternative perspective on the capability approach. She tries to find a "minimum core that is shared by all capability theories and accounts". The two most important concepts within the capability approach are capabilities and functionings. In 2011 Robeyns – following Sen – already defines capabilities as "a person's real freedoms or opportunities to achieve functionings". Functionings are simply a person's "beings and doings". Her definition of these terms in 2016 does not differ much from this. To explain it even more clearly, Sen states that capability is "a person's ability to do valuable acts or reach valuable states of being" (2009, 30). With this we can already draw a connection to the research at hand: becoming a valued member in society can be identified as one of the main goals of the children with disabilities who participated in my study.

Sen defined capability as "the ability" to reach these goals. Hence, having the ability does not automatically lead to the real functioning. In other words, most of the children in my study had the ability – hence the capability – to reach the goal of becoming a valued member in society through education, but were not sufficiently supported by their environment. Education, in their view, was one of the major motors to achieve their goals (e.g. being able to support their family by getting a job), which also meant doing valuable acts. From the perspective of "receiving quality education – having better job opportunities – supporting family (reducing poverty) – being valued by society", it becomes clear that educational equity and equal possibilities in education are of major importance, leading to a better quality of life for the individual and, in the particular case of the results of my study, also for the community (supporting the family, contributing to society). Over the last years, the capability approach has been criticised for being too individualistic and neglecting groups and social structures (Robeyns 2005, 109). However, as regards equity in education, the capability approach adds another valuable perspective on the issue. We know that education can lead to better job opportunities. Consequently, not having the possibility to receive quality education can lead to an exclusion from the labour market. "As it happens, the rejection of the freedom to participate in the labor market is one of the ways of keeping people in bondage and captivity […]" (Sen 1999, 7).

More than 80% of the people that I interviewed came from very poor backgrounds. This means that most of the parents were daily labourers and lived on less than 1$ per day. Consequently, poverty was one of the additional challenges that accompanied the children through their day-to-day life.

Poverty is identified as a twofold barrier in this book. Firstly, it influences the children's parents in supporting their children in their education, which can have far-reaching consequences. Secondly, it constitutes a threat to the children with disabilities themselves in cases where their education does not help them to become economically independent after school (or they are not able to go to school at all[1]). Thus, poverty compromises the children's goals that are inherent in their "feeling like a family", amongst which are supporting the parents and "developing a sense of belonging" (to society). It constitutes yet another barrier towards equal opportunities. Thereby opportunities can be seen in possibilities of finding jobs, receiving quality education and participating in social life. Equality in opportunities of participation is the most challenging aspect, as this is "about real life". Michailakis sees an economic aspect within this real life that gains importance for people with disabilities (1997, 28). And this is what is of high relevance for the book at hand when

---

[1] Such cases were not included in the sample as the research only focused on children with disabilities who were already attending a school.

talking about poverty and education: it is about the real life of children with disabilities, about their economic independence and about their possibilities to economically support their families. This, together with possibilities of social participation, will define their well-being and quality of life to a great extent.

In this context, the capability approach "[…] offers a broad normative framework to conceptualize and evaluate individual well-being and social arrangements in any particular context or society" (Walker and Unterhalter 2007, 3).

In other words, leading a good life and being able to participate in society as a valued member greatly depend on equity issues during one's life and on the possibilities which are available or unavailable in each individual case. Considering the subject matter of this book, it is a priority to address the goal of reaching educational equity through inclusive education. In my study, I learnt that inclusive education is the goal of the Ethiopian Ministry of Education and that the schools are still far from making such an endeavour reality.

Looking back on Ethiopian history with a focus on children with disabilities, only subtle hints can be found in the literature in connection with education; evidence of a clear development towards education for children with disabilities appears only towards the end of the twentieth and at the beginning of the twenty-first century. Tirussew (2005) states that schools for educating children with disabilities during the last 40 years were mainly managed by foreign missionaries. Most of the children who attended these schools had visual or hearing impairments. The late 1980s saw the beginning of schools for intellectually[2] disabled children (Tirussew 2005, 84). The question arises what aspects led to these developments and what hampered them. Attitudes of people and society in general certainly play an important role. What I want to highlight in this respect is that the cultural background becomes highly relevant – a focus on disability and culture can reveal many interesting things about the people in the respective society: What are people's attitudes towards disability and towards people with disabilities? Where do these attitudes come from? Have they ever changed – and if so, why? And finally, what consequences do certain attitudes have for people with disabilities living in this society? Asking questions like these can be very revealing when looking at children with disabilities and equity in education.

One of the objectives of this book is to answer such questions, aiming to identify barriers and facilitators for children with disabilities in their environment in the area of education. The results of this research only allow a limited insight into complex contexts. Therefore, there is no claim of providing a complete picture of the processes that can be observed within the setting of primary school children with disabilities in their educational environment.

---

[2] In this book, the term "intellectual disability" is used instead of the term "learning disability", which personally I would prefer because I think it is more about learning issues than about intellectual issues. This is because in the whole research, the former has been in use much more by the interviewees themselves.

References

Cohen, G. A. (2009). Equality of what? On welfare, goods and capabilities. In M. C. Nussbaum & A. Sen (Eds.), *The quality of life*. (original work published 1993 (pp. 9–29). New York: Oxford University Press.

Michailakis, D. (1997). When opportunity is the thing to be equalised. *Disability & Society, 12*(1), 17–30.

Robeyns, I. (2005). The capability approach: A theoretical survey. *Journal of Human Development, 6*(1), 93–117.

Robeyns, I. (2016). *Capabilitarianism*. Retrieved November 23, 2016, from https://www.ris.uu.nl/ws/files/18205164/Capabilitarianism_final.pdf

Sen, A. (1979). *Equality of what, The Tanner Lecture on Human Values held on 22nd of May 1979.* Stanford: Stanford University.

Sen, A. (1992/2009). *Inequality reexamined* (Original work published 1992). New York: Oxford University Press.

Sen, A. (1993/2009). Capability and well-being. Nussbaum, M. C., Sen, A.: *The quality of life* (Original work published 1993, pp. 30–53). New York: Oxford University Press.

Sen, A. (1999). *Development as freedom*. New York: Oxford University Press.

Sen, A. (2004). Disability and Justice. Keynote Speech. Paper presented at the Disability and Inclusive Development Conference. Retrieved June 6, 2016 from http://siteresources.worldbank.org/DISABILITY/214576-1092421729901/20291152/Amartya_Sen_Speech.doc

Sen, A. (2009). *The idea of justice*. Cambridge: The Belknap Press of Harvard University Press.

Tirussew, T. (2005). *Disability in Ethiopia: Issues, insights and implications*. Addis Ababa: Addis Ababa University Printing Press.

UNICEF. (2013). Educating teachers for children with disabilities. Mapping, scoping and best practices exercise in the context of developing inclusive education. *Rights, education and protection (REAP) project*. (UNICEF) Retrieved November 23, 2016, from https://dl.dropboxusercontent.com/u/8608264/UNICEF%20Educating%20Teachers%20for%20Children%20with%20Disabilities1a.pdf

Walker, M., & Unterhalter, E. (2007). *Amartya Sen's capability approach and social justice in education*. Basingstoke: Palgrave Macmillan.

Chapter 2
How to Make Sense of "Developing a Sense of Belonging" Through "Feeling Like a Family" in the Light of Cultural and Societal Backgrounds

Abstract In this chapter, I first provide the reader with geopolitical and historical information which is meaningful for the study that is presented. It enables potential readers to deepen their background information and hence get a view on the results of the study that is rich in content.

Regarding history, this chapter goes back to the time before the "modern" Ethiopia. It has been regarded as important to present glimpses into the rich Ethiopian history and political developments as this explains lots of the current developments, values, attitudes and the main characteristics of the Ethiopian society. These aspects are of major importance to the main topic of this book which is disability and education.

Furthermore, the chapter is discussing the main results of the study in the light of relevant literature. Thereby aspects like belonging and ethnicity, self-concept, disability and collectivist cultures, family and disability, special needs education, teachers' attitudes and community, religion and belief and last but not least the role of poverty are considered. This leads towards a broader picture regarding the most important results of this investigation. Additionally, it embeds the single outcomes into the framework of cultural and societal realities.

In this chapter, I introduce the main outcomes of my study in order to illustrate how important it is to look at the background of certain phenomena like the meaning of belonging and family but also religion and other essential aspects in a different culture and especially in the context of disability. My study was an in-depth exploration of the situation of children with disabilities in their educational environments in Addis Ababa. Looking at barriers and facilitators in their daily lives helped to get a clearer picture of cultural issues influencing inclusion. In this context, it is very important not to settle for generalisations about the differences within certain cultures, as Sen states: "The recognition of diversity within different cultures is extremely important in the contemporary world. Our understanding of the presence of diversity tends to be somewhat undermined by constant bombardment with oversimple generalizations about 'Western civilisation', 'Asian values', 'African cultures' and so on" (Sen 1999, 247).

© The Author(s) 2017
M. Schiemer, *Education for Children with Disabilities in Addis Ababa,
Ethiopia*, Inclusive Learning and Educational Equity 4,
DOI 10.1007/978-3-319-60768-9_2

With this in mind, the results of my research proved once more the importance of looking closely at cultural and societal aspects when it comes to disability and education. The core category which finally emerged from the data was *feeling like a family*. This reflects the positive aspect which was described especially by teachers and parents referring to their relations at school. In some schools, this feeling helped the parents greatly to cooperate and to support the child in being successful at school, even if they were illiterate themselves. In the context of the core category, the children with disabilities mostly referred to the internal family relations. In other words, the children spoke very much about their goals of being able to support their families after school and the importance of being able to help their parents. The final title of my theory was "Developing a sense of belonging". This refers to belonging to a family, to school, to a community and to society as such. I will go into more detail about the development of the theory and the different perspectives of the participants later in the book.

In regard to culture, the following quotation helps to understand the specific aspects on which I want to place my focus:

> Cultural conceptualizations of difference must be seen in relation to social contexts. Cross-cultural literature on disability employs two general ways of doing this: examining features of social organization, and focusing on the implications of specific social characteristics (gender, age, class) within a society. (Ingstad and Whyte 1995, 12)

This is precisely what I aim at: to identify special cultural, social and societal characteristics that influence perceptions of disability in the environment I studied. Seeing the results within the social context makes the model of "developing a sense of belonging" more specific. Thereby, the cultural conceptualisation of disability is also further clarified. I undertook a literature review in order to be able to discuss and embed the theory in the already existing research environment related to important aspects like belonging, family, attitudes, self-concept, beliefs, etc. in the light of cultural and societal aspects in the Ethiopian and the majority world context.

The following discussion of literature demonstrates how the book at hand adds new dimensions to existing research rather than verifying the results (Stern 2007, 123). However, the reviewed literature often also confirms the findings, which strengthens the backbones of the theory developed in this book.

While going through existing research, it became evident that studies about Ethiopia often refer to single ethnic groups. Looking for the above-mentioned main topics of this research (family, belonging, religion, etc.) in relation to Ethiopia led to considerably fewer results than when adding different ethnicities in the search fields (e.g. Amhara, Oromo, Tigrinya and Gurage, which also represent the different ethnicities of the parents interviewed in this study). Published research on disability and culture in Ethiopia could not be found extensively in peer-reviewed journals. Yet, I know that students at the Department for Special Needs Education at the University of Addis Ababa conduct a lot of unpublished research in the field for their Master theses, Bachelor theses or Seminar papers etc., which is a resource that is not yet widely accessible. Finally, I am also addressing historical aspects. This is the case because cultural and societal factors usually have to be elaborated starting from their historical roots.

Regarding the aim of this chapter, which is to discuss the results against the background of societal and cultural aspects of Ethiopia, one challenge becomes essential. Ethiopia is a country that unites people of various ethnicities, religions, language families, etc. Therefore, it is also difficult to speak of "the" Ethiopian culture or society, as Ethiopia exhibits a colourful set of these aspects, comprising people from various ethnicities and cultural characteristics. Also in the capital, Ethiopia's ethnic, linguistic and religious diversity is reflected by its inhabitants. Even though the results of this book can only be seen in relation to Addis Ababa, considering some topics a restricted perspective only on the capital is not sufficient for explaining certain cultural or societal aspects that have grown historically within one or the other ethnic group. Therefore, the development of the whole country had to be regarded.

Even though strong policies exist in the field of inclusive education, Ethiopia has failed to implement these policies satisfactorily to date. The problem – like in other countries – is "a disconnect [sic] between what is taught to pre-service teachers and actual knowledge and skills necessary to implement inclusive education in the classroom" (UNICEF 2013, 2). This is the case because the understanding of inclusive education often varies on the different levels (government, teacher training institutions, schools, teachers, etc.) (UNICEF 2013). Yet, the education of children with disabilities in the existing settings (integrative and special) still led to changes in attitudes and opportunities.

By starting with Ethiopian history, I want to emphasise the fact that I consider it as indispensable to become familiar with the history of a country and a people in order to be able to understand the particular features. This brief historical excursus will open a new window to look at the people, their country and their way of life.

Understanding the Context: Ethiopian History, Politics and Education

In Ethiopia,[1] geographical, social, and cultural differences between people and regions that are typical for the whole continent of Africa are united in a unique way. Christianity, Islam and a high number of animist cults can be found here as well as technical know-how and illiteracy, nomadism and urbanism. It seems as if the geographical variety of the country supports this diversity. Ethiopia has mountains of up to 4000 m, lake areas in the African Rift Valley and the salt desert in the Danakil

---

[1] The Ethiopian year consists of 365 days, divided into 12 months of 30 days each plus one additional month of 5 days (six in leap years). The Ethiopian year starts on September 11 and ends the following September 10, according to the Gregorian (Western) calendar. From September 11 to December 31, the Ethiopian year runs 7 years behind the Gregorian year; thereafter, the difference is 8 years. Hence, the Ethiopian year 1983 began on September 11, 1990, according to the Gregorian calendar, and ended on September 10, 1991. This discrepancy results from differences between the Ethiopian Orthodox Church and the Roman Catholic Church as to the date of the creation of the world.

Depression. All these geographical features reflect the beauty and the richness of the country as well as its problems and possibilities (Wartenberg and Mayrhofer 1999, 69). This short description of Wartenberg and Mayrhofer offers a vivid picture of the country at the focus of this research. The ambivalence between advantages and disadvantages of the rich and diverse culture and landscape of the country becomes particularly clear.

I am using the name Ethiopia throughout the text instead of changing between Abessinia and Ethiopia even if the denomination "Ethiopia" was not known or used in the early periods when Ethiopia was still called Abessinia. Abessinia actually comes from the word "habashat", a tribe living in the regions of Ethiopia during the times before Christ. The term "Ethiopia" originates from Greek and was used to describe the approximate landmass in the South of Egypt (Bahru 2001, 1). Ethiopians still call themselves "Habesha" today.

In connection with the history of the country, King Solomon plays an important role. It has been told that the Queen of Sheba (also Saba or Shaba[2]) had a son, David, together with Solomon. David later became the king of Ethiopia with the name Menelik I.

Accompanied by the first-born sons of the Israeli tribes, he travelled to his father's court to get the ark of the covenant and bring it to Ethiopia (Phillipson 1998, 141). Now, so Ethiopians believe, the ark is situated in Axum, in the North of Ethiopia, sheltered by one monk, and no one but he is to see the ark.

King Solomon can be seen as the embodiment of wisdom. Even though wisdom and education are different terms with different meanings, there is a certain connection between them: knowledge. Throughout the history of Ethiopia, one always stumbles across the importance of this aspect and the connection to growth, prosperity but also poverty in the country.

The story of Solomon and Queen of Sheba, which takes place in the tenth century B.C., represents an important aspect for most Ethiopians in connection with the history of their people. This is the reason why the time around the tenth century B.C. will be discussed briefly. Nevertheless, the underlying historical framework for this book starts with the "modern Ethiopia" (Bahru 2001, 270). The modern Ethiopia begins in the second half of the nineteenth century.

I want to present a general overview of the "modern Ethiopia", which is the most important part. Within this time frame, the Ethiopian history can be illustrated also regarding important political and educational developments that are relevant here.

---

[2] The vowels of names and certain terms, are translated differently from the Amharic in diverse publications. This is the reason why translated names and terms differ slightly when used by different authors.

The Time Before "the Modern" Ethiopia

The fact that Ethiopia looks back on 3000 years of history can be explained by the overall accepted tracing back of the beginning to Queen of Sheba and her visit to Solomon, king of Israel. However, the scientific foundations for this story are very low (Bahru 2001, 7). Many chronicles lead to the assumption that the Abyssinians are one of the oldest civilisations of the nations existing today. Although they constituted their own kingdom, they were geared to the Egyptian religion and were using the same language and script (Erlich 2005, 84). Even though there are clear connections from Ethiopia to Arabia and the Middle East, Ethiopia does not count as part of these regions. Also regarding other aspects, it cannot be classified into many of the existing categories. As a consequence, Ethiopia, situated at the Horn of Africa, is mostly viewed separately from the rest of Africa. Ethiopia sustains one of the oldest Christian civilisations. Alone for that matter the history of the country is a very meaningful one. The fact that it was not known in "the West" for thousands of years, up to the nineteenth century, makes this kingdom even more interesting. Only a few travellers made it to Ethiopia before the second quarter of the twentieth century (Phillipson 1998, 7).

History, Politics and Education During "the Modern" Ethiopia

A vast diversity of people, speaking many different languages, live in the country. These languages are separated into four groups: Kushitic, Omotic, Semitic and Nilo-Saharan. All of them can be traced back to the common mother tongue of the "Proto-Afroasiatic". Three of them, Kushitic, Omotic and Semitic languages, are spoken in Ethiopia and are seen as the oldest language families in Ethiopia. Semitic languages are the younger ones. The fourth group, Nilo-Saharan, developed independently from the others (Bahru 2001, 5). It is important to point out this diversity at this point, as language diversity is still an issue in Ethiopia.

At the beginning of the nineteenth century, Ethiopia was in a state of political fragmentation. Bahru sees this disunity together with the presence of the Europeans, who were in Africa during this period, as determining factors for the development of the history of the modern Ethiopia. During this period, the ruling kings of Ethiopia reacted in different ways, and with different outcomes, to the internal and external challenges of the country. The political emphasis had been put on centralisation and consolidation of the country (Bahru 2001, 270).

While the nineteenth and twentieth centuries have been described by historians as the modern period of Ethiopian history (Bahru 2001, xvii), Tekeste Negash (2006, 12) adds that in regard to education, the golden era of modern education has to be seen in the years between 1941 and 1970.

Nevertheless, the time before this golden era for modern education has to be considered as well. Until the time of Menelik II (1889–1913), education was determined mainly by the church (Pankhurst 1990; Tekeste 2006). In most sub-Saharan countries, education and school meant learning from books in big classes. The traditional primary schools in the churches taught how to read and write in Ge'ez and Amharic. Some basic arithmetic was also taught. Nevertheless, the focus was on reading and writing in Ge'ez, as this was the original language of the religious rituals. School lasted for 6 years and was for children aged 4–10. The six school years were divided into four phases:

Learning the syllabus (similar to the Western alphabet).
"Fidel Hawaria" (alphabet of the apostles): the letters of the apostles were read, and writing and arithmetic were taught.
"Gabre Hawaria": the deeds of the apostles were studied, and writing and arithmetic continued.
"David" (Dawit): psalms of David were read by children and explained by the teachers.

The beginning of the last phase (David) by the child was always celebrated by the parents (Pankhurst 1955, 234f.).

Young people who decided to undergo higher education through the church had to leave their home and move into the school of their choice. There, they shared their life with other students, learnt to fast, etc. (Pankhurst 1955, 237). Until the end of the nineteenth century, the church had the strongest influence on education in Ethiopia. Curricula did not develop or change a lot and were based on old standards for quite a long time.

The following Tables 2.1 and 2.2 developments regarding education against the background of historically and politically relevant events in modern Ethiopia (second half of the nineteenth to beginning of the twenty-first century) (Tables 2.1 and 2.2).

Table 2.1 Overview of developments regarding education on the background of historically and politically relevant incidents in the modern Ethiopia

Year	King/ emperor	Policies/event	Consequences/meaningful events regarding education
1855–1868	Tewodros II first modern king of Ethiopia	The king is seen as a uniting, reconstituting and modernising power of Ethiopia (imperial idea). He founded a school in Gafat	He was very impressed by the European technologies and the military power that these technologies would give him. Hence, he had teachers teach techniques of production of arms in school. (After the battle of Adwa in 1896, it was possible to have more intensive relations with Europe. Therefore, modern education was also spread in Ethiopia)

(continued)

Table 2.1 (continued)

Year	King/ emperor	Policies/event	Consequences/meaningful events regarding education	
1872–1889	Yohannes IV	He follows a "politics of controlled regionalism"; like Tewodros II, he also has friendly relationships with the European powers	He also supported Catholic missionaries, as he saw their teaching as a basis for support from powers outside the country	Education is determined and influenced mainly by the church
1886		Addis Ababa (new flower) was founded		
1889–1913	Menelik II	He successfully combines the imperial idea of Tewodros and the tolerance of Yohannes		
1889		Treaty of Wuchale	Ethiopia is subdued to the Italian protectorate	
1892		Addis Ababa becomes the capital of Ethiopia		
1892		Famine "Kefu Qan", thousands of people die because of hunger	Because of the adversity, Italians are experiencing fewer difficulties to get access to the Ethiopian kingdom	
1896		Italy attacks, battle of Adwa, Ethiopia defeats Italy	Treaty of peace of Addis Ababa in October 26. October 1896: Independence	
1898		End of the consolidation of Ethiopia and of its expansion		
1908				Menelik founds the first school according to modern terms of reference: Menelik II school. The medium of instruction is French
1913–1916	Iyyasu	He is Muslim and therefore dangerous for the hegemony of the Orthodox Christians in Ethiopia	Iyyasu is dispossessed in 1916	

(continued)

Table 2.1 (continued)

Year	King/emperor	Policies/event		Consequences/meaningful events regarding education
1916–1928	Zawditu	The daughter of Menelik takes over the regency. Ras Tafari Makonnen (later Haile Selassie) becomes fully authorised crown prince	Zawditu does not seem to be dangerous for the nobility. Tafari on the other hand, with all his relations abroad, is	In the 1920s new phase: many students are sent to foreign countries, mostly to France
1923/1924		In 1923 Ethiopia becomes part of the United Nations	In 1924 Tafari leaves for his tour in Europe	
1928–1930	Zawditu + Ras Tafari (Haile Selassie)	Zawditu shares regency with Haile Selassie		
1930–1935	Haile Selassie	Absolutism, 1931 new constitution	The absolute power of the king is legalised in the constitution	Many schools are built in the provinces and in Addis Ababa
1931				Queen Menen, wife of Haile Selassie, founds the first modern school for girls. The medium of instruction is French
1935/1936–1941	Italians in power	Italy attacks Ethiopia under Mussolini. Fascism	5 years of Italian occupation. Exploitation, Italians as "Herrenrasse" feel superior. More than 760,000 Ethiopians die	Educational efforts are stagnating. Ethiopians are prevented from being educated
February 19–20, 1937		Big massacre	Innocent and educated citizens are killed	75% of the educated class of Ethiopians are killed by the Italians
1941/1942–1974	Haile Selassie (last king)	Imperialistic phase, the majority of the budget goes to the Ministry of Education	Italy has to leave Ethiopia. Haile Selassie resumes governmental work	Educational efforts are resumed; schools, uniforms and food are usually free

(continued)

Table 2.1 (continued)

Year	King/ emperor	Policies/event	Consequences/meaningful events regarding education	
1940s/1950s				A surplus of schools can be observed. Western education systems and teachers are coming to the country
1950s/1960s			Universities try to usurp students with vocationally and technically oriented education. There are sufficient jobs and salaries are oriented on academic qualification. In this period, high investments seem to be very understandable	
1958			First voices notice that the way curricula are developed does not create citizens who will be able to interpret the heritage of the country, to enrich it and to adapt it to the new conditions and needs	
1960s			The golden era of education is over	Many school leavers cannot be accommodated by the labour market. The consequences are unemployment and demand for reforms
1974		Revolution of students and military	Downfall of Haile Selassie I. – last king	
1974–1991	Dictator Mengistu Haile Mariam	DERG, socialist–communist regime, Ethiopia is proclaimed republic	Endeavours for education are rising, as is poverty	Alphabetisation is rising, whereas quality of education is getting worse. While there was a little number of students with a good education under Haile Selassie, now there are many with a bad quality of education

(continued)

Table 2.1 (continued)

Year	King/emperor	Policies/event	Consequences/meaningful events regarding education	
1980		Many wars are fought within the country, as the spectrum of political groups and independent movements reaches from monarchists to Marxists	Consideration of changing from Amharic to English as language of instruction	
End of the 1980s		Kokebe Tsibah primary school is the first one to offer education for children with "developmental retardation"		Children with intellectual disabilities are gaining first possibilities for education. More schools are developing which are offering special programmes for those children
1990				In 1990, English is only to be found in textbooks, but no more as the language of instruction
1991		Insurgents overwhelm the socialist government; EPRDF (Ethiopian People's Revolutionary Democratic Front) comes into power	Mengistu Haile Mariam flees after 17 years of military dictatorship; end of civil war between the Amharic dominated central power in Addis Ababa and the rebellious people of 80 nationalities. Eritrea leaves state alliance. Ethiopia becomes the "Federal Democratic Republic of Ethiopia". Reconstruction of the educational system is getting utmost priority	
1994		Proclamation of new constitution; federal system; design of "Education and Training Policy"	Decentralisation and democratisation	Respective ethnical languages are introduced in primary schools as language of instruction
1996		"Education Sector Development Programme"		

(continued)

Table 2.1 (continued)

Year	King/ emperor	Policies/event	Consequences/meaningful events regarding education	
2004		Implementation of "Ethiopian Satellite Education Programme" (ESEP)	450 schools get 8000 plasma screens	Difficulties at the beginning, as lots of teachers in television are speaking English. At primary schools, local language is spoken
Beginning of the twenty-first century		Efforts to develop inclusive education aiming at the inclusion of children with disabilities in the regular school system	There is an increase in special classes in regular schools for children with visual/hearing and intellectual disabilities	Most special schools as well as regular schools suffer from a high number of students, limited material for support and lack of teachers with appropriate education

Bahru (2001), Bartnicki and Mantel-Niećko (1978), Brogini Künzi (2006), Dawit (1994), Donham (2002), Haile Selassie I (1937), Hrbek (1993), Krylow (1994), Mockler (2003), Mulugeta (2009), Ottaway and Ottaway (1978), Pankhurst (1955), Rønning Balsvik (1994), Rubenson (1976), Tekeste (2006), Tirussew (2005), Wartenberg (1999a, b), Wartenberg and Mayrhofer (1999), and Zegeye and Pausewang (1994a, b)

Relevant Legacies and Developments in Ethiopia Today

Article 10 of the Ethiopian Constitution from 1994 clearly states the human and democratic rights of the people. "Human rights and freedoms are inviolable and inalienable. They are inherent in the dignity of human beings. Human and democratic rights of Ethiopian citizens shall be respected" (Federal Democratic Republic of Ethiopia (FDRE) 1994). Article 25 additionally underlines the equality of all citizens. Education is considered to be a fundamental human right. Hence, the state of Ethiopia commits to providing education as a human right to all citizens, who also have to be considered as equal.

The next chapter examines the year 1994 (see table above). This year is of importance for the current developments of policies regarding education in Ethiopia.

1994: The Training and Education Policy of Ethiopia

The policy of 1994 has been chosen as the starting point for this chapter as this policy was to be implemented after the fall of the military DERG regime in 1991 and hence marks a new era in Ethiopian history.

After 1991, the Ethiopian government changed and educational reforms were one important step the transitional government had included in its agenda. "The educational reforms include a new education policy, decentralization of educational administration, new school curricula, and the use of vernacular languages of nationalities as media of instruction" (Belete 2011, 35). Amongst the changes, the media of instruction was one very important aspect as children could study using their mother tongue. Other major reforms of the policy included:

- Extension of primary education from 6 to 8 years in all schools, to increase the schooling received by the majority who do not go beyond the
- primary level,
- Automatic promotion of children in primary grades up to grade 3, to reduce repetition and dropouts,
- [U]se of local languages as media of instruction in primary grades to facilitate children's adjustment to school, increase the relevance of school work to their home environment, and facilitate cognitive growth,
- Development of a new teaching career structure based on professional growth, performance, and experience to motivate teachers,
- Elimination of fees for grades 1–10 to reduce the financial burden on parents,[3]
- Development of cost sharing for grades 11–12 and higher education. (Mamo 2000, 85)

Additionally, the education policy mentioned special education as one main point to be specially regarded. "The policy encompasses overall and specific objectives, implementation strategies, including formal and non-formal education, from kindergarten to higher education and special education" (Transitional Government of Ethiopia (TGE) 1994, 4). The terms used here show that on the one hand special education is seen as separate from other education levels. On the other hand, the term inclusive or special needs education had not yet found its way into the new policy. In chapter 3.2 "Educational structure" on the policy for training and education, the last point 3.2.9 declares: "Special education and training will be provided for people with special needs" (TGE 1994, 17). Furthermore, the chapter on "Teachers" includes point 3.4.11: "Teacher training for special education will be provided in regular teacher training programmers [sic]" (TGE 1994, 22). The last point where special education is mentioned can be found in the chapter "Educational support inputs" point 3.7.6: "Special attention will be given in the preparation and utilization of support input for special education" (TGE 1994, 29). Having such acknowledgements by the government on paper in the three areas of educational structure, teachers and educational support inputs reflected a change in the general

---

[3] "Free primary education was introduced with the adoption of the new Education and Training Policy in 1994 as a major strategy towards achieving the EFA goals. This has led to rapid increase in the net enrolment rate, which currently stands at 83% of primary school aged children" (Ethiopian Ministry of Education 2011b, 13).

approach towards education for people with disabilities. Still, the implementation can be seen as problematic and did not lead to general changes of attitudes in society (which might not be surprising).

All in all, the 1994 policy for training and education mentions special education on four occasions and special needs only once. Still, the concessions of the Ethiopian government did not involve the teaching profession as an employment possibility for persons with disabilities. Article 3 point 4.1 clearly excludes people with disabilities from this occupation. It says that teachers have to have "physical and mental fitness" as a requirement for being able to teach (TGE 1994, 20). Furthermore, the whole policy lacks detailed directives for implementation. Even though this led to major problems considering implementation, the Ethiopian Ministry of Education (MoE) tried to make the goals of the new policy accessible for its people in 2002. This was the year in which the Ministry developed a handbook where it explained the education and training policy and its implementation. The intention was to bring it close to the people, as without the people's participation, implementation would not be possible.

> Education is all about people. It is, therefore, imperative that students, teachers, parents, and the public in general have a firm grasp of the essence of the policy. Hence, this booklet has been prepared to help the public understand the education and training policy, grasp its basic concepts, realize its background and over all contexts, comprehend its content, its merits as well as its practical application. (Ethiopian Ministry of Education 2002, f.)

This shows that the government has been aware of the problematic aspects of implementation. It furthermore highlighted the challenges of a policy statement:

> Since a policy statement never spells out all the elements factored in its formulation, but only indicates the salient strategic directions and objectives couched in the concept-laden language of short phrases, it is difficult to grasp its basic rationale. The 1994 education and training policy statement is no exception to this general truth. In fact, the inadequacy of all previous work done to raise public awareness of the education policy has compounded the problem. As a result, numerous accurate and inaccurate statements regarding the policy are heard from time to time. (Ethiopian Ministry of Education 2002, 2)

The MoE's statements had been reactions to some ongoing displeasure throughout the population. Obviously, there had been public discontentment throughout the process of development of the 1994 policy. In the booklet of the Ministry, it reads: "Contrary to what certain people and groups allege, the process of formulating the education and training policy was not shrouded in secrecy. It was rather conducted in a transparent fashion where the draft proposal was openly submitted for the consideration of representatives of a wide sector of the society" (Ethiopian Ministry of Education 2002, 6).

The Ministry emphasises that a big group of people contributed and participated in the process and that it was a democratic and public discussion (Ethiopian Ministry of Education 2002). It is interesting that this issue seems to require special attention. It indicates that there were tensions around the government that had to be dealt with.

Since 1996: "Education Sector Development Programme"

The last chapter illustrated the beginnings of the new era regarding changes in education policy on the level of the new Ethiopian government. More important developments in this process have to be mentioned like the ESDP (Education Sector Development Programme) starting in 1996.

> The five year plan (ESDP) is said to be comprehensive for it consists of all components, in particular primary, secondary, adult and non-formal, special needs, distance and tertiary education, technical and vocational education and training, teacher education and training, instructional materials, curriculum reform, capacity building, educational assessment, information management and policy analysis. (Mamo 2000, 86)

Since its first version, the ESDP has been under constant development. The latest version before this book that was ready for publication was ESDP IV, which was used for the years 2010/2011–2014/2015. It focuses on areas like achievement, reaching the unreached and disadvantaged, adult literacy, higher education and technology as well as an improvement of administration in educational environments. In short, these are merged under the priority themes: quality, equity and improved management. Furthermore, there is an emphasis on female students (Ethiopian Ministry of Education 2011b, 9). The goal of ESDP IV is "[…] to make sure that all children, youngsters and adults […] acquire the competencies, skills, values and attitudes enabling them to participate fully in the social, economic and political development of Ethiopia […]" (Ethiopian Ministry of Education 2011b). When highlighting social, economic and political participation as a main goal of education in Ethiopia, emphasis must also be placed on children with disabilities. Otherwise, they would most probably be excluded from the possibility of participating in forming the state of Ethiopia in the future. Even though gender and equal rights are already a very known and famous topic in this respect in Ethiopia and the agendas of different organisations, the aspect of disability is not considered enough. The mechanisms that exclude girls from schools are in some regards the same for children with disabilities: attitudes, traditions and beliefs usually put a barrier to children's school access.

Looking at the UNESCO country information on Ethiopia, we find that there are special schools run by government and religious organisations. "In 1996/97 there were twenty-two schools for the blind (1,020 pupils enrolled with ninety teachers), twenty-eight schools for the deaf (1,274 pupils enrolled with 136 teachers) and nineteen schools for the mentally retarded (411 pupils enrolled with fifty-seven teachers)" (UNESCO 2006). Thus, in some regions, there are no special schools at all (Afar, Ethio-Somali, Benishangul–Gumuz, Gambella, Dire Dawa) (UNESCO 2006). These data were collected two decades ago, meaning that the number of special schools might have changed. In the report on the implementation of the UNCRPD of Ethiopia, we find that "[…] most parents tend to prefer to send their children to such schools [special schools] for lack of facilities in their localities" (FDRE 2012, 2/40). It is further stated that special schools only allow a small number of students to access education, while the rest have to stay at home because of a lack of options (FDRE 2012). These facts show that a special school system has already started to develop. However, we cannot say that these developments are the basis of a strongly institutionalised separating system and comparable to some Western countries.

The Ethiopian Education System Today

This chapter intends to give a short overview of the prevailing Ethiopian education system. Currently there are five types of schools in Ethiopia for children from 7 to 19 years of age:

The two cycles of the 8 years of primary education (each 4 years) provide basic education (years 1–4) and general education (years 5–8). The earlier existing junior secondary schools do not exist any longer (years 7–8) as they have been integrated in the second cycle of the primary education. The secondary education also consists of two cycles: general secondary education (grades 9–10) and preparatory secondary education (grades 11–12).

> Since the education reform, completion of Grade X results in the Ethiopian School Leaving Certificate Examination (ESLCE). It used to be at the end of Grade XII. The second cycle prepares students to continue their studies at the higher education level or select their profession. It offers a science option and a social science option. (Ethiopian Ministry of Education 2011a)

After completion of the preparatory secondary education (second cycle of secondary education), the Ethiopian Higher Education Entrance Examination entitles students to access higher education systems. Institutions for technical and vocational education are separated from the regular education system (Ethiopian Ministry of Education 2011a).

Table 2.2 Ethiopian education system (Ethiopian Ministry of Education 2011a)

Type/level of education	Type of school providing this education	Duration of programme in years	Age level	Certificate/diploma awarded
Primary	Primary school	8	7–14	–
First cycle secondary	General secondary school	2	15–16	Ethiopian General School Leaving Certificate Examination (EGSLCE)
Second cycle secondary	Preparatory secondary school	2	17–18	Ethiopian Higher Education Entrance Examination (EHEEE)
Technical	Technical school and junior college	3	17–19	
Vocational	Vocational school and junior college	3	17–19	

Special Needs Experts in the Ministry of Education

The Ethiopian Ministry of Education (MoE) has reacted on the high number of children with disabilities that is excluded from primary education. Within the MoE, it has established a team of special needs experts. Especially the Finnish government supports this department with additional experts and further support.[4] Even though there has been considerable investment in the educational sector in general, problems remain.

> In spite of this desirable trend, the education system is still facing the challenges which were identified before the policy reform. To repeat the essentials: most of the problems associated with the sector, such as low enrolment, disparity between the two sexes and high dropout and repetition rates, still remain pressing issues. Poorly trained and unqualified teachers, lack of supportive structural leadership and capacity, scarcity of resources and lack of interest in education on the part of parents and students, are also associated with the low quality of education. (Mamo 2000, 89)

In an interview I conducted on November 23, 2011, Ato Demeke Mekonnen, the Ethiopian Minister of Education, stated that the main goal of Ethiopian education politics is quality assurance. For him, the three main challenges regarding education are quality assurance, equity issues in pocket areas like the pastoral areas of Ethiopia and realising inclusive education. The Minister further mentioned the high number of students that have to be managed and the sustainment of the capital intensive programmes in general (personal interview, November 23, 2011). The Ethiopian special needs expert in the Ministry, Ato Alemayehu, spoke about the main problems for the implementation of inclusive education. His first point was the attitude of people. Furthermore, he mentioned a lack of budget and a lack of commitment as main barriers for the education of people with disabilities (personal interview, December 16, 2011). Another interview with the Finnish[5] senior advisor in the Ethiopian Ministry of Education showed that the main reason for the low access to schools for children with disabilities is also to be found in parents' attitudes. Secondly, she mentioned teacher education as a big problem. According to the senior advisor, the compulsory course on special needs education for students in teacher training institutions does not give enough information to be able to teach in an inclusive classroom. The last challenge she mentioned is the financial situation of the schools. They often do not have the budget to supply classrooms with adequate material (personal interview, December 16, 2011).

In his opening speech of the ninth UNESCO high-level group meeting on education for all in February 2010, the Ethiopian Minister of Education, Ato Demeke Mekonnen, stated: "In conclusion, may I assure you that the Government of Ethiopia remains unequivocally engaged and committed to meet all the aims and goals of

---

[4] For further information, see the homepage of the Finnish foreign ministry at http://formin.finland.fi/public/default.aspx?contentid=78516&contentlan=2&culture=en-US

[5] She is working in the Finnish funded "Special needs education programme in Ethiopia".

Education for All" (Demeke 2010). Hence, the MoE seems to be very engaged regarding issues of the inclusion of people with disabilities.

The Department of Special Needs Education at Addis Ababa University

In 2007, the Department of Special Needs Education was established at Addis Ababa University. Before, issues concerning special needs and disability had been allocated in the Department of Psychology (Addis Ababa University 2011). Through the step of devoting a separate department to the topic of special needs, the University showed a clear move towards taking the challenges of people with special needs as a serious issue.

All in all, it can be observed that there are positive developments and attitudes towards a more inclusive society through approaching inclusive education also on the governmental level in Ethiopia. However, the implementation is still held back by several barriers.

Disability and Poverty

> Disabled people have lower education and income levels than the rest of the population. They are more likely to have incomes below poverty level, and less likely to have savings and other assets than the non-disabled population. These findings hold for both developing and developed countries. (Elwan 1999, iv)

The following elaboration of the interconnectedness between poverty and disability and its consequences explains why disability and poverty are often referred to as a "vicious circle". This is how it is known that poverty can cause disability and disability can cause poverty as well (Barnes and Sheldon 2010; Campbell 2010; Elwan 1999; Lustig and Strauser 2007; Palmer 2011; Peterson et al. 2011; Skiba et al. 2005). It makes the results of this study more meaningful, as children with disabilities want to break free from such repressions by supporting their families and developing a sense of belonging to society. In their "poverty disability model", Lustig and Strauser (2007) define four aspects that increase the risk of disability: environmental risk factors, social role devaluation, negative group membership factors and a weakened sense of coherence. All of these factors lead to exclusion and loss of income (Lustig and Strauser 2007, 195). Consequently, poverty leads to "disempowerment at all levels of daily life [...]" (Lustig and Strauser 2007, 199). Disability in this context poses even more challenges to an already difficult situation if society is not able to build inclusive environments.

Parents who were involved in the study at hand but who were not experiencing supporting structures in the schools were often struggling with more problems resulting from the situation of their child with a disability attending a school than the other parents, who received support in the school. However, poverty played a major role for both groups. "Without income maintenance and other programs available in developed countries, the disabled in poor communities are usually the responsibility of their families; without family support, a disabled person's condition can be very precarious" (Elwan 1999, v). This is an interesting point, as this book is concerned with feeling like a family. The difference is that the focus of my research lies on educational environments. In both cases, however, the main aspect lies in supportive structures.

Being poor in some cases meant that time was needed to earn a living and could not be invested in the "luxuries" of education for the child with a disability or education in general. Therefore, poverty prevented parents from going to school. This, according to my theory of "developing a sense of belonging", had an influence on parental support and on the quality of education for the child. In these "nonsupportive" cases, teachers and parents were not able to develop a *feeling like a family* amongst themselves within the school context. However, as the research shows, most parents from poor backgrounds were able to come to the schools and develop a *feeling like a family* towards the institution and its staff.

Hypothetically, in the cases where parents did not have the possibility to be involved in school, the result would probably be a lower quality of education and hence less opportunities for the child on the labour market and thus, again, poverty. However, the fact that a child with a disability could attend a school at all also relieved those parents who did not get involved in school-related issues at all. Hence, education also supported those parents in such a way. In the cases where it was poverty that prevented parents from, e.g. going to schools, developing a closer relationship with the teachers, etc. – which is what mostly applied – it can be identified as a major barrier for "developing a sense of belonging".

Yet, poverty can also prevent children with disabilities from going to school, which has further consequences for the general opportunities in their lives. The labour market offers better opportunities for people with disabilities who are educated. Hence, contributions to the community are less likely without education. Additionally, such barriers will lead to social exclusion (Elwan 1999, v).

This emphasises the importance of the children's striving for being a valued member of society by contributing to it. This adds not only to the "development of a sense of belonging" for their psychological well-being but also to possibilities of earning income, becoming independent and avoiding poverty.

Belonging and Ethnicity

The topic of belonging is a very old one in the Ethiopian context. There are a number of different ethnic groups living in the landmass that today is known as the Federal Democratic Republic of Ethiopia (Markakis 1998; Poluha 1998; Salih and Markakis 1998).

In North Ethiopia, the highlands of Eritrea and Tigray are currently occupied by the Tigrayans and others. The Amhara, to the south, are in the majority in the highlands of Wollo, Gonder, Gojam and northern Shoa. Further south, Ethiopia's largest ethnic group is found: the Oromo and the Southern Nations. These three major ethnic groups have not always lived under the same rule. (Michael 2008, 394)

Considering that Ethiopia is a conglomerate of different ethnic groups and nationalities (far higher in number than the mentioned ones), conflicts and challenges can appear. Oromo people, for example, have often felt excluded from the Ethiopian polity as they did not adapt to the mainly Amharic coined system. They developed a national identity with "a distinctive shared memory and history" (Michael 2008, 399). Elements of this identity are the common language, Gada[6] tradition and democratic values. According to Michael, some Ethiopian nationalists are not ready "to accept the existence of a separate Oromo nation and promote an image of ethnic harmony" (2008, 399). The tensions that still exist in the country amongst different ethnic groups are not to be underestimated (Markakis 1998). This also became visible in the latest unrests in the Oromo region near Addis Ababa, which started in November 2015 and were still ongoing by the end of the year 2016. Consequently, a state of emergency for 6 months was declared in the country on October 8, 2016 (for further information, see media reports and comments on Al Jazeera, BBC, CNN, etc.).

But how did Ethiopia come to be what it is today? The expansion from Northern Ethiopia to the South can be related to the Solomonic dynasty. Various ethnic and religious groups were integrated in what later came to be Ethiopia (Michael 2008, 394). This shows that regions that had been inhabited by different populations belonging to different ethnicities and peoples were conquered.

Throughout the Ethiopian history, kings and emperors tried to unite the country. The aim of creating a multiethnic state that provides a feeling of belonging to one nation for every ethnicity rather than belonging to a certain ethnic group has not worked satisfactorily up to this day. The reason for this failure might be found in the fact that "there was no clear sense of ethnic national identity" (Michael 2008, 394). Additionally, Michael states that the "question of ethnic equality has never been answered" (Michael 2008, 394). These explanations make the basic issues clear. It is hence not surprising that people of different ethnic groups have different feelings of belonging regarding the state of Ethiopia. In this context, Michael distinguishes between "ethnic identity" and "ethnic consciousness".

Ethnically a person can be an Oromo, Tigray or Amhara, but may have no nationalist consciousness or may consciously reject the nationalist construction per se. In other words, a person who is an Amhara by birth may not subscribe to Amhara identity and the Amhara nationalist consciousness. Amhara identity can be defined from the ethnic perspective at the level of consciousness. (2008, 403)

---

[6]Gada is the traditional political organisation system of the Oromo. It is based on the "age-set system […] with five grades, each lasting 8 years. Males initiated together constituted a distinct group which passed as a bod from one grade to the next. Each group, when it reached the fifth grade, exercised governing power for 8 years" (Markakis 1998, 76).

The complexity of ethnicities and their influence on building up identities becomes visible at this point. What I want to highlight here is that a question of belonging related to ethnicity and nation prevails. The problematic aspect in this context is the fact that "several ethnically identifiable peoples assert their ethnic identity, not as part of a cohering nation-building enterprise but, on the contrary, to seek a collective identity that will ultimately be recognised as a sovereign nation-state" (Michael 2008, 394). Due to the historical developments, the Amhara are often characterised as a dominating and oppressive ethnic group.

> Amhara became the culture of an educated elite. To advance in administration one had to be educated and those who had an Amharic education had the best chance of administrative advancement. (Michael 2008, 96)

These historical developments often led to conflicts amongst different ethnic groups. Poluha also states that people who aimed at being powerful and becoming members of the ruling class had to fulfil certain requirements like adopting the Orthodox Christian religion. Furthermore, she remarks that class interests continued to be an essential factor regarding political alliances throughout the centuries (1998, 31). This indicates the pre-eminence of ethnicity in Ethiopia that, according to Markakis, rose to be such an important factor during the political changes in 1974 and led to "a period of political instability, economic dislocation and social unrest in Ethiopia [...]" (1998, 136). He mentions the Eritrean revolution as a first incident during this period which was followed by several other rebellious and armed movements amongst ethnic groups like the Tigray, Oromo, Afar and Sidama striving for ethnic liberation. Simultaneously, changes took place also in the field of religion. While the Christian Church lost some of its significance and power, the Islam gained recognition. Amharic was kept as the official language but other indigenous languages started to be used in broadcast and print (Markakis 1998, 136). "[F]irst tentative attempts to study the history and culture of subordinate groups were made. Ethnic cultural associations proliferated. The celebration of cultural diversity was officially encouraged, and a season of cultural festivities, featuring mostly songs and dances, followed" (Markakis 1998, 136). This could also be observed in the schools of the sample of this study, as they celebrated the day of nations and nationalities where children were encouraged to wear their traditional clothes.

Hence, the question of belonging to a certain ethnic group in Ethiopia grew important historically. Doornbos (1998) sees two sides of ethnicity. On the one hand, enforcing ethnic identities can be perceived as positive because it might lead towards a "rediscovery of meaning, a recapturing of cultural identity and recreation of solidarity [...]" (Doornbos 1998, 28). On the other hand, ethnicity is sometimes used in a negative way and "presents itself in narrowly parochial terms over which powerful political patrons claim to be the sole legitimate interpreters" (Doornbos 1998, 28). However, there seems to be a need to create a shared identity in Ethiopia which is the "pan-Ethiopian" identity. In this context, Tegegne emphasises the importance of common symbols that are able to build a democratic culture as a basis for a peaceful and enduring Ethiopian future incorporating different ethnic groups

in one nation (1998, 124). However, the ethnic group which an individual belongs
to might be more important for some than for others.

> [...] [That] everybody belongs to one ethnic group or 'nation', whose language they speak
> and with which they identify, seems to be relevant for certain groups in Ethiopia. For others
> it would be remote from, even contradictory to their life experience, especially since the
> meaning and implications of ethnic belonging have changed over time and continue to do
> so. (Poluha 1998, 37)

The same is true for the participants in my study. For some people, ethnicity
might have more meaning than for others. Nevertheless, it is a feature loaded with
significance in certain situations. When seeing the result of this research against this
background, "developing a sense of belonging" for children with disabilities gets
even more complex. It means that belonging to society can have different shapes if
ethnicity is considered additionally. In other words, identity and self-concept are
influenced by a historically grown significance of belonging to a certain ethnicity.

At this point, it might be interesting to mention that the fact that they conquered
the Italians in the battle of Adwa in 1896 and have never been colonised is very
meaningful for the people of Ethiopia. It can be observed that regarding this aspect,
"Ethiopians" feel like "Ethiopians" regardless of any ethnical background. Another
uniting factor can be seen in the international success of Ethiopian sports men and
women (e.g. the marathon runner Haile Gebrselassie). Also Tegegne concludes that
"[b]eing Ethiopian is not an identity that only the Amhara carry. It is an identity
shared by many Ethiopians, despite language differences. Hence, one can argue that
it is an identity which is a synthesis of many cultures" (1998, 124). Michael states
that ethnicity, identity and nationality have to be discussed openly to enable "a better society by managing conflicts and differences" (2008, 397). Discussing issues
and differences openly can also be applied to issues of exclusion regarding people
with disabilities. It would lead to a better society by managing conflicts and differences also in this case. Additionally, it would prepare the grounds for children with
disabilities to be accepted and respected as well as treated equally. Hence, differing
ethnicities add a further domain of complexity to the process of children with disabilities finding a place in society. Thereby identity, self-concept and belonging are
influenced to a great extent. To enable the social inclusion of people with disabilities
focusing on equality and equity, a change of attitudes in society is required. "The
common objective is to build a society based on mutual respect and equality, a society that is responsive to the interest of all. It is essential to redress the social, economic, political and cultural imbalances inherited from the past" (Tegegne 1998,
125). Even though Tegegne refers to ethnic groups in this quotation and pleads for
a society which recognises the rights of different ethnicities, the same wording
could be applied for differences regarding people with disabilities, as inclusion and
rights of persons with disabilities need similar developments. In other words, a society built on mutual respect, equity and equality should be able to include persons
with disabilities on these same grounds as integrating different ethnicities. Similarly,
to see differences in people and make normative distinctions is usually learnt by
growing up in a certain environment and community with certain attitudes. Ethnic

differences as well as disabilities are issues that can be referred to in this same context; children become members of different groups by exhibiting certain features, be it aspects of ethnicity (language, culture, traditions, etc.) or disability (observed differences that do not fulfil the expectations of people in a certain culture). Hence, belonging to certain groups leads to the experience of different barriers or facilitators in society. Poluha (1998) describes the development of belonging to certain ethnic groups as a process of enculturation. "From birth they [individuals] learn to recognize similarities and differences and in this context develop a specific competence of behavior, sometimes consciously and sometimes unconsciously. The unconscious, on the other hand, is often made up of norms and values that have become part of our way of being" (Poluha 1998, 32). Such norms and values also influence attitudes towards people with disabilities. Therefore, belonging to an ethnic group and belonging to society can be considered as highly related and hence important regarding the children's process of "developing a sense of belonging" by *feeling like a family*.

Self-Concept, Disability and Collectivist Cultures

"Everyone, disabled or not, who interacts with disability is engaged in producing its meaning and its social identity. A 'disability identity' does not belong strictly and only to those of us who are identified as disabled" (Titchkosky 2003, 4). The whole community as well as the society in which the children with disabilities live produce their disabilities. This influences the children's self-concept to a great extent. Wei and Marder (2012) criticise the lack of research that is conducted on the role of self-concept and learning regarding children with disabilities. They emphasise that typically research is done on students with learning disabilities compared to non-disabled peers. Other types of disabilities are usually left out although it is known that the development of a positive self-concept is important for many aspects of life for all children, amongst them academic achievement, social and emotional competence, mental health, etc. (Wei and Marder 2012, 247).

This chapter does not elaborate theories on self-concepts as such. This would be too extensive and go beyond the scope of this book. Instead it aims at exploring how the self-concept of children with disabilities is influenced and how the outcomes of the research at hand contributes to and can be integrated into existing research.

Support at school (teachers) and family life (parents) helps children to build up a positive self-concept (Wei and Marder 2012, 253ff). Aspects that are listed as supportive in this context are "positive feedback, express acceptance and a nonjudgmental attitude, listen, care, respect, and support the child and reduce social comparison" (Wei and Marder 2012, 255). The question now is how such findings can be related to Ethiopia as a country of the South that can differ to a great extent from Western cultures especially regarding topics such as self-concept and identity. Referring to Hofstede (2001), Eaton and Louw state that self-concepts of people from collectivist cultures might be more concrete and interdependent than self-concepts of people from individualist cultures (2000, 210). In this way, according to Triandis (1989), African cultures can usually be defined as collective cultures (see also Eaton and Louw 2000). However, Eaton and Louw limit this statement, as "the [African] continent has been ignored almost entirely, and assertions of collectivism have not been empirically tested" (2000, 211). In the case of Ethiopia and the sample studied, it became clear that community, family and relationships played major roles in the lives of the participants. This leads to the assumption that a collectivist culture prevails. Yet, it cannot be assumed that this is true for the whole population of the country.

> People in collectivist cultures, compared to people in individualist cultures, are likely to define themselves as aspects of groups, to give priority to in-group goals, to focus on context more than the content in making attributions and in communicating, to pay less attention to internal than to external processes as determinants of social behavior to define most relationships with in-group members as communal, to make more situational attributions, and tend to be self-effacing. (Triandis 2001, 907)

Such generalisations are problematic as they might tempt to simply adopt them to own research, without closer examination. Triandis also makes a relativising statement in noting that individuals do not possess all the characteristics of either a collectivist or an individualist culture. He describes that people, depending on the situation, rather refer to the "cognitive structures" of both types (Triandis 2001, 909). Additionally, also within cultures, there might be domains that can be characterised as being collectivist, whereas others might be individualist.

Regarding the research at hand, the result has many features that can be related to collectivism, and the core category *feeling like a family* clearly points into this direction. This means that in the situation of education for children with disabilities, especially parents but also teachers refer to the cognitive structures of a collectivist culture. My conviction that such a culture prevails in the situations analysed in the book at hand was enforced by the aspects mentioned by Triandis (in-group goals, communication and relationships) (Triandis 2001) as they are overwhelmingly applicable in my research. Aspects like supporting parents and people in need (from the children's perspective) and the way in which parents and teachers communicate were pivotal. On the other hand, the importance of relationships, which is reflected especially in the core category *feeling like a family,* was very clear. Eaton and Louw also stress that "members of collectivist cultures tend to [...] experience relatedness with others as a fundamental part of themselves, to the extent that the self is defined very specifically (i.e. concretely) and uniquely within each social relationship" (2000, 211). Furthermore, it has to be stated that the kind of sample that is studied in the respective culture usually determines the social affiliation to a collectivist or individualist culture. "Specifically, age, gender, social class, education, amount of contact with other cultures, and exposure to the modern mass media can change the position of a sample on any of these dimensions of cultural variation" (Triandis 2011, 7). Triandis furthermore explains that "lower class" samples are usually more collectivist than "upper class" samples from the same culture. This leads to the situation that people that are well off might be more individualist in a collectivist culture than people that are not that well off in an individualist culture (2011, 7). This is important as the sample of the study at hand included almost only people – and principally parents – from lower classes, of whom, according to Triandis' argument, one could expect more collectivist tendencies. As "[p]eople in collectivist cultures are especially concerned with relationships" (Triandis 2001, 909), it makes sense that the *feeling like a family* emerges more easily.

Following this discourse, the results of the study can be seen in a new light. Given that the children of the sample grow up in a collectivist environment, the aims of being part of the society and developing a sense of belonging receive a new meaning. It becomes clear that being part of society and contributing to the community are of major importance. These are also aspects that constitute the children's self-concept to a considerable extent. Thus, in contrast to individualist cultures where one's own goals and achievements are more important, being excluded from participating in society has quite a different influence on children's self-concepts, even though exclusion also has major influences on the self-concept of children with disabilities in individualist cultures. "In individualist societies people are autonomous and independent from their in-groups, they behave primarily on the basis of their attitudes rather than the norms of their in-groups, and exchange theory adequately predicts their social behaviour" (Triandis 2001, 909). Hence, norms of people's in-groups are more important for members of collectivist cultures. Consequently, "developing a sense of belonging" and *feeling like a family* within a certain group or society become comparably more significant for developing a positive self-concept for children with disabilities in a collectivist culture. Combining this with the aspects discussed in the previous chapter on ethnicity and belonging, the picture of social and cultural influences on children with disabilities in Addis Ababa becomes even more complex. Certainly, future research on the specific aspects that are of importance in making a difference in collectivist or individualist contexts for the self-concept and feeling of belonging for children with disabilities in the majority world – but also in the minority world – would be very interesting. In such a context, ethnicity would also have to be considered.

Family and Disability

In Ethiopia, it is common to have the father's name in addition to the name one is called by; hence, descent is reckoned to be patrilineal. However, the use of a first and a second name, as is customary in most Western cultures, is not common there (Crummey 1983; Hoben 1973). This is also the reason why Ethiopian scholars are usually cited by using their own (first) name and not their father's (second) name.

Article 34 of the Ethiopian Constitution states that the family is the basic unit in society and deserves special attention and protection by society and the state. Furthermore, a family is conceived of as natural and fundamental in the state of Ethiopia (Federal Democratic Republic of Ethiopia 1994). What actually is defined as family (extended or not) does not become clear here. The family, being such an important entity, however, must receive special attention also regarding disability.

> I think we need to think harder about the role of families. The CRPD [Convention on the Rights of People with Disabilities] hardly mentions the non-disabled family members whom most of us rely on, wherever we live in the world. When someone has an impairment, often the whole family is disabled, not just the individual. None of us wants to be dominated by or spoken for by our family. But I think that our parents and partners and children and siblings need to be supported and included and listened to, as well as us disabled people. (Shakespear 2014)

Naturally, families react differently to a disability in their family. Yet, for most families, the disability of a child poses serious challenges. In cases where negative attitudes and lack of awareness prevail and neither coping strategies are available nor additional support is given, sometimes violence against children with disabilities can also be observed.

In her study on violence against children with disabilities in Ethiopia, Boersma found that many children reported that they were treated unequal to their siblings and that they felt excluded. Furthermore, the parents seemed to try not to involve their child with a disability in the immediate community because of feelings of shame (2008, 48f). "The lack of access of the child to the social networks of the family relates to the fear of the family to damage their networks with the community around them because of their disabled child" (Boersma 2008, 49). Furthermore, conflicts are described between the families taking the side of their child and at the same time trying to maintain good relationships with their neighbours (Boersma 2008). In my study, some examples also reflect conflict laden relationships with neighbours and community. One of those examples is described by a mother, who spoke about fighting with her neighbour and losing one eye in the fight. Another mother told a story of young people in the community who made her son drunk and her arguing with them about that. In these cases, the violence was not directed against the child with a disability in the family but in relation with the community. It was argued earlier that shame develops especially in regard to the nearby community. Hence, it is clear that tensions might develop and make life in the community difficult.

In this paragraph, the category *walk of shame*, which emerged during the analysis of my data, receives special attention. The feeling of shame and having to decide whether to profess to the child with a disability or not lead to a great conflict for parents. Belonging is an important aspect in this context. Parents sometimes believe that they risk their place in the community and hence their place of belonging if they officially give their child with a disability a place in their family. This again supports the theory of parents developing the *feeling like a family* and looking for a place of belonging at school if the situation in the community and neighbourhood gets complicated. In the South-African/American study of Yssel et al. (2007), the authors emphasise that the philosophy of inclusive education stands for exactly this: the sense of belonging and shared ownership. This applies to all people involved in an inclusive setting. Furthermore, they state that this "yet has to be experienced by many of the parents in our study" (Yssel et al. 2007, 363). One could say that some parents in my study already experienced the sense of belonging in the schools their children attended. In this way, the sense of belonging can be experienced by the children as well as by the parents. What is interesting in this context is that I observed the feeling of belonging and the *feeling like a family* mainly in special settings. Not many integrative[7] settings seemed to exhibit such feelings. One reason for such developments might be that it was not inclusion that was practiced but integration, and hence the main issues of the mentioned philosophy of inclusion (sense of belonging and shared ownership) could not unfold in those schools. The reasons why it developed anyway in the special settings are elaborated in the chapter on the core category *feeling like a family*.

Changing the point of reference and moving back into the families, we already know that children with disabilities, like other children, need their place in their family and need the feeling of being valued. "Not being part of family life can result in a child that feels useless to the family" (Boersma 2008, 28). An example from my research that is interesting in this context is about a child with an intellectual disability who was already able to prepare everything for his mother to make coffee for the family. It became clear that he was very proud of the fact that he could contribute to daily life in the family. It was his task, and he felt needed in this specific situation because he was helping his mother. Furthermore, culturally, there are certain expectations of children to undertake certain tasks. What is interesting in this case is that it was a boy doing the tasks that are culturally assigned to girls. According to Camfield and Tafere (2011), there are differences between urban and rural environments. In an urban environment, girls are expected to start working at the age of 5. Tasks at this age are taking messages, carrying babies and the like. From the age of 7, girls help at home. They clean the house, fetch water and carry babies. Between 7 and 9 years of age, girls usually start to cook; they make stew and coffee. Only at the age of 10 are girls expected to be able to bake injera.[8] As soon as they are around 12 years old, girls are considered as mature enough to take on responsibility and perform all household activities (Camfield and Tafere 2011, 255). It is important to mention that drinking coffee is a cultural tradition in Ethiopia and has its own ceremony. Preparing coffee therefore is more meaningful for children.

> The Ethiopian traditional coffee ceremony, which is one of the most respected and colorful social rituals, gives the local people both a frivolous entertainment and congenial atmosphere to get together and discuss about various issues ranging from politics to minor personal issues. As an essential and an integral part of almost all Ethiopian social life coffee is drunk not only for its stimulating effect but also for getting together and having conversations. While the coffee ceremony is liked and cherished by all people regardless of differences in culture, social class, age and sex, in many cases it is women who spend much of their time on it. Many women make coffee and call each other turn by turn and exchange information. In the Ethiopian society, where male chauvinism seems to exist, coffee ceremonies give women the chance of discussing issues with men relatively on equal basis. (Tesfaye 2011, 123f)

In the above-illustrated case, preparing coffee seemed to give the boy satisfaction. This illustrates the significant meanings that a traditional coffee ceremony can

---

[7] The author does not use "inclusive" at this point, as the schools involved usually had not reached the levels of inclusion but rather integration.

[8] Traditional Ethiopian bread made of teff, a special Ethiopian grain.

have for the people involved. Even if children "only" help to prepare coffee at home for their family, they are aware of the cultural significance of drinking coffee, as it is a very visible tradition practiced a lot in daily life in Addis Ababa. This also led to the fact that the coffee ceremony as a social ritual was employed by lots of organisations (NGOs and GOs) to "foster participatory problem-solving schemes at the grassroots level" (Tesfaye 2011, 122). How is education for children with disabilities related to this aspect? Lots of parents – mostly, but not only of children with intellectual disabilities – reported that they observed the children improving in doing house chores but also in dressing and washing themselves when instructed by the parents after they started attending a school. Thus, parental support was an important aspect in this process of supporting children in acquiring more functionings. From the perspective of the capability approach, as the capability to do certain tasks was there, it only required the environment (support) to turn the capability into a functioning. It seems that often children discovered their potentials by getting access to school as their self-esteem got promoted at the same time. These potentials are obviously not restricted to capabilities related to school education.

However, in the already cited study involving parents from South Africa and the United States, the researchers found that parents from both countries were critical towards teachers who lacked training and preparation (Yssel et al. 2007, 361f). The same cannot be said of the sample of my study. Instead, the parents were very content with the teachers and did not complain very much. On the other hand, the study on South Africa and the United States also reports about parents' praise for teachers. The reason for this result in Ethiopia is above all the meaning that it had for parents that their child with a disability had the possibility to attend a school. In other words, for most parents in the Ethiopian sample, it was already overwhelming that their child was attending a school at all. Teachers were one of several important factors making this possible. The question about the quality of education might not have come to their mind at all at this point – especially in cases where they had not received education themselves.

Special Needs Education, Teachers' Attitudes and Community

"In countries like Ethiopia, teachers are the main indispensable resources for promoting special needs education. If teachers have a positive attitude towards the teaching profession and children and are able to attend to all children, then the requirements of inclusive education can more or less be fulfilled" (Mamo 2000, 84). First it has to be stated that teachers are probably indispensable resources for special needs education in most countries. However, the problematic part of this quotation is the "more or less", as even with positive attitudes it is problematic for teachers to implement inclusive education without proper training, knowledge and material, as the research at hand shows. "I am new, only three years. Still, I don't know how to write and how to read Braille. This is one barrier for them [the children]. Just I am teaching them orally and […] we have, we have […] Braille teachers, they help them not in their class [but] in the resource room. But for me this is a barrier. I don't know how to teach them with Braille" (Mamite, 2E–VI-E-10-GIT).[9]

In other words, lack of support and possibilities hinders the successful implementation of inclusive education. "More or less" does not exist in inclusion. Education either is or is not inclusive. Yet, positive attitudes are still the first step towards making inclusive education happen at all.

In the development of the categories for teachers and consequently in the model of "developing a sense of belonging", it can be seen that *feeling like a family* leads towards a positive attitude regarding the teaching profession. This statement is supported by other studies undertaken in different countries of the South. Ingrid Marais (2010), for instance, conducted research in two primary schools in South Africa focusing on the school community. "One of the reasons that teachers at these two schools remain in the profession is that they have a sense of belonging in the school, a sense of community [...]" (Marais 2010, 27). Relating this to the results of this study, it becomes clear that the same is true for the teachers of the Addis Ababa sample but that *feeling like a family* seems to reach even beyond a sense of community. In the chapter on the teachers' perspective, it becomes clear that solidarity, exchange and mutual understanding amongst teachers might be the most important aspects for teacher motivation. Furthermore, the thus produced feeling of togetherness and belonging becomes crucial. What became visible through this research, however, is that especially the feeling of family and community between teachers and parents is important for enhancing teachers' commitment to quality education for children with disabilities.

Looking at another study that focused on the quality of education in Ethiopia, the results show that quality depends on resources, teachers and the community. In this context, the importance of including parents was emphasised:

> They [teachers and principals] view community involvement as an important determinant of quality education, including teachers' interactions with parents as well as the communities' financial and other contributions to schools. (Barrow and Leu 2006, 2)

Hence, community involvement is seen as supportive for quality education. The building of strong relationships with students and communities was also emphasised in all the interviews with teachers and headmasters of that study (Barrow and Leu 2006, 2f). This points towards the importance of community in Ethiopia. It could be argued that community and parental involvement is an important aspect of education also in Western societies. The subtle distinction in the case of this research is the *feeling like a family*, which might not prevail in such dimensions in Western cultures. However, building up relationships with students was not emphasised as much as building up relationships with parents in the results of my research. This might be due to the fact that this study had a focus on children with disabilities, whereas Barrow and Leu focused on regular classrooms. That would indicate that there might still be differences in how children with disabilities are perceived and included compared to children without disabilities. This is not really surprising. As

---

[9] Interview conducted in English.

regards the establishment of relationships between teachers and students, it is actually a fact that children with disabilities usually cannot be included as much as students without disabilities.

In the South-African study that was mentioned before, Marais states "how social integration can be enabled through the school as a community" (2010, 19). Even though the focus was not on the disability in her research, the aspect that Marais raises here is of major importance. Schools might support social integration in the school communities as children are enabled to build up relationships with peers.

In many of the schools of the sample, the attitudes towards disability have already changed. Especially teachers tend to develop positive attitudes towards children with disabilities during the teaching learning process. Thereby, also the school climate – which is definitely influenced by *feeling like a family* – plays an important role (Peters 2007, 127).

Referring to Arbeiter and Hartley (2002), Peters states that "[i]n Uganda, teachers reported that ignorance, fear, and a lack of confidence were the causes of their attitudes towards children with disabilities before these children entered their classrooms. As they 'got used to' these children, they reported increased confidence, coping strategies, and a positive attitude change [...]" (2007, 127).

Next to attitudes, as discussed before, appropriate teacher training is essential for enabling inclusive classrooms. By referring to research that includes countries from around the world, UNICEF reports that "the level and standard of learning for children with disabilities rises, and so do the levels of their non-disabled peers" (2013a, 2) if teachers get equipped with knowledge about how to manage inclusive classrooms. In Ethiopia, teacher education for inclusive education is still not sufficient. General teacher training starts after the completion of the 10th grade. For the lower grades in primary schools, until 2008, 1 year of training and, for the upper grades, 3 years of training were allotted. In 2008, however, the duration for the lower grades was also raised to 3 years (Alemayehu and Temesgen 2011).

> Because of the low level of awareness of the field of special education and a shortage of professional educators and institutions until recently there was not any organized system of special needs teacher training in the country. From our own experiences, we know that the teacher training for special needs education was dependent on intermittently organized short seminars, workshops almost totally based on the support of donors from various voluntary organizations, and scholarships from abroad. (Alemayehu and Temesgen 2011, 132)

This again illustrates the challenging situation in which teachers find themselves when suddenly having to teach in a so-called inclusive classroom, meaning that they have to think about how to integrate one or more students with disabilities in their regular classroom. Without proper training in the teacher education programmes, teachers are usually overburdened. However, also regarding teacher training, an "atmosphere of departure" can be observed in Ethiopia regarding special needs education. "There have been recent encouraging developments with the initiation of new programs on special needs education in different universities and colleges as well as a mainstream course in special needs education across all teacher education and training institutes in the country" (Alemayehu and Temesgen 2011, 132). The quality of education strongly depends on the quality of the teachers. That is the reason why it is essential to train teachers in teaching and managing inclusive classrooms. This is the only way in which children with disabilities will have the possibility to receive educational equity and quality education.

Religion and Belief

> […][T]he very notion of disability as a cultural concept, comprising a wide range of cognitive, physical, sensory, and psychological states of being, is understood quite differently in varying religious communities and even within those communities. The very notion of disability as a cultural concept may be unfamiliar to a range of communities; in fact, some languages do not have a word for disability. (Stoltzfus and Schumm 2011, xiii)

It is interesting to discover that diversity and not uniformity is a common aspect of religion *and* disability (Stoltzfus and Schumm 2011, 12). It became visible in my research that religion and traditional beliefs can have a great influence on attitudes towards disability in Ethiopia. Disability, as a concept that cannot really be unified on a global level, manifests itself in a number of ways, depending on the respective culture that defines in which cases, how and why people's expectations of what people should be able to do are disappointed (Weisser 2007). Disability is a topic in different religions but also traditional beliefs that is typically addressed in multiple ways. Thus, the perspective on disability in each religion is difficult to grasp. "Disabilities and disabled people appear in Christian contexts and literature across a wide spectrum, generating a plethora of views, in an on-going, accelerating process. It is even more difficult to summarise confidently how the major Eastern religions of Hinduism, Buddhism or Islam have addressed disability" (Miles 1995, 50). At the same time, religion as an essential aspect of culture influences views on disability.

> It is widely recognized that religious teachings and practices help to establish cultural standards for what is deemed 'normal' human physical and mental behaviour and in establishing a moral order for the fit and healthy body and mind. Religion, in its multiple manifestations, plays a critical role in determining how disability is understood and how persons with disabilities are treated or mistreated in a given historical-cultural context. (Stoltzfus and Schumm 2011, xi)

This means that while views on disability in different religious traditions and texts take on varying forms, the religious beliefs define disability to a great extent for certain groups and communities. Thereby, it can be observed that religion and ethnicity are usually interconnected. However, in the Ethiopian context, it is interesting that "[w]hile in many countries outside Ethiopia, religion is an important ethnic criterion, as it provides yet another tie between members of the same ethnic groups, this is not yet the case in Ethiopia where many ethnic groups remain religiously divided" (Poluha 1998, 31). This means that in one ethnic group people can be members of different religions. Therefore, people can also have the same religion while belonging to different ethnicities. Furthermore, it is interesting to state that in certain aspects religion is more important than ethnicity in Ethiopia. As a consequence, marriages between couples from different ethnicities take place quite frequently. "[M]arriages between Christian Amharas and Christian Oromos [are] more frequent than between Christian Oromos and Muslim Oromos" (Poluha 1998, 37). Poluha concludes that this proves that "homogeneity and similarity of interests" is not a given fact within one ethnic group (Poluha 1998, 37). This indicates that religiously influenced perceptions of disability might coincide also between different ethnic groups in Ethiopia when they follow the same religion. In this book, the Ethiopian Orthodox Church received more attention than other religious traditions in the country. Even though some participants of this research were members of the Islam and other religions, the majority were followers of the Orthodox Church. Therefore, I concentrate on the Ethiopian Orthodox Tewahedo Church. The Ethiopian Tewahedo Church "is the only pre-colonial Christian Church in sub-Saharan Africa; it has been formed from a distinct mix of cultural traditions and has developed in comparative isolation from the rest of the Church for most of its history. As a result it has taken a very different shape and way of life from other churches" (Binns 2013, 34). In this quotation, one interesting aspect for this chapter is the "mix of cultural traditions". This suggests that already during the development of the Ethiopian Church, traditional beliefs were involved in the doctrine. Furthermore, it is oriented on the Semitic culture and follows the Old Testament's suggestions for daily life (circumcision, dietary laws, etc.) (Binns 2013).

Religion and traditional beliefs have a great influence on attitudes towards people with disabilities in Addis Ababa. In this respect, it could be observed that especially parents of children with disabilities combined what seemed to be traditional and religious beliefs. Looking for explanations for the fact that disability is perceived as a curse by people who are deeply religious, even though the Church does not teach such a misconception (according to my interview with a representative of the Orthodox Church), various sources were found.

Addis Ababa is located in an Amhara region, surrounded by Oromo area. The main Amhara regions, though, are located in the central and northern provinces in the highlands of Ethiopia (Young 1977). Even though the sample of the research does not only consist of people of Amhara descent, I put my focus on this ethnicity because it is the predominating one in the area of research. Additionally, the majority of participants were of Amhara descent. Young's study on Amhara Ethiopian medical divination, conducted in the 1970s, resulted in the outcome that "[a]ccording to Amhara, people can tap extra-ordinary powers with which it is possible to perform certain medical works" (Young 1977, 185). These medical works include divining events, healing or preventing sickness and misfortune, etc. What was interesting for the research at hand is the fact that ecclesiastic persons are mentioned as one of the four categories of people who were able to possess these powers: "Any ecclesiastic can anoint sick people with sanctified water, with the hope that this will repel sickness causing demons [...]" (Young 1977, 185.). The mention of holy water in this context makes it clear how religious beliefs and traditional "medical works" might be connected. Hence, it makes sense for parents to use holy water for a child with a disability if disability is perceived as something that should be healed. This is the case even though disability is generally not considered as an illness but as a misfortune and curse. Following the interview in the Orthodox Church, however, this view on disability being a curse is not held by the Church. But the logic behind combining the Church, "holy waters" and "healing" becomes transparent. Additionally, it is obvious that parents' hopes, needs and desires enforce their believing in the healing powers of holy water and holy springs and, beyond that, in God. Triandis states that "God is an excellent example of self-deception. What would be more consistent with our hopes, needs, and desires than to have an omnipotent entity support our battles, whether they are to grow better crops, to reach health and happiness, or to eliminate our enemies?" (2011, 4). Most of the parents of the sample felt that God was almighty and deciding about disability, health, fortune and misfortune. It is not my intention to judge how much of this might be self-deception and what might not be. It is a fact that God seemed to exist in the views of the participants and had great influence on their lives. The quotation above emphasises the hidden persuasion that lies in believing in God as almighty and in healing powers for parents of children with disabilities who cannot accept their child's impairment. It can be understood as support to keep up hopes for their child, as disability constitutes a challenge and a disturbance in their lives. Therefore, I defined going to holy waters as support for the children with disabilities in the category *parental support*, as the parents experienced it as something that they did *for* the child.

References

Addis Ababa University. (2011). *Department of special needs education.* Retrieved August 27, 2013, from http://www.aau.edu.et/index.php/special-needs-overview (not online anymore, alternativley look at: http://www.aau.edu.et/cebs/academics/special-needs-department/overview/. Retrieved November 23, 2016).

Alemayehu, T., & Temesgen, F. (2011). Special needs education in Ethiopia. In M. A. Winzer & K. Mazurek (Eds.), *International practices in special education: Debates and challenges* (pp. 125–137). Washington, DC: Gallaudet University Press.

Arbeiter, S., & Hartley, S. (2002). Teachers' and pupils' experiences of integrated education in Uganda. *International Journal of Disability, Development and Education, 49*(1), 61–78.

Bahru, Z. (2001). *A history of modern Ethiopia 1855–1991.* Oxford et al.: Currey et al.

Barnes, C., & Sheldon, A. (2010). Disability, politics and poverty in a majority world context. *Disability & Society, 25*(7), 771–782.

Barrow, K., & Leu, E. (2006). Issue paper. *Perceptions of Ethiopian teachers and principals on quality of education.* Report for USAID.

Bartnicki, A., & Mantel-Niećko, J. (1978). *Geschichte Äthiopiens. Vom Beginn des 20. Jahrhunderts bis zur Gegenwart.* Berlin: Akad. Verl.

Belete, M. (2011). An investigation of multicultural provisions of the Ethiopian education policy. *Journal of Contemporary Issues in Education, 6*(1), 35–41.

Binns, J. (2013). Out of Ethiopia – A different way of doing theology. *International journal for the Study of the Christian Church, 13*(1), 33–47.

Boersma, M. (2008). *Violence against Ethiopian children with disabilities. The stories and perspectives of children.* University of Amsterdam.

Brogini Künzi, G. (2006). *Italien und der Abessinienkrieg 1935/36. Kolonialkrieg oder totaler Krieg?* Paderborn/Wien u. a.: Schöningh.

Camfield, L., & Tafere, Y. (2011). Community understandings of childhood transitions in Ethiopia: Different for girls? *Children's Geographies, 9*(2), 247–262.

Campbell, C. (2010). Disability and international development: Towards inclusive global health. *Psychology, Health & Medicine, 15*(5), 622–623.

Crummey, D. (1983). Family and property amongst the Amhara nobility. *The Journal of African History, 24*(2), 207–220.

Dawit, A. (1994). The end of crises? Or crises without end? The evolving dynamics in post-derg Ethiopia. In A. Zegeye & S. Pausewang (Eds.), *Ethiopia in change. Peasantry, nationalism and democracy* (pp. 280–308). London: British Academic Press.

Demeke, M. (2010). Opening statement. In *UNESCO ninth high level meeting on education for all.* Ministry of Education, Addis Ababa.

Donham, D. L. (2002). Introduction. In W. James et al. (Eds.), *Remapping Ethiopia. Socialism & after* (pp. 1–8). Oxford et al.: Currey et al.

Doornbos, M. (1998). Linking the future to the past – ethnicity and pluralism. In M. A. M. Salih & J. Markakis (Eds.), *Ethnicity and the state in Eastern Africa* (pp. 17–29). Stockholm: Nordiska Afrikainstitutet.

Eaton, L., & Louw, J. (2000). Culture and self in South Africa: Individualism-collectivism predictions. *The Journal of Social Psychology, 140*(2), 210–217.

Erlich, H. (2005). The Copts and Ethiopia – "A Literal-Historical Lecture", 1895. In S. Brüne & T. Bairu (Eds.), *Auf dem Weg zum modernen Äthiopien. Festschrift für Bairu Tafla* (pp. 80–94). LIT-Verl: Münster.

Elwan, A. (1999). *Title, Social Protection Discussion Paper Series.* Washington, DC: Social Protection Unit. Human Development Network. The World Bank.

Ethiopian Ministry of Education. (2002). *The education and training policy and its implementation.* Addis Ababa: Ethiopian Ministry of Education.

Ethiopian Ministry of Education (2011a). About the Ethiopian education system. (Addis Ababa, Federal Democratic Republic of Ethiopia) Retrieved March 7, 2014, from http://info.moe.gov.et/ates.shtml

Ethiopian Ministry of Education. (2011b). *Education sector development program IV (ESDP IV). 2010/2011–2014/2015.* Addis Ababa: Ethiopian Ministry of Education.

Federal Democratic Republic of Ethiopia (FDRE). (1994). *Constitution of the Federal Democratic Republic of Ethiopia.* Ethiopia, Addis Ababa.

Federal Democratic Republic of Ethiopia (FDRE) (2012). Implementation of the UN convention on the rights of persons with disabilities (CRPD). (Addis Ababa, FDRE) Retrieved November 23, 2016, from http://www.molsa.gov.et/English/SWD/Documents/ETHIOPIA%20 Implementation%20of%20the%20UN%20Convention%20on%20the%20Rights%20of%20 Persons%20with%20Desabilities%20Initial%20Report.pdf

Haile Sellassie, I. (1937). *The autobiography of emperor Haile Sellassie i. 'My life and Ethiopia's progress' 1892–1937.* Oxford: Oxford University Press.

Hoben, A. (1973). *Land tenure among the Amhara of Ethiopia. The dynamic of cognatic descent.* Chicago: The University of Chicago Press.

Hofstede, G. (2001). *Culture's consequences. Comparing values, behaviors, institutions and organizations across nations.* Thousands Oaks: SAGE.

Hrbek, I. (1993). North Africa and the Horn. In A. A. Mazrui (Ed.), *General history of Africa/ UNESCO international scientific committee for drafting of a general history of Africa. Africa since 1935* (pp. 127–160). London u. a.: Heinemann u. a.

Ingstad, B., & Whyte, S. R. (Eds.). (2007). *Disability in local and global worlds*. Berkeley: University of California Press.

Krylow, A. (1994). Ethnic factors in post-Mengistu Ethiopia. In A. Zegeye & S. Pausewang (Eds.), *Ethiopia in change. Peasantry, nationalism and democracy* (pp. 231–241). London: British Academic Press.

Lustig, D. C., & Strauser, D. R. (2007). Causal relationships between poverty and disability. *Rehabilitation Counseling Bulletin, 50*(4), 194–202.

Mamo, M. (2000). Special needs education: Emerging in Ethiopia. In H. Savolainen (Ed.), *Meeting special and diverse educational needs: Making inclusive education a reality* (pp. 84–94). Helsinki: Ministry for Foreign Affairs of Finland & Niilo Mäki Institute.

Marais, I. (2010). Together in their school gemeinschaft – Faithfully: An ethnographic study of two primary schools in Johannesburg. *Education as Change, 14*(1), 19–32.

Markakis, J. (1998). The politics of identity – The case of the Gurage in Ethiopia. In M. A. M. Salih & J. Markakis (Eds.), *Ethnicity and the state in Eastern Africa* (pp. 127–146). Stockholm: Nordiska Afrikainstitutet.

Michael, M. (2008). Who is Amhara? *African Identities, 2008, 6*(4), 393–404. Vol., 393.

Miles, M. (1995). Disability in an Eastern religious context: Historical perspectives. *Disability & Society, 10*(1), 49–70.

Mockler, A. (2003). *Haile Selassie's war*. Oxford: Signal Books.

Mulugeta, S. (2009). *Ethiopian education via SA TV* (MediaClubSouthAfrica) Retrieved November 23, 2016, from http://www.mediaclubsouthafrica.com/index.php?option=com_content&view=article&id=1218:Ethiopian-education-via-sa-tv&catid=47:africa_news&Itemid=116

Ottaway, M., & Ottaway, D. (1978). *Ethiopia. Empire in revolution*. New York et al.: Africana Publishing Company.

Palmer, M. (2011). Disability and poverty: A conceptual review. *Journal of Disability Policy Studies, 21*(4), 210–218.

Pankhurst, E. S. (1955). *Ethiopia – A cultural history*. Woodford Green: Lalibela House.

Pankhurst, R. (1990). *A social history of Ethiopia. The Northern and Central highlands from early medieval times to the rise of emperor Tewodros II*. Huntingdon: Institute of Ethiopian Studies, Addis Ababa University [u. a.].

Peters, S. (2007). Inclusion as a strategy for achieving education for all. In L. Florian (Ed.), *The sage handbook of special education* (pp. 117–130). London/Thousand Oaks/New Delhi: Sage.

Peterson, C. A., et al. (2011). Identification of disabilities and service receipt among preschool children living in poverty. *The Journal of Special Education, XX*(X), 1–13.

Phillipson, D. W. (1998). *Ancient Ethiopia. Aksum: Its antecedents and successors*. London: British Museum Press.

Poluha, E. (1998). Ethnicity and democracy – A viable alliance? In M. A. M. Salih & J. Markakis (Eds.), *Ethnicity and the state in Eastern Africa* (pp. 30–41). Stockholm: Nordiska Afrikainstitutet.

Rønning Balsvik, R. (1994). An important root of the Ethiopian revolution: The student movement. In A. Zegeye & S. Pausewang (Eds.), *Ethiopia in change. Peasantry, nationalism and democracy* (pp. 77–94). London: British Academic Press.

Rubenson, S. (1976). *The survival of Ethiopian independence*. London et al.: Heinemann et al.

Salih, M. A., & Markakis, J. (1998). *Ethnicity and the state in Eastern Africa*. Stockholm: Nordiska Afrikainstitutet.

Sen, A. (1979). *Equality of what, The Tanner Lecture on Human Values held on 22nd of May 1979*. Stanford: Stanford University.

Shakespear, T. (2014). *My top five disability rights and wrongs* (Online, CBM Christoffel Blind Mission) Retrieved June 20, 2014, from http://www.cbm.org/My-top-five-disability-rights-and-wrongs-445675.php?utm_source=CBM+International+-+IAA+Newsletter&utm_campaign= 7c901be7a4-IAA_March+2014&utm_medium=email&utm_term=0_3827112f1a-7c901be7a4-46829129

Skiba, R. J., et al. (2005). Unproven links: Can poverty explain ethnic disproportionality in special education? *The Journal of Special Education, 39*(3), 130–144.

Stern, P. N. (2007). On solid ground: Essential properties for growing grounded theory. In A. Bryant & K. Charmaz (Eds.), *The sage handbook of grounded theory* (pp. 114–126). London/New Delhi/Thousand Oaks/Singapore: Sage.

Stoltzfus, M., & Schumm, D. (2011). Editor's introduction. In D. Schumm & M. Stoltzfus (Eds.), *Disability and religious diversity*. New York: Palgrave Macmillan.

Tegegne, T. (1998). Amhara ethnicity in the making. In M. A. M. Salih & J. Markakis (Eds.), *Ethnicity and the state in Eastern Africa* (pp. 116–126). Stockholm: Nordiska Afrikainstitutet.

Tekeste, N. (2006). *Education in Ethiopia. From crisis to the brink of collapse*. Uppsala: Nordiska Afrikainstitutet.

Tesfaye, A. M. (2011). Piggybacking the traditional coffee ceremony as a participatory communication strategy to resolve social problems: An assessment of practices in Addis Ababa, Ethiopia. *Online Journal of Communication and Media Technologies, 1*(4), 121–149.

Tirussew, T. (2005). *Disability in Ethiopia: Issues, insights and implications*. Addis Ababa: Addis Ababa University Printing Press.

Titchkosky, T. (2003). *Disability, self, and society*. Toronto [u. a.]: University of Toronto Press.

Transitional Government of Ethiopia (TGE). (1994). *The training and education policy of Ethiopia*. In. Addis Ababa: Ethiopia, St. George Printing Press.

Triandis, H. (1989). The self and social behaviour in differing cultural contexts. *Psychological Review, 96*, 506–520.

Triandis, H. C. (2001). Individualism-collectivism and personality. *Journal of personality, 2001, 69*(6), 907–924. Vol. 907.

Triandis, H. C. (2011). Culture and self-deception: A theoretical perspective. *Social Behavior and Personality, 2011, 39*(1), 3–13. Vol. 3.

UNESCO. (2006). *Ethiopia. Principles and general objectives of education*. Retrieved November 23, 2016, from http://www.ibe.unesco.org/fileadmin/user_upload/archive/Countries/WDE/2006/SUB-SAHARAN_AFRICA/Ethiopia/Ethiopia.htm

UNICEF. (2013). Educating teachers for children with disabilities. Mapping, scoping and best practices exercise in the context of developing inclusive education. *Rights, education and protection (REAP) project*. (UNICEF) Retrieved November 23, 2016, from https://dl.dropboxusercontent.com/u/8608264/UNICEF%20Educating%20Teachers%20for%20Children%20with%20Disabilities1a.pdf

Wartenberg, D. (1999a). Äthiopien – ein Land geht neue Wege. Ein kommentiertes Interview mit Dr. Tekle Haimanot Haile Selassie (Vice-Minister of Education). In D. Wartenberg & W. Mayrhofer (Eds.), *Bildung in Äthiopien. Ein Land geht neue Wege* (pp. 9–16). Hamburg: Kovac.

Wartenberg, D. (1999b). Äthiopiens Aufbruch in eine neue bildungspolitische Zukunft. In D. Wartenberg & W. Mayrhofer (Eds.), *Bildung in Äthiopien. Ein Land geht neue Wege* (pp. 66–98). Hamburg: Kovac.

Wartenberg, D., & Mayrhofer, W. (Eds.). (1999). *Bildung in Äthiopien. Ein Land geht neue Wege*. Hamburg: Kovac.

Wei, X., & Marder, C. (2012). Self-concept development of students with disabilities: Disability category, gender, and racial differences from early elementary to high school. *Remedial and Special Education, 33*(4), 247–257.

Weisser, J. (2007). Für eine anti-essentialistische Theorie der Behinderung. *Behindertenpädagogik, 46*(3/4), 237–249.

Young, A. (1977). Order, analogy, and efficacy in Ethiopian medical divination. *Culture, Medicine and Psychiatry, 1*(2), 183–199.

Yssel, N., Engelbrecht, P., Oswald, M. M., Eloff, I., & Swart, E. (2007). Views of inclusion: A comparative study of parents' perceptions in South Africa and the United States. *Remedial and Special Education, 28*(6), 356–365.

Zegeye, A., & Pausewang, S. (1994a). *Ethiopia in change. Peasantry, nationalism and democracy*. London: British Academic Press.

Zegeye, A., & Pausewang, S. (1994b). Introduction: Looking back into the future. In A. Zegeye & S. Pausewang (Eds.), *Ethiopia in change. Peasantry, nationalism and democracy* (pp. 1–11). London: British Academic Press.

Chapter 3
Three Reasons for Dealing with Disability, Education and the Majority World

Abstract This chapter covers aspects of relevance for the topic regarding scientific, disciplinary and methodical relevance, political and developmental relevance (including educational equity) and terminological relevance. This illustrates the importance of the topic regarding the necessity of conducting research on disability, education and the majority world as well as research that includes disability and culture. Thereby, international developments and discussions about disability-specific issues (like discussions on inclusive education) are reflected. A final summary of these diverse aspects, which are all meaningful to this work, provides the reader with a first introduction to the topic in a broader framework. Last but not least, the chapter concludes by approaching the field with a question.

The topic of interest for this research comprises a multitude of aspects such as disability, education and children; other aspects of relevance are countries of the majority world,[1] development and poverty, as well as culture, human rights, inclusion, equity and equality.[2] I give terms like "majority world" or "global South" general preference as they are not loaded with so-called "lag-behind" assumptions like "third world" or "developing countries", which are often discriminating and suggest that "developed countries" are where "developing countries" should develop towards (Fujiura et al. 2005). Several authors refer to this terminology within the field of disability (Barnes and Sheldon 2010; Grech 2011; Turmusani 2004). Yet, the term "developing country" has not been abandoned completely.

Regarding the research as a whole, even more issues can certainly be found when looking more closely at the subject. However, from my perspective, the most relevant aspects for this book are covered. In order to provide you with a clear overview, this chapter is split into three discourses which I consider as relevant: "scientific, disciplinary and methodical", "political and developmental" and "terminological". Naturally, the three aspects are interconnected and overlap; hence, a clear delimitation between these three discourses is not possible.

---

[1] The terms used here interchangeably for so-called developing countries are "majority world" and "countries of the South". So-called developed countries are also referred to as "Western countries", "countries of the North", "minority world", etc.

[2] The order in which these aspects are listed is not meant to be in line with their relevance.

© The Author(s) 2017
M. Schiemer, *Education for Children with Disabilities in Addis Ababa,
Ethiopia*, Inclusive Learning and Educational Equity 4,
DOI 10.1007/978-3-319-60768-9_3

Reason 1: Scientific, Disciplinary and Methodical Relevance

Research on Disability and the Majority World

In regard to issues of research in and knowledge about countries of the South, some alarming facts have to be mentioned. "The imbalance between the sheer size of the developing world and what little is known about the lives and life circumstances of persons with disabilities living there should command our attention" (Fujiura et al. 2005, 295). This statement is important in many regards. It is known that the greater part of people with disabilities can be found in the majority world. Around 80% of the world's people with disabilities live in countries of the South. Furthermore, the life conditions for this group of people are far worse in those countries than in the so-called developed countries (UN Enable 2013; WHO 2011). Regarding the knowledge acquired about the life situations, the challenges and related problems faced by people with disabilities and how these might be solved, much more research has been done in Western countries than in countries of the South. Additionally, it has to be mentioned that Western-led research projects and international funding organisations play an important role in this context. This leads to constructions of disability which are mainly coloured by knowledge based on Western norms and cultures.

A study of projects on inclusive education in the majority world revealed that "in developing countries the implementation of inclusive education is basically undertaken by the NGOs instead of a country's government" (Srivastava et al. 2015, 190).

This distorts global debates about disability in general and issues on how to deal with poverty and disability in particular in countries of the majority world. These facts exemplify the need for research to use Southern knowledge and include people and researchers from countries of the South when looking at people with disabilities and their needs in so-called developing countries. The aspect of education and educational equity deserves special consideration, as it is regarded as one of the most important political issues concerning development (see, e.g. Miles et al. 2012).

Looking at equity in education, clarifying words have to be said regarding the meaning of this concept. According to the OECD policy brief (OECD 2008), two dimensions can be found by looking at equity in education: fairness and inclusion. In more detail, the first aspect refers to circumstances (social as well as personal) that should not interfere with "achieving educational potential" (OECD 2008), whereas inclusion "implies ensuring a basic minimum standard of education for all – for example that everyone should be able to read, write and do simple arithmetic" (OECD 2008). This goal is not compatible with the goals of the capability approach, which are more about having real possibilities to reach goals that can be defined individually than about achieving the same things.

At the same time, both aspects (fairness and inclusion) can't be approached separately: "The two dimensions are closely intertwined: tackling school failure helps to overcome the effects of social deprivation which often causes school failure" (OECD 2008). The OECD does not have so-called developing countries amongst their members. However, inclusion and fairness can be taken as aspects which are of similar importance for countries of the global South when moving towards educational equity, as they can (and have to) be defined according to the prevailing culture. Therefore, I want to emphasise the fact that inclusive education is a Western concept which might lead to problems when it comes to its implementation in the global South. Mutua and Swadener state that "a [W]estern definition of inclusion requires that it is implemented in the same way that it is done in the West without taking into account conditions in local communities. Additionally, it illustrates how colonial practices devalued and erased indigenous inclusive practices that did not necessarily mimic [W]estern conceptions of inclusion" (Mutua and Swadener 2011, 213). It is therefore important to approach the concept of inclusion from a different angle. I want to refer to a statement which will appear again later in the book: Inclusion aspires to shape environments in such a way that no one is excluded. Additionally, inclusive education tries to avoid classifications of children with disabilities. Instead it is aimed to switch towards descriptions of the environment in the child's educational surrounding (Biewer 2009a, b). It is of utmost importance to read these sentences with different cultural environments in mind. Feeling like a family may be much more important for people in one culture compared to another. We may not be able to imagine or understand the different values which people with backgrounds different from ours give to certain aspects. But we can try to gain as much knowledge as possible about that culture in order to be able to understand at least a small part of it. By being open to and immerging into other value systems and by leaving out Western approaches and knowledge as far as possible, I am helping to make inclusion meaningful for countries of the South. As an example, it might be interesting to look at the meaning of goals set for an individual person compared to goals set for a community. This also requires questioning the Western concept of inclusion as such. Grech, too, sees the discussing of transferring Western knowledge to the South, especially in relation to development, as an urgent matter:

> The inclusion of disability in development is approached as one of incorporation in the existent structure, without considering the implications of this structure for disabled people, notably its colonial and neoliberal foundations and practices. [...]
>
> Overall, the epistemological disengagement from majority world disability not only sustains the little knowledge about disability in the global South (Miles and Ahuja 2007) but also has given rise to a discourse characterised by inferences and generalisations from North to South, where the Western knowledge and practices homogenise, assume and dictate, and where critical issues related to context, culture, economy, history, community and relationships of power among others are often bypassed or reframed to accommodate a minority world view. (Grech 2011, 88)

This underscores the importance of taking a critical stance towards the knowledge which we have gained from our own cultures when dealing with other parts of the world. Aspects like "developing a sense of belonging" and "feeling like a family" can only be seen in the context of the culture where they are observed. Hence, the meaning of those values can only be understood by gaining more knowledge about a society, community and/or culture. We therefore also have to ask ourselves what inclusion and/or inclusive education means in a particular environment and to what extent we have to change preconceived convictions. I discuss the issues mentioned by Grech, as well as other aspects, in depth in Chap. 11 on the United Nations Convention on the Rights of Persons with Disabilities (UNCRPD).

In the aforementioned study about projects on inclusive education, it is stated that "there is insufficient empirical evidence on the effects of projects under the aegis of international organisations. It is alarming that governments and other organisations proceed in developing or implementing inclusive education without actual knowledge on possible outcomes" (Srivastava et al. 2015, 190). This is a very critical point. It is especially important to know what inclusive education aims at and how to implement it in a particular environment as well as to be informed about possible consequences. People with disabilities play the main role in proceeding in this way. The need to include people with disabilities in educational efforts must be emphasised especially when referring to development and goals like the Sustainable Development Goals (SDGs). Goal number 4 claims to "ensure inclusive and equitable quality education and promote lifelong learning opportunities for all" (UN 2015). We know that education and development are very strongly interconnected. Different measures have been taken to strengthen and further develop education systems in different countries, amongst them, the gathering of data on the educational situation, in order to decide on further action.

> By the late twentieth century, quantitative data had gained enormous influence in education systems through the work of the OECD, the European Commission and national system agencies. The creation and flow of data has become a powerful governing tool in education. […] Comparison between pupils, costs, regions and states has grown ever more important. The visualization of this data, and its range of techniques, has changed over time, especially in its movement from an expert to a public act. Data began to be explained to a widening audience to shape its behaviors and its institutions. (Lawn 2013, abstract)

From a quantitative perspective, the quality and scope of available statistics on populations in the majority world have to be viewed critically. Differing results, for example, restrict authentic references to numbers of people with disabilities. This refers to the fact that statistics of different investigations on the same topic frequently reach different results (Fujiura et al. 2005). Numbers are often the most important aspect for governments or organisations to react to certain conditions. Additionally, when regarding disability statistics in particular, they comprise a myriad of challenges. For example, definitions of what is and what is not to be "identified" as a disability and to what extent these definitions confront researchers with problems must not be underestimated (Fujiura et al. 2005, 295). In 2001, the United Nations published a paper on "Guidelines and Principles for the Development of Disability Statistics".[3] The suggestions address managers of disability programmes as well as researchers. There is a clear recommendation of using the International

---

[3] It is very problematic to try to classify people by referring to disabilities. It strengthens a deficit-oriented approach rather than looking at capabilities and the environment that is often responsible for barriers and hence deficits.

Classification of Functioning, Disability and Health (ICF)[4] (WHO 2001) as a tool for investigation and as an orientation for definitions of disabilities (UN 2001). Different critical references to the ICF already exist, predominantly – but not only – concerning terminological issues (see, e.g. Badley 2008; Biewer 2002; Chapireau 2005; Hirschberg 2003; Hollenweger 1998). I am examining the ICF itself in more detail in the chapter on "International Development regarding Access to Education", in the chapter on "Models of Disability" and especially in the chapter on "Facts and Challenges regarding Grounded Theory, the ICF and Ethical Issues". As indicated above, a lack of knowledge and tools for collecting information about disability and the situation of people with disabilities in the majority world leads to disadvantage and invisibility of the topic as such. The search for appropriate tools and methods in research is therefore of utmost importance and must not be restricted to quantitative data.

Methodical Aspects

The focus of this book is on qualitative methods for gathering data and information about the situation of children with disabilities in Ethiopia. In their report on using qualitative methods in studying the link between disability and poverty, Ingstad and Grut state that "[t]here are several reasons for choosing a qualitative design. A qualitative approach is likely to be chosen when the focus involves an interpretive approach in which the aim is to understand and interpret the meaning the different experiences have to the individuals" (Ingstad and Grut 2005, 6). As this research focuses explicitly on different perspectives on how children experience the aspect of inclusion, exclusion and participation, it seemed most logical to me not to resort to quantitative methods for answering emerging questions.

Another reason why to put emphasis on qualitative research is that qualitative methods allow the researcher to explore people's experiences, their personal perspectives and convictions. In the field of research which this study belongs to, with children with disabilities at its centre, delicate and sensitive issues (especially regarding the children and parents) can come up during the research. This means that the phenomenon under research is difficult to study. In these cases qualitative methods are more useful instruments for research than quantitative instruments (Denzin and Lincoln 2005; Ingstad and Grut 2005). On the other hand, there is the challenge of conducting qualitative research in a foreign culture in a country of the majority world. In their book, which was originally published in 1983, Bulmer and Warwick state:

---

[4] The International Classification of Functioning, Disability and Health (ICF) will be presented in more detail in later chapters. It has to be acknowledged that the ICF and ICF-CY (child and youth version) will appear in different contexts: in political contexts (international classification), terminological contexts (models of disabilities) as well as in the context of being used as a language for starting the investigation at hand (framework).

> The conduct of social research in developing countries is an important issue. For Third World countries rely increasingly upon social science methods to gather data which is used by governments both for development planning and in day-to-day administration. The results of social inquiry are not just fed back to fellow academics, but are used to influence the life chances of millions upon millions of people. The means by which social data are collected, and the quality of the data which result, are therefore issues of major importance […]. (Bulmer and Warwick 1993, 3)

It might be ambitious to expect social research to have an impact on millions of people, but it is certainly realistic for some research. It is a fact that qualitative methods can lead to insights into people's lives that are capable of identifying conditions that are affecting their quality of life. Consequently, this can allow interventions that might improve the respective life situations (and hence affect millions of people).

At this point I have to state that the research at hand is classified as basic research rather than implementing new ideas or interventions and studying how they affect certain situations. It hence has to be understood as research that analyses the situation of children with disabilities as such. This can provide a basis for further research. Consequently, the importance of conducting quality research on social issues has to be emphasised as a major tool for elucidating the situations of people living under problematic conditions. In this context it has to be pointed out that it is not exclusively the "developed" countries who should initiate research and who are going to change the life situations of people and point at directions of development. The research must rather be conducted by the countries in question and their people themselves to identify their own needs. Although the research at hand was initiated by a Western university and Western researchers, I accomplished it in partnership with Addis Ababa University, involving a team of researchers from the Department of Special Needs Education throughout the research process. Additionally, I consulted and involved the expertise of ministries, schools, teacher education institutions as well as NGOs and associations for people with disabilities. In this way, I tried to obtain emic as well as etic perspectives on the topic and to uncover my possible biases.

Research Including Culture and Disability

As mentioned above, only a small number of qualitative studies on people with disabilities in the majority world are available (McEwan and Butler 2007). Within these, at the beginning especially, studies in the field of anthropology started to engage in the topic (Ingstad and Grut 2005; Ingstad and Whyte 1995, 2007; Neubert and Cloerkes 2001; Kohrman 2005). Regarding cultural diversity and disability, Ingstad and Whyte realised already during their first meeting in 1983 that a big gap existed in the literature on people with disabilities in so-called developing countries. Most of the existing research had been related to Europe and North America (Ingstad and Whyte 1995, 9f). It can be assumed that this situation has changed to a certain extent and more research can be found on the topic (e.g. Barnes and Sheldon 2010;

Beyene and Abate 2005; Braithwaite and Mont 2008; Campbell 2010; Elwan 1999; Fujiura et al. 2005; Grech 2011; Leonhardt 2002; Mengistu 1994; Peresuh and Ndawi 1998; Tomlinson and Abdi 2003; Zehle 2008 etc., just to mention a few).

What is important to note in this regard is that usually the research studies are initiated and led by Western researchers.

Hatton (2004), however, addresses one aspect regarding existing gaps in research in the context of disability and the majority world. He criticises the unsatisfactory attention which research papers pay to culture, basing themselves on a picture of average cultural norms. This approach can lead to the wrong assumption that those norms are interculturally applicable. Arzubiaga et al. (2008) state that researchers from the fields of psychology and special needs education work mainly in "culture-blind" areas. When looking at systematic analyses of empirical studies that have been published over a longer period, it is striking that researchers have been neglecting the role of culture in human development in journals for psychology, special needs education and school psychology. Furthermore, the authors note that analyses and documentation of data that focus on this aspect are missing. Such data could provide researchers and the public with new findings about achievements and behaviour patterns of students which are not only based on the students' deficits (Arzubiaga et al. 2008, 311). According to Neubert and Cloerkes (2001), this gap in research can be explained by the topic's position in a pocket area. The subject that is delimited by the terms "culture" and "disability" is usually dealt with in the areas of sociology of disability and ethnology. It hence constitutes an interdisciplinary field of research. In both of these areas, however, the subject is not the main interest of research. Connections are more likely to be found in the areas of ethnopsychology and obsession (Neubert and Cloerkes 2001, 6). An interdisciplinary approach towards the topic of the book at hand is therefore regarded as desirable as it could broaden the perspectives on disability including cultural aspects. In fact Neubert and Cloerkes are looking at the situation that can be found in the area of ethnology. Thereby, they are criticising first and foremost the low consideration of disability within the research area. In the third edition of their publication, the authors mention that they still feel reassured regarding their assumptions of a gap within research on disability and culture. Hence, they criticise that research does not involve the subject by conducting further research (Neubert and Cloerkes 2001, 7). However, the book at hand aims at paying special attention to the aspect of culture related to disability in Ethiopia.

Even though a mainstream culture exists, the population in Ethiopia is heterogeneous in social and cultural dimensions through external and internal migration processes. As a result, social inequalities are problems faced by the educational systems in different ways. Generally, it can be stated that cultural diversity as well as cultural transformation processes influence certain developments in an educational system (Luciak and Khan-Svik 2008; Tirussew 2005). Therefore, culture has to be regarded as a variable that on the one hand influences education and on the other hand determines perspectives on disability. "Culture" itself cannot be regarded as static (Holzer et al. 1999, 15) as it changes over time. There are geographical as well as historical differences regarding the meaning of culture. The concept of culture is therefore very difficult to identify and to describe (Mason 2007, 175). The concept of Nieke (2008) will be used for the purposes of the book at hand. His concept is a heuristic one that is open for changes. For Nieke, culture is the overall sum of collective patterns of orientation in a lifeworld (Nieke 2008, 50). It has to be assumed that a person is influenced fundamentally by his or her culture and the culture of its predecessors. The idea of "lifeworld" (Lebenswelt) is introduced as an essential term to Nieke's discussion of culture. He states that the lifeworld of a person or group is mainly constituted by the patterns of orientation which are used for orientation in the respective lifeworlds (Nieke 2008, 65). Furthermore, the term lifeworld represents an explanatory approach that is able to describe elementary interpretations within a culture as the only possible and true ones (Nieke 2008, 52).

Hence, the term culture is understood as the availability of patterns of orientation for a person that help her to adjust within a community. The mentioned patterns of orientation are passed on to that person by her environment from the very beginning of her life. In the context of research within an intercultural framework, relevant patterns of orientation have to be identified. These patterns have to be analysed regarding their specific meanings in order to be able to obtain access to the lifeworlds of the participants (Schiemer 2013).

In brief, in the book at hand, culture is seen as a concept that is not static, that is passed on from generation to generation, that influences the people who live in that culture, that changes also through the influence of its people and that provides people with patterns that enable them to orient themselves in their lifeworld.

Finally, the relation between culture and disability is a very important one in the research at hand. On the one hand, I am a foreigner in the culture under investigation, and on the other hand, Ethiopia is a country with a great ethnical diversity. It therefore has to be analysed how disability is perceived and constructed within this culture and which patterns of orientation are offered to the members of the community in order to be able to deal with it.

Reason 2: Political and Developmental Relevance

The Economic and Social Council of the United Nations "expressed concern about the persistent gap that continued to exist between policy and practice regarding mainstreaming the perspective of persons with disabilities in realizing the Millennium Development Goals" (UN 2009, 3). These words can be found in the report of the secretary general on mainstreaming disability in the development agenda. Millennium Development Goal number two strived for achieving universal primary education(UNDP 2010).

The aforementioned report of the secretary general furthermore highlights that the mentioned policy and practice gap have to be filled by taking "concrete measures to incorporate the perspective of persons with disabilities and accessibility requirements in relation to such issues as poverty eradication, education and training, employment and the allocation of resources" (UN 2009, 3). It becomes clear that the topic of disability has started to be taken more seriously during the last years, also regarding development cooperation. In September 2013, for example, the outcome document of the UN General Assembly High-Level Meeting in New York on disability and development was approved.[5] Even more important in this context is for it to mention the Sustainable Development Goals which follow the Millennium Development Goals and show a clear development towards including disability as an important issue. The UN developed an infographic about disability-inclusive SDGs. In relation to education, it says: "Guaranteeing equal and accessible education by building inclusive learning environments and providing the needed assistance for persons with disabilities" (UN 2015).

International Developments Regarding Access to Education

> The legacy of inequality generated by imperialism and sustained through unequal global progress has left the majority of children and youth with disabilities and their families in the global South living in stark conditions of inequity and deprivation in almost every sphere of their lives, including education and health care. (Singal and Muthukrishna 2014, 294)

With this statement in mind, it is even more important to look with a critical lens at international agreements, documents, etc. which should actually prevent such developments but often seem to fail to do so.

Next to a number of international declarations and conventions, important developments within the scientific landscape of special needs and inclusive education can be observed. Debates on principles as well as on shifts of paradigms have opened new possibilities and perspectives. One significant development can be seen in the establishment of the International Classification of Functioning, Disability and Health (ICF) (WHO 2001), which is also discussed in Chap. 4.

The predecessor of the version published in 2001 had been published in 1980 under the title "International Classification of Impairments, Disabilities and Handicaps" (ICIDH) (WHO 1980). Following a number of critical statements, the old version has been revised and renamed ICIDH2 and ICF, respectively. The new version differs significantly from the original ICIDH.

Two years before the publication of the initial ICIDH, the so-called Warnock Report had been published (Warnock 1978; Wedell 2008). This report became a benchmark for further developments within special needs and inclusive education. The concept of special needs education represents the most important aspect of the report and was introduced as an alternative to the categories of disabilities which were in use at that time. Consequently, a reorientation in focus took place from whether a child was disabled to whether a child had special needs and how those needs could be reacted to (Dyson 2007). In this context the topic of inclusive education comes up quite often (UNESCO 2005).

---

[5] Further information can be found at http://www.un.org/disabilities/default.asp?id=1590 (accessed September 25, 2013).

Throughout the mentioned developments, classifications and categorisations have been rejected increasingly also on an international level (Norwich 2007). This process has been called "de-categorisation" and "de-stigmatisation" by different experts (Benkmann 1994; Cloerkes and Markowetz 2003; Stein 2006; Weisser 2003). The ICF is meant to support this process as a framework and to provide a tool for researchers to achieve internationally comparable results.

In general, it can be stated that the use of the ICF and ICF-CY (child and youth version), respectively, for the area of education has certain advantages. The problem of identifying syndromes in educational environments and of clearly defining the scopes of the problems is a serious one. Potential problems are usually complex and influenced by the environment (Hollenweger 2003, 5). The ICF is often expected to be the adequate tool for making those aspects visible. Hollenweger sees further opportunities for special needs education and science in general through the ICF. She mentions common discourses in research, teaching and practice as aspects that can be improved by using the ICF as a basis. Furthermore, she speaks of the standardisation and operationalisation of terminologies and indicators as benefits (Hollenweger 2003, 4). The updated version of the ICF seems to be promising. By revealing alternative possibilities to describe disability, the classification rejects only medical and deficit-oriented models, and the special consideration of environmental factors plays a major role. The special version for children and youth – the ICF-CY – was only published in the year 2007 (WHO), as it was impossible to satisfactorily describe functions, needs and environmental conditions regarding children through the ICF before that. Generally, the concept of the ICF showed deficits in many areas regarding the environment and life situations of children. The ICF-CY was developed to correct these insufficiencies. These are positive developments regarding the classification. It must be stated nevertheless that the research at hand takes a critical stance towards the ICF/ICF-CY.

Active participation in activities that are relevant for education can be considered as essential for school-aged children, their development and future. Possible barriers that hinder participation must be identified and, if possible, be removed. In regard to the discussion on human rights, in which education is viewed as a fundamental right, as well as in the 1960 "Convention against Discrimination in Education" (UNESCO 1960) and the goals of the "Education for All" programme at the World Education Conference 1990 in Jomtien (Thailand) and 2000 in Dakar (Senegal), disability-related efforts concerning education receive special attention. In Dakar, for instance, the set goal was to ensure access to primary education for everyone by 2015 (UNESCO 2000). This is particularly important for people with special needs, as research shows that children and adults with disabilities generally experience restricted access to education (Lindqvist 1999 cited in Peters 2007b, 98). As children who don't have access to primary education often have limited possibilities in their life later on, it is important to offer education without barriers. It is only in this way that equal opportunities can be secured.

The 1994 Salamanca statement framework for action is one of the most important documents in this context (Ainscow 2007a, 147; Peters 2007b). It indicates that regular schools which follow an inclusive approach are the most effective in combating discriminatory attitudes, building an inclusive society and achieving education for all (UNESCO 1994). In relation to the Salamanca declaration, Peters remarks that inclusive measures for education are first and foremost built on the concept of social equation (Peters 2007b, 99). Furthermore, she criticises that inclusion was perceived as one of the leading principles and a basic philosophy for UNESCO in 2002 but decreased in importance during the year 2004. Hence, the topic of disability was not as present as expected in the "Education for All" observation report in 2004 (Peters 2007b, 98). However, the big goal of "Education for All" does not only contain the principle of inclusion, it even determines it. "The philosophy of inclusive education is based on the right of all individuals to quality education with equal opportunities – one that develops their potential and respects their human dignity" (Peters 2007b, 99). Insofar, inclusion must be a constant principle of the goal of "Education for All".

Furthermore, as a human right, education is eligible to contribute to human dignity. Tekeste Negash (2006, 10) argues that the only solution for unworthy life conditions and poverty would be a new definition of human rights. Missing education is often seen as one of the factors that contribute to poverty. If people have to live under degrading life conditions because of poverty, this might also affect their human dignity. Education has been identified as one of the key aspects for solving many of the problems that exist today for minorities and other marginal groups all over the world (Peters 2007b, 105). It therefore has to receive special attention.

At the World Summit for Social Development 1995 in Copenhagen, it was confirmed that poverty is one basic barrier for education (Peters 2007b). Therefore, initiatives for supporting access to education are of special importance in the area of fighting against poverty, particularly in countries of the majority world (Zehle 2008, 56). In this context, the inclusion of people with disabilities plays a major role, since there are also interdependencies between poverty and disability:

> There is a close relationship between poverty and disability: malnutrition, mothers weakened by frequent childbirth, inadequate immunisation programmes, accidents in overcrowded homes, all contribute to an incidence of disability among poor people that is higher than among people living in easier circumstances. Furthermore, disability creates and exacerbates poverty by increasing isolation and economic strain, not just for the individual but for the family: there is little doubt that disabled people are among the poorest in poor countries. (Coleridge 1993, 64)

On this background, it becomes apparent that fighting against poverty can also affect the appearance of disability. Education can definitely be viewed as one instrument against poverty. However, there are many documents and international declarations that contain the implementation of the right to education (UN 2006; UNESCO 1994, 2000). Starting with the "General Declaration of Human Rights", resolution 217 A (III) of December 10, 1948 (UN 1948), lots of situations have already improved. However, the overall goals have seldom been reached satisfactorily.

Education and Development

> One of the greatest problems facing the world today is the growing number of persons who
> are excluded from meaningful participation in the economic, social, political and cultural
> life of their communities. Such a society is neither efficient nor safe. (UNESCO 2003b, 3)

To minimise exclusion and to strengthen societies, education is one of the key elements. It is widely acknowledged that education is one of the most important aspects for human beings to follow the developments of modern societies and to be able to participate in society.

This does not mean that education alone can change a whole society. However, it can provide important impulses for discussions and enable people to participate in fundamental political discussions which can be of great importance to the individual. Similarly, the International Commission on Education for the twenty-first century states for UNESCO that education is "no miracle cure or magic formula" for development. It is rather seen as one of the resources that can lead to appropriate human development which could decrease miseries like poverty, exclusion, ignorance, oppression and war in this world (UNESCO International Commission on Education for the twenty-first century 1996). In this context "feeling like a family" and "developing a sense of belonging" clearly show ways to improve the lives of people (with disabilities) living in poverty (in Addis Ababa) by enabling them to receive quality education. The keyword here is "quality education", as in the schools in which "feeling like a family" was an important value, the quality of education was higher compared to schools without this feeling.

Having identified education as a contributing tool for human development and hence for the improvement of the life situations of many people, it has to be regarded as essential to make education accessible for everyone. Through education, information will be accessible, which is of major importance. "Access to information and means of communication are essential for anyone to realise their rights as a citizen. Without ways to gather knowledge, express opinions or voice demands, it is impossible to obtain an education, find a job or participate in civic affairs" (Krishneer 2013, 20). Knowledge about human rights is difficult to access for people who are illiterate and do not have other possibilities to get information about their rights as citizens and human beings. This deprives them of opportunities for claiming their rights, which might have massive impacts on their lives.

Especially in the majority world, people with disabilities experience a high level of exclusion from education. Particularly in sub-Saharan Africa, education is not a reality for every child (Johnson 2008). For children with disabilities, the situation is even worse. "In principle, all children have the same right to education. In practice, children with disabilities are disproportionately denied this right. In consequence, their ability to enjoy the full rights of citizenship and take up valued roles in society [...] is undermined" (UNICEF 2013c, 27).

The reasons for this degree of exclusion can be found on the one hand within general facilities or teaching methods, as they are usually not accessible for children with disabilities (e.g. multi-storey buildings, use of spoken language not sign language, use of written material and no Braille devices, difficulties in understanding complex issues, teachers' knowledge about special needs, etc.). On the other hand, most of these barriers exist due to a lack of awareness and commitment and due to discriminatory attitudes within a society. As a consequence, people with disabilities are often excluded from various possibilities because barriers do not allow them to access buildings, information, discussions, knowledge, societies, etc.[6]

Johnson articulates that beside the fact that major problems can be found in the educational systems of sub-Saharan countries, there are also problems for children who attend primary schools. He states that less than half of the children enrolled complete their primary education. Furthermore, the skills and knowledge they obtain are at a very low level. Lastly, there is a big gap between rural and urban areas concerning the accessibility of education in general and a difference between the wealth of the families of the children and between girls and boys (Johnson 2008, 7). Children with disabilities are not mentioned by the author. Nevertheless, this group of children has to be referred to especially when talking about discrimination regarding the access to education. The Ethiopian Ministry of Education points out this problem in the following statement:

> Ordinary schools tend to refuse to enrol children with special educational needs, particularly those with apparent disabilities. The school management and teachers are unaware of the universal right to primary education. Instead of reporting about children with special needs to kebele[7] education boards and woreda[8] education officers to search for solutions and support, schools simply send children back home. The need for guidelines and capacity building is evident. (Ethiopian Ministry of Education 2006, 7)

The Ministry brings up very important issues here. The need of awareness, knowledge and guidelines is highlighted. Nevertheless, it is not only the school management and the teachers who must be blamed for refusing to grant access to school for children with disabilities. The parents and the community as such are also responsible. And last but not least, the government has to find further ways to implement the policies and regulations for inclusive education that exist on paper. The

---

[6] According to the report on the state of the world's children regarding children with disabilities, in Ethiopia, gross enrolment in primary schools is 106% for male and 97% for female. The net enrolment rate is 85% male and 80% female. Net attendance is m 64% and f 65%; and survival until the last class of primary school is m 47% and f 84% (UNICEF 2013b, 116).

According to the Ethiopian Ministry of Education, 43,132 children with disabilities (24,825 boys, 18,307 girls) were enrolled in primary schools (levels 1–8) in the year 2011/2012. Distinctions are made between visually, physically, hearing, mentally impaired and others (Ethiopian Ministry of Education 2012, 37). There is no conversion to percentages of the number, so interpretation is difficult.

[7] "Popular term used to describe a cooperative urban neighbourhood association. *Kebeles* were formed after the nationalisation of all urban land and rentable dwellings in July 1975. These cooperatives became the counterpart of the peasant associations developed under the military government's Land Reform Proclamation of March 1975. After their introduction, *kebeles* became the basic unit of urban government and served as instruments of socio-political control in urban areas" (Library of Congress *Glossary Ethiopia*).

[8] Kebele and woreda refer to a certain division of parts of the city into neighbourhoods and districts. Kebele is the smaller unit compared to the woreda.

problem that has been identified by the government regarding special as well as inclusive schools and units is: "All of them are under-resourced. In 2006, there are 17 special needs education schools, 11 of them run by non-governmental organizations" (Ethiopian Ministry of Education 2006, 7). In other words, the government states that it does not have enough resources for establishing the basics for offering special education and even less for supporting special needs and inclusive education. The problem is that such conditions affect children for whom it is difficult to access school in the first place: "Children living in poverty are among the least likely to enjoy the benefits of education and health care, for example, but children who live in poverty and have a disability are even less likely to attend their local school or clinic" (UNICEF 2013c, 1).

Research into disability, culture and education has the possibility to reach beyond superficial problems and obstacles and try to identify anchor points where first steps towards change can start to be effective. It therefore has to be regarded as essential for reaching goals like "Education for All".

Reason 3: Terminological Relevance

The term "disability" cannot be understood as a self-explaining one. In the last decades, there have been many different perspectives and discourses on how to define disability. The same is true for culture amongst others. Therefore, in the following, some insight will be provided into the discussions on the different terms that are of relevance for this book. This illustrates the importance of putting effort into terminological issues within academic research, as it can add to the discussion by revealing important aspects that might have been neglected before.

Disability

The uncertainty regarding the phenomenon of disability leads to different ways of solving the dilemma. In this research, the first reference was the ICF-CY with a biopsychosocial model of disability that was used as a language for starting the development of research instruments. Leaving this first point of orientation behind, disability has to be defined from a different perspective so as to be of use for the understanding of the further research process.

"[…] [O]ne is not born a disabled person, one is observed to be one" (Michailakis 2003, 209). This quotation provides an excellent basis for the discussion of disability for this research study. This sentence represents the main issue which the book at hand has been concerned with: it is predominantly the social environment and specific circumstances that are involved in the construction and deconstruction, respectively, of disability. Disability is not a fact but is observed as such by the surrounding. Hence, this book concentrates on the social environment and attitudes which children with disabilities are exposed to when undergoing education. The tendency to see in persons with disabilities something that is not "normal", something that does not meet expectations, can be observed in different cultures and societies. In observing differences, Weisser (2005) points out that it is necessary to include the fact that differing expectations exist. He defines disability as an experience that results from a conflict between capabilities and expectations. This means that first disability is perceived as an irritation, as something that does not conform with certain expectations, and is later reinforced through repetition (2005, 16). In other words, disability becomes manifest through repeated disappointment of the expectations of a counterpart. In this way, persons with disabilities differ from other persons by continuously irritating the observer. What these expectations are and how they are disappointed differ in various cultures depending on cultural codes, concepts and understandings.

The book at hand focuses on children at school that have been observed by their surroundings to have a disability. Regarding education, the children's social environment has different expectations of children with and without disabilities. Consequently, the former are often expected not to be able to learn. This is of great importance, as education for children with disabilities is essential for opening possibilities of educational equity, social and economic participation and hence a more inclusive society. Therefore, in this book, I understand disability as a phenomenon that is mainly constructed by the (social) environment and influenced by cultural and historical aspects.

In 1995, in their book *Disability and Culture*, the anthropologists Benedicte Ingstad and Susan Reynolds Whyte state that the term "disability" does not exist as an accepted category in all cultures (also see Stoltzfus and Schumm 2011, xiii). Disability can be seen as something that is constructed, for example, by the members of a community.

In this context, I want to mention an important publication which focuses on disability as more than a social category in late-twentieth-century China. It explores how disability "has been emerging and metamorphosing in China as a social, political, and somatic sphere of existence in recent decades" (Kohrman 2005, xi). Kohrman's book thus gives valuable insights into constructions of otherness and related developments in governmental bureaucracies in China.

Different models of disability have been identified to be able to differentiate between different approaches. Nevertheless, not every model is per se explanatory enough for the concepts and pictures of disability that exist in the world. "Obviously, it would be convenient to have a model of disability that is found superior to others, but the multitude of models that have been developed may in fact reflect the multifaceted nature of disability" (Mitra 2006, 236). This statement describes the problem when trying to define disability for an international or intercultural audience. There is no definition that can satisfactorily define disability on a global level. How disability is seen depends on too many different aspects in too many different cultures in this world. Hence, it is obvious that it does not make sense to look for a globally accepted definition of disability. Instead, it is important to get an idea of the concept of disability in the area in which research is conducted. This will enable researchers to interpret data on the basis that has been created on-site.

Disabilities of all kinds can be found in cultures all over the world, in all stages of life. In many cultures in the majority world, the image of disability has been influenced by external perspectives. Very often, a medical concept of disability is prevalent. This can be traced back to international organisations that have worked in that area, research projects, but also to political measures taken by the respective countries (Ingstad and Whyte 1995; Neubert and Cloerkes 2001). In this context it is difficult to deduce the original perception of disability. Therefore, it is essential to get a deep understanding of the way disability is perceived and dealt with in a society. In Ethiopia, aspects like physical limitations, learning abilities, independence, family life and inclusion into sociocultural and leisure time activities as well as the person's contribution to society might play a major role (Tirussew 2005, 7). Additionally, a society's knowledge and awareness of disability are of great importance. The state's actions and policies towards an inclusive society do not necessarily reflect so much the general attitudes of a society as the goals pursued by its government. The failure to achieve a more inclusive society is often rooted in socio-political and historical developments.

In regard to Ethiopia, Tirussew states: "There have been as many different views and understandings of disability and persons with disabilities in the history of mankind as there are today in Ethiopia" (Tirussew 2005, 92). This indicates that not only different nations have different perspectives on disability but also within a nation there are different views on disability. Not surprisingly, the people's perception of disability in different contexts is hence more related to the respective community, culture and ethnicity than to the simple boarders of a land mass. In this book I attempt to elucidate the way disability has been constructed by the participants of the research study. Furthermore, I will show that perceptions of disabilities are not static but can change during the lifetime of an individual.

Models of Disability

Disability is a concept that has been discussed and negotiated for a very long time. Throughout this process of discussion, different directions and models have developed.

The 1960s serve as a starting point to enter the discussion about disability, as this was the time when disability began to become a socio-political issue (in the Western world). During the 1970s the establishment of an international disability movement can be observed. Additionally, the social model of disability started to have an impact on academics, politics and law (Samaha 2007). In the 1980s the formation of the Disabled People's International (DPI) and the establishment of the disability studies (Oliver 1990) followed (Waldschmidt 2005). The year 2001 marks the time when through the publication of the ICF, representing the biopsychosocial model, disability became an issue of mainstreaming in development discussions (WHO

2001). Many more developments and discourses could be mentioned at this point, but this chapter intends to give a brief insight rather than a broad overview of those discussions. At the same time, I want to put emphasis on the fact that Western knowledge plays a major role also in this context. As Singal and Muthukrishna state very clearly: "Undoubtedly, disability is a hugely debated and politicised issue, especially in relation to how it is defined. However, the models which frame these discussions are exclusively anchored in the industrialised, liberalised and individualistic scripting of the North" (Singal and Muthukrishna 2014, 294).

For this exact reason, I consider it as important to look at those models of disability – Western in origin – as this enables us to understand the biases that cloud and influence our view when looking at disability in the global South.

In the literature, the biomedical model, the social (or socio-political) model and the biopsychosocial model are some of the most discussed ones and will therefore be discussed here as examples (Altman 2001; Bickenbach et al. 1999; Burchardt 2004; McEwan and Butler 2007; Samaha 2007; Smart 2009; Waldschmidt 2005). Approaches towards a cultural model, an individual model, a moral model or a religious model of disability (Smart 2009; Waldschmidt 2005), amongst others, can also be found.

Within these approaches, disability has been described from different perspectives including medical, economic, socio-political and administrative points of view (Altman 2001, 98). It can be quite confusing to try to get an orientation within the different approaches, perspectives and schools of definitions and models. The aim of this chapter is, however, to illustrate briefly the importance which the decision on a certain model of disability can have and to exemplify three of the models in order to provide the readers with an idea of existing differences in models of disability from a Western point of view.

The *medical model* of disability has been very strong and predominant for a long time and is still referred to in many areas. "Definitions that have been developed for clinical circumstances and administrative implementation are those most commonly known among the total population and have had the greatest influence on our understanding of this phenomenon until recent years" (Altman 2001, 98). It is also a model that has been fought against by institutions and organisations that think in a more holistic way, as it reduces a person to its biological functions and does not include environmental and social factors in the definition of disability.

The *social model* on the other hand considers society as the one main factor in the construction of disability. "A social model of disability relates a person's disadvantage to the combination of personal traits and social setting" (Samaha 2007, 1251). One of the main actors of this approach is Michael Oliver (1990) and the field of disability studies. Samaha further states: "The model has the potential to knock out ill-considered defences of the status quo based on nature and necessity, just as legal realism and other reform advocacy attempted to unsettle assumptions in the past" (2007, 1308). However, the author finishes by noting that this model is also incomplete and in need of more reflection and a broader perspective on disability (Samaha 2007, 1308).

Last but not least, the biopsychosocial model can be found in the International Classification of Functioning, Disability and Health (WHO 2001). The approach chosen in the classification aims to include medical as well as psychological and social perspectives on disability. This can be considered as a rather ambitious attempt, as the ICF also claims international and intercultural applicability (Üstün et al. 2001). I already mentioned the classification several times and will examine it under a critical lens in Chap. 4.

It can be stated that models of disability have always had and still have a major influence on people's perceptions of disability.

> […] [T]he daily lives of people with disabilities, if and how they are educated, if and where they work, and their social and familial life, in large part are determined by models of disability. Perhaps, most important, models of disability exert a powerful influence on the public perception of disability and public's response to people with disabilities. (Smart 2009, 3)

Smart (2009) also mentions that models of disability go as far as having the power to influence and shape the self-identity of people with disabilities. Generally, models of disability define disability; they are not a reality or a fact but human made. None of the models is morally neutral and all of them are time- and culture-bound. Furthermore, each model of disability is reductionist or incomplete (Smart 2009). These aspects spell out the critical stance that should be taken when choosing a model of disability for working on the topic of disability – especially in the context of countries of the majority world.

Special Education, Special Needs Education and Inclusive Education

> Within many schools, the predominant approach to teaching and learning is still based on the grouping of pupils into classes. The rigidities this imposes on children and young people, and the problems it creates for teachers, have been widely recognised. (Wedell 2005, 4)

Special education represents a concept of educating people with disabilities by placing them in separate schools or classrooms in order to be able to implement interventions. It is a concept that has been criticised from its beginning but has also been seen as a solution to the right to education for everyone. Special education has increasingly been seen as a practice excluding rather than including children with disabilities in society and providing them with quality education. Hence, marginalisation is still seen as a consequence of special education practices (Florian 2007, 8f.). Referring to Minow (1990), Florian states that "the laws and policies that are created to protect vulnerable groups also serve to marginalize them" (Florian 2007, 10). She calls it a vicious cycle that is created by the approach of special education, where rights should be protected but at the same time stigmatisation is created (Florian 2007). This problem has been referred to as the "dilemma of difference" by several authors (Florian 2007; Minow 1990; Norwich 2008; Terzi 2008, amongst others). Furthermore, Florian identifies two main problems regarding special education: the concept of "normal" that is perceived as common and positive on the one hand and the already mentioned dilemma of difference on the other hand. The most promising approach to tackling these problems would be a change in the discourse about difference (Florian 2007, 12).

The term "special education" was changed into "special needs education" by the International Standard Classification of Education in 1997. According to Florian, a distinction between the two terms is essential. The former has been associated with the need of placement in special schools or classes in order to be able to make an intervention and receive provisions. However, the new term addresses educational interventions and support that aim at special educational needs and are not bound to special classrooms and applicable at any location[9] (Florian 2007). The "central dilemma", as Florian calls it, remains regardless of which term is used. As soon as there is a deviation from the mainstream like an additional need (support, provisions, etc.), the children in question differ from the rest. This is often assumed to indicate a lower quality as a learner, which makes it the central dilemma (Florian 2007, 13).

> The idea of special education as a parallel or separate system of education to that which is provided to the majority of children has been challenged by notions of inclusion in which all children are part of one education system. The problem, of course, is that inclusive education is not a denial of individual difference, but an accommodation of it, within the structures and processes that are available to all learners. (Florian 2007, 10)

The concept of inclusive education follows international developments, which abandon one-dimensional, mainly medically influenced and deficit-oriented models of disability (Altman 2001) and take on a social and multidimensional perspective (Hollenweger 2006, 48ff.). Inclusion aspires to shape environments in such a way that no one is excluded. Additionally, inclusive education tries to avoid classifications of children with disabilities. Instead it is aimed to switch towards descriptions of the environment in the child's educational surrounding (Biewer 2009a, b).

However, the insufficient knowledge about successful implementation of inclusive programmes regarding children with disabilities in schools confronts scientists with serious challenges. It is important to be able to identify the degree of inclusion which students with disabilities are enabled to achieve or not. This would lead to possibilities of identifying aspects that might be responsible for successful or unsuccessful inclusion. Judith Hollenweger (2006) puts the emphasis on studying children's activity and participation in order to identify degrees of successful inclusion. Yet she states that we do not have enough information about the processes in school that possibly affect participation and the acquirement of competencies (Hollenweger 2006, 52). This lack of information describes a gap in research that can also be attributed to other countries, including Ethiopia.

When talking about participation, the question of equal opportunities especially regarding people with disabilities moves into the centre of attention. Hence, barriers

---

[9] See Section "International Developments Regarding Access to Education" for more information on special needs education and the Warnock Report (Warnock 1978).

that hinder participation in private, public and everyday life have to be diminished (Hollenweger 2006). One significant aspect when analysing a problematic situation in a given society is the perception of the problem in the respective culture (Hollenweger 2006, Holzer et al. 1999, 12). In other words, it has great influence where people localise the problem. Regarding the topic of disability, the question would be: do people see the problem located within the person with disability, within society, within the environment or within immediate surroundings and the lifeworld of the person or somewhere else? One could also ask which model of disability is the prevailing one. Additionally, it has to be elucidated which other influencing factors (personal situations, economic aspects, etc.) are considered when people with disabilities and problems they are confronted with get attention. This discussion is of special interest for special needs and inclusive education, as it helps determine problems that cause exclusion. The clarification of perceptions of a problem shows at which points initiatives for improvement have to start.

Inclusive education is mentioned as one of the aspired goals of the Ethiopian government. In other words, inclusion is one of the keywords for the Ethiopian government regarding future developments in the area of education. However, there are difficulties concerning the definition of inclusive education. "Whilst recent years have seen an increased interest in the idea of inclusive education, the field remains confused as to what this implies" (Ainscow 2007b, 3). It is clear that an agenda aiming at inclusive education comes about with "economic and political contexts underpinned by cultural values" (Peters 2007a, 128). One important motor for striving towards inclusive education in Ethiopia is the signing and ratification of the "Convention on the Rights of Persons with Disabilities" (UN 2006) by the Ethiopian government in 2010. But even before this, Ethiopia aimed towards making schools accessible for children with disabilities following the principle of inclusive education.

The UNESCO offers a clear statement on the meaning of inclusive education which should be applicable internationally as it is drawn from the Salamanca Framework of Action which was developed by an international consortium:

> The fundamental principle of the inclusive school is that all children should learn together, wherever possible, regardless of any difficulties or differences they may have. Inclusive schools must recognize and respond to the diverse needs of their students, accommodating both different styles and rates of learning and ensuring quality education to all through appropriate curricula, organizational arrangements, teaching strategies, resource use and partnerships with their communities. There should be a continuum of support and services to match the continuum of special needs encountered in every school. (1994, 11f.)

The Salamanca Framework has been mentioned to have further consequences pointing towards a positive development regarding inclusive education. Ainscow states that it has been used "to formulate strategies that will support movements towards inclusive schooling" (Ainscow 1997, 3). Another paper that cannot be ignored in this context is the index for inclusion (Booth and Ainscow 2002), which has been cited as the "most detailed explanation available about what an inclusive school looks like [...][10]" (Ainscow 2007b, 4).

---

[10] Details can be obtained from http://www.csie.org.uk/

In the context of Ethiopia, a developmental aspect which is also connected to the Sustainable Development Goals has to be added. In this context, Peters describes inclusive education as a complex issue with overlapping areas (e.g. health, education, social welfare and employment sectors). This might lead to certain problems for the development of appropriate policies (Ainscow 2007a, 117). She furthermore highlights the problematic aspect of identifying special needs by using classification systems that are not the same between and within countries (Peters 2007a), 118). Generally, it can be stated that inclusive education has been identified as "one of the key strategies to address issues of marginalization and exclusion for vulnerable children, notably girls and disabled children" by the Education for All agreement (Peters 2007a,117). Ainscow sees a difference in the perceptions of inclusive education within countries compared to the international level:

> In many countries, inclusive education is still thought of as an approach to serving children with disabilities within general education settings. However, internationally, it is increasingly seen more broadly as a reform that supports and welcomes diversity amongst all learners (United Nations Educational, Scientific and Cultural Organization (UNESCO, 2001). (Peters 2007b, 3)

It has been demonstrated that there are definitions of inclusive education that might not coincide with views on inclusive education taken by different countries. Different processes within countries and on a global level might influence the meaning and aims of inclusive education in a constant process. However, the UNESCO sees a high potential in the concept of inclusive education:

> Inclusive education encourages policy-makers and managers to look at the barriers within the education system, how they arise and how they can be removed. These barriers usually include:
>
> * inappropriately-designed curricula
> * teachers who are not trained to work with children who have a wide range of needs
> * inappropriate media for teaching
> * inaccessible buildings. (2003a, 2)

These aspects are certainly some of the most prevailing barriers within different education systems that produce obstacles for people with disabilities to access education. Finally, there are also positive developments regarding the improvement of inclusive education. Different assessments of needs and feasibility studies are taken seriously and are used as contributions to the enhancement of inclusive education. Consequently, these steps lead to sustainability (Peters 2007a, 127).

Inclusive education has been presented as a programme for education that should enable every child to access education on the basis of equal opportunities and emphasis on competencies rather than on deficits. This means that children could be taught together by using their diversity as a potential for the whole class. Special needs therefore have to be identified for every child in the class to be able to support the individual child according to his/her needs.

Summary of Relevant Aspects

This study is considered to be of high relevance within the field of international special needs and inclusive education with emphasis on a country of the majority world. By conducting research in the area of disability and education, I want to contribute to filling a gap regarding knowledge about people with disabilities in educational systems in the majority world. This will also contribute to gathering information about what further steps must be taken regarding development, especially considering international goals like the Sustainable Development Goals as well as the "Education for All" framework (UNESCO 2000). The book at hand aims at adding new perspectives to the issue of special needs and inclusive education by concentrating on the experiences and topics raised by participants. It focuses on people who are directly involved in the educational process. Furthermore, the book raises awareness and underscores the importance of improving inclusive education in primary schools in Ethiopia. Last but not least, working on the subject of disability in an international context enriches critical perspectives on classifications and categorisations and contributes to a perspective on disability which includes the environment as one of the main players in constructing disability. Thereby, the aspect of culture is given special emphasis. My research thus contributes to an international discussion about disability, special needs and inclusive education, development and culture.

Approaching the Field with a Question

On the basis of the previous explanations and illustrations, the book at hand examines the issue of inclusion and exclusion, participation and activity of children with disabilities in an educational environment. The formulation of a research question usually determines the methods that can best answer the question. In qualitative research, a research question can be open for change during the investigation. The primary question about a topic or phenomenon may not be the question that is eventually answered (Ingstad and Grut 2005, 6). In this research study, I am especially interested in processes that can be identified in the interviews. I therefore need to follow the main issues raised by the participants. Phenomena that are of importance to the interviewees can be identified and become significant for the whole research. The most appropriate approach for this is grounded theory. Therefore, in this research, I use grounded theory for approaching the area of research. Birks and Mills note that "[i]n grounded theory, it is the research process that generates the question" (Birks and Mills 2011, 20).

The research question I used to start into the field was:

Which environmental factors facilitate or restrict activity and participation of school-aged children with disabilities in the field of education in Addis Ababa, Ethiopia?

This question addressed an extensive field that had to be narrowed down at later stages of the investigation. Furthermore, the relatively open formulation allowed me to go more into depth during the research following the content provided by the participants. The enquiry had to be refined in the course of the research according to the ongoing process of interviewing, analysing and interpreting. The question which developed in the course of the research process is the synthesis of different questions which arose in the process of working with the data and in the field:

> In which ways does the school access of children with disabilities support or hinder children, parents and teachers in dealing with emotional stress situations which are created through negative cultural and societal attitudes towards disability?

This shows that the focus was placed on three phenomena which proved to be the most meaningful to the participants: the fact that the child with a disability was attending school, the teaching profession as such and the negative societal attitudes towards disability.

References

Ainscow, M. (1997). Towards inclusive schooling. *British Journal of Special Education, 24*(1), 3–6.

Ainscow, M. (2007a). From special education to effective schools for all: A review for progress so far. In L. Florian (Ed.), *The sage handbook of special education* (pp. 146–159). London/Thousand Oaks/New Delhi: Sage.

Ainscow, M. (2007b). Taking an inclusive turn. *Journal of Research in Special Educational Needs, 7*(1), 3–7.

Altman, B. M. (2001). Disability, definitions, models, classification schemes, and applications. In G. L. Albrecht, K. D. Seelman, & M. Bury (Eds.), *Handbook of disability studies* (pp. 97–122). Thousand Oaks/London/New Delhi: Sage.

Arzubiaga, A. E., et al. (2008). Beyond research on cultural minorities: Challenges and implications of research as situated cultural practice. *Exceptional Children, 74*(3), 309–327.

Badley, E. (2008). Enhancing the conceptual clarity of the activity and participation components of the international classification of functioning, disability and health. *Social Science & Medicine, 66*, 2335–2345.

Barnes, C., & Sheldon, A. (2010). Disability, politics and poverty in a majority world context. *Disability & Society, 25*(7), 771–782.

Benkmann, R. (1994). Dekategorisierung und Heterogenität – aktuelle Probleme schulischer Integration von Kindern mit Lernschwierigkeiten in den Vereinigten Staaten und der Bundesrepublik. *Sonderpädagogik, 24*(1), 4–13.

Beyene, B., & Abate, S. T. (2005). Access to information and communication technology (ICT) and education for visual impaired people in Ethiopia. In S. Brüne & B. Tafla (Eds.), *Auf dem Weg zum modernen Äthiopien. Festschrift für Bairu Tafla* (pp. 29–47). Münster: LIT-Verl..

Bickenbach, J. E., et al. (1999). Models of disablement, universalism and the international classification of impairments, disabilities and handicaps. *Social Science & Medicine, 48*, 1173–1187.

Biewer, G. (2002). Ist die ICIDH-2 für die Heilpädagogik brauchbar? In K. Bundschuh (Ed.), *Sonder- und Heilpädagogik in der modernen Leistungsgesellschaft. Krise oder Chance?* (pp. 293–301). Bad Heilbrunn/Obb.: Klinkhardt.

Biewer, G. (2009a). *Grundlagen der Heilpädagogik und Inklusiven Pädagogik*. Bad Heilbrunn: Klinkhardt.

Biewer, G. (2009b). Vom Verschwinden der Etiketten zum Verlust der Inhalte. Heilpädagogische Klassifizierung im internationalen Vergleich. In A. Bürli, U. Strasser, & A. D. Stein (Eds.), *Integration/Inklusion aus internationaler Sicht* (pp. 169–176). Bad Heilbrunn: Klinkhardt.

Birks, M., & Mills, J. (2011). *Grounded theory. A practical guide.* Los Angeles/London/New Delhi/Singapore/Washington, DC: Sage.

Booth, T., & Ainscow, M. (2002). *Index for inclusion. Developing learning and participation in schools.* London: CSIE Centre for Studies on Inclusive Education.

Braithwaite, J., & Mont, D. (2008). *Disability and poverty: A survey of World Bank poverty assessments and implications.* (Discussion Paper No. 0805).

Bulmer, M., & Warwick, D. P. (1993). *Social research in developing countries. Surveys and censuses in the Third world.* London: UCL Press.

Burchardt, T. (2004). Capabilities and disability: The capabilities framework and the social model of disability. *Disability & Society, 19*(7), 735–751.

Campbell, C. (2010). Disability and international development: Towards inclusive global health. *Psychology, Health & Medicine, 15*(5), 622–623.

Chapireau, F. (2005). The environment in the international classification of functioning, disability and health. *Journal of Applied Research in Intellectual Disabilities, 18,* 305–311.

Cloerkes, G., & Markowetz, R. (2003). Stigmatisierung und Entstigmatisierung im gemeinsamen Unterricht. *Zeitschrift für Heilpädagogik, 54*(11), 452–460.

Coleridge, P. (1993). *Disability, liberation and development.* Oxford: Oxfam.

Denzin, N. K., & Lincoln, Y. S. (Eds.). (2005). *The sage handbook of qualitative research.* Thousand Oaks/London/New Delhi: Sage.

Dyson, A. (2007). Sonderpädagogische Theoriebildung im Wandel – ein Beitrag aus Englischer Sicht. In C. Liesen, U. Hoyningen-Süess, & K. Bernath (Eds.), *Inclusive education: Modell für die Schweiz? Internationale und nationale Perspektiven im Gespräch* (pp. 93–121). Bern: Haupt.

Elwan, A. (1999). *Title, Social Protection Discussion Paper Series.* Washington, DC: Social Protection Unit. Human Development Network. The World Bank.

Ethiopian Ministry of Education. (2006). *Special needs education program strategy. Emphasising inclusive education to meet the UPEC and EFA goals.* Addis Ababa: Ethiopian Ministry of Education.

Ethiopian Ministry of Education. (2012). *Education statistics annual abstract. 2004 e.C (2011/2012).* Addis Ababa: Ethiopian Ministry of Education, EMIS, Planning and Resource Mobilization Directorate.

Florian, L. (2007). Reimagining special education. In L. Florian (Ed.), *The sage handbook of special education* (pp. 7–20). London/Thousand Oaks/New Delhi: Sage.

Fujiura, G. T., et al. (2005). Disability statistics in the developing world: A reflection on the meanings in our numbers. *Journal of Applied Research in Intellectual Disabilities, 18*(4), 295–304.

Grech, S. (2011). Recolonising debates or perpetuated coloniality? Decentring the spaces of disability, development and community in the global South. *International Journal of Inclusive Education, 15*(1), 87–100.

Hatton, C. (2004). Cultural issues. In E. Emerson et al. (Eds.), *The international handbook of applied research in intellectual disabilities* (pp. 41–60). Chichester: Wiley.

Hirschberg, M. (2003). Wie wird Behinderung beurteilt? Anmerkungen zum Menschenbild der Klassifikation von Behinderung der Weltgesundheitsorganisation. *eWi Report* (Vol. 28).

Hollenweger, J. (1998). "Behinderung" neu denken: Ein Schritt nach vorne? Die Revision der Internationalen Klassifikation der Schädigungen, Funktionsstörungen und Beeinträchtigungen (ICIDH). *Schweizerische Zeitschrift für Heilpädagogik, 12,* 24–29.

Hollenweger, J. (2003). Die Internationale Klassifikation der Funktionsfähigkeit, Behinderung und Gesundheit (ICF) und ihre Bedeutung für Bildungssysteme (Teil II). *Schweizerische Zeitschrift für Heilpädagogik, 11,* 40–46.

Hollenweger, J. (2006). Der Beitrag der Weltgesundheitsorganisation zur Klärung konzeptueller Grundlagen einer inklusiven Pädagogik. In M. Dederich, H. Greving, & P. Rödler (Eds.), *Inklusion statt Integration? Heilpädagogik als Kulturtechnik* (pp. 45–61). Gießen: Psychosozial.

Holzer, B., et al. (Eds.). (1999). *Disability in different cultures: Reflections on local concepts.* Bielefeld: Transcript.

Ingstad, B., & Grut, L. (2005). *Using qualitative methods in studying the link between disability and poverty. Developing a methodology and pilot testing in Kenya.* Report for SINTEF, Oslo.

Ingstad, B., & Whyte, S. R. (Eds.). (1995). *Disability and culture.* Berkeley/Los Angeles/London: University of California Press.

Ingstad, B., & Whyte, S. R. (Eds.). (2007). *Disability in local and global worlds.* Berkeley: University of California Press.

Johnson, D. (Ed.). (2008). *The changing landscape of education in Africa: Quality, equality and democracy.* Oxford: Cambridge University Press.

Kohrman, M. (2005). *Bodies of difference. Experiences of disability and institutional advocacy in the making of modern China.* Berkeley/Los Angeles/London: University of California Press.

Krishneer, S. (2013). Perspective: For deaf young people, language is the key. In UNICEF (Ed.), The state of the world's children 2013. *Children with disabilities* (pp. 20–21). New York: UNICEF.

Lawn, M. (Ed.). (2013). *The rise of data in education systems. Collection, visualization and use.* Oxford: Symposium Books.

Leonhardt, A. (2002). Hörgeschädigtenpädagogik in einem Entwicklungsland – dargestellt am Beispiel der Alpha School for the Deaf in Addis Abeba (Äthiopien). *Die neue Sonderschule, 47*(5), 333–347.

Luciak, M., & Khan-Svik, G. (2008). Intercultural education and intercultural learning in Austria – Critical reflections on theory and practice. *Intercultural Education, 19*(5), 493–504.

Mason, M. (2007). Comparing cultures. In M. Bray, B. Adamson, & M. Mason (Eds.), *Comparative education research. Approaches and methods* (pp. 165–196). Hong Kong: Springer.

McEwan, C., & Butler, R. (2007). Disability and development: Different models, different places. *Geography Compass, 1*(3), 448–466.

Mengistu, L. G. (1994). *Psychological classification of students with and without handicaps. A test of Holland's theory in Ethiopia.* Jyväskylä: University of Jyväskylä.

Michailakis, D. (2003). The systems theory concept of disability: One is not born a disabled person, one is observed to be one. *Disability & Society, 18*(2), 209–229.

Miles, S., & Ahuja, A. (2007). Learning from difference: Sharing international experiences of developments in inclusive education. In L. Florian (Ed.), *The sage handbook of special education* (pp. 131–145). London/Thousand Oaks/New Delhi: Sage.

Miles, S., Fefoame, G. O., Mulligan, D., & Haque, Z. (2012). Education for diversity: The role of networking in resisting disabled people's marginalisation in Bangladesh. *Compare: A Journal of Comparative and International Education, 42*(2), 283–302.

Minow, M. (1990). *Making all the difference: Inclusion exclusion and American law.* Ithaca: Cornell University Press.

Mitra, S. (2006). The capability approach and disability. *Journal of Disability Policy Studies, 16*(4), 236–247.

Mutua, K., & Swadener, B. (2011). Challenges to inclusive education in Kenya: Postcolonial perspectives and family narratives. In A. Artiles, E. Kozleski, & F. Waitoller (Eds.), *Inclusive education. Examining equity in five continents* (pp. 201–222). Cambridge, MA: Harvard Education Press.

Neubert, D., & Cloerkes, G. (2001). *Behinderung und Behinderte in verschiedenen Kulturen. Eine vergleichende Analyse ethnologischer Studien.* Heidelberg: Winter "Edition S".

Nieke, W. (2008). *Interkulturelle Erziehung und Bildung. Wertorientierungen im Alltag.* Wiesbaden: VS Verlag für Sozialwissenschaften.

Norwich, B. (2007). Categories of special educational needs. In L. Florian (Ed.), *The sage handbook of special education* (pp. 55–66). London/Thousand Oaks/New Delhi: Sage.

Norwich, B. (2008). *Dilemmas of difference, inclusion and disability.* Routledge: London/New York.

OECD. (2008). *Policy brief: Ten steps to equity in education.* Retrieved November 23, 2016, from http://www.oecd.org/education/school/39989494.pdf

Oliver, M. (1990). *The politics of disablement: A sociological approach.* New York: Macmillan.

Peresuh, M., & Ndawi, O. P. (1998). Education for all – The challenges for a developing country: The Zimbabwe experience. *International Journal of Inclusive Education, 2*(3), 209–224.

Peters, S. (2007a). Inclusion as a strategy for achieving education for all. In L. Florian (Ed.), *The sage handbook of special education* (pp. 117–130). London/Thousand Oaks/New Delhi: Sage.

Peters, S. (2007b). "Education for all?" A historical analysis of international inclusive education policy and individuals with disabilities. *Journal of Disability Policy Studies, 18*(2), 98–108.

Samaha, A. M. (2007). What good is the social model of disability? *The University of Chicago Law Review*, 1251–1308.

Schiemer, M. (2013). Zur Problematik der Interpretation von Daten aus fremden Kulturen. In E. O. Graf (Ed.), *Globale Perspektiven auf Behinderung* (pp. 129–146). Berlin: epubli GmbH.

Singal, N., & Muthukrishna, N. (2014). Education, childhood and disability in countries of the South – Re-positioning the debates. *Childhood, 21*(3), 293–307.

Smart, J. F. (2009). The power of models of disability. *Journal of Rehabilitation, 25*(2), 3–11.

Srivastava, M., de Boer, A., & Pijl, S. (2015). Inclusive education in developing countries: A closer look at its implementation in the last 10 years. *Educational Review, 2015, 67*(2), 179–195.

Stein, R. (2006). Beeinträchtigungen und Behinderungen. In G. Hansen & R. Stein (Eds.), *Kompendium Sonderpädagogik* (pp. 9–24). Bad Heilbrunn: Klinkhardt.

Stoltzfus, M., & Schumm, D. (2011). Editor's introduction. In D. Schumm & M. Stoltzfus (Eds.), *Disability and religious diversity*. New York: Palgrave Macmillan.

Tekeste, N. (2006). *Education in Ethiopia. From crisis to the brink of collapse*. Uppsala: Nordiska Afrikainstitutet.

Terzi, L. (2008). Beyond the dilemma of difference. The capability approach in disability and special educational needs. In L. Florian & M. J. McLaughlin (Eds.), *Disability classification in education. Issues and perspectives* (pp. 244–262). Thousand Oaks/London/New Delhi/Singapore: Corwin Press.

Tirussew, T. (2005). *Disability in Ethiopia: Issues, insights and implications*. Addis Ababa: Addis Ababa University Printing Press.

Tomlinson, S., & Abdi, O. A. (2003). Disability in Somaliland. *Disability & Society, 18*(7), 911–920.

Turmusani, M. (2004). An eclectic approach to disability research: A majority world perspective. *Asia Pacific Disability Rehabilitation Journal, 15*(1), 3–11.

UN. (1948). *"Allgemeinen Erklärung der Menschenrechte" Resolution 217 a (III) vom 10. 12. 1948*. Genf: United Nations.

UN. (2001). *Guidelines and recommendations for the development of disability statistics*. New York: United Nations.

UN. (2006). *Convention on the rights of persons with disabilities and optional protocol*. New York: United Nations.

UN. (2015). *Sustainable Development Goals (SDG)*. Retrieved November 23, 2016, from https://sustainabledevelopment.un.org/topics

UN Enable. (2013). *Factsheet on persons with disabilities*. Retrieved November 23, 2016, from http://www.un.org/disabilities/documents/toolaction/pwdfs.pdf

UN Secretary General. (2009). *Mainstreaming disability in the development agenda, Report for the United Nations Commission for Social Development*. New York: United Nations.

UNDP. (2010). *The path to achieving the millenium development goals: A synthesis of MDG evidence from around the world*. New York: UNDP.

UNESCO. (1960). *Convention against discrimination in education*. Paris: UNESCO.

UNESCO. (1994). *The Salamanca statement and framework for action on special needs education. World conference on special needs education. Access and quality*. Paris: UNESCO.

UNESCO. (1996). *International commission on education for the twenty-first century. Education: The necessary utopia, Report for UNESCO*. Paris: UNESCO.

UNESCO. (2000). *The Dakar framework for action. Education for all: Meeting our collective commitments*. Paris: UNESCO.

UNESCO (2001). International Bureau of Education. The Development of Education. National Report of Ethiopia by Ethiopian National Agency for UNESCO (Final Version) March 2001. Retrieved on June 6, 2016 from: http://www.ibe.unesco.org/International/ICE/natrap/Ethiopia.pdf

UNESCO. (2003a). *Open file on inclusive education. Support materials for managers and administrators*. Paris: UNESCO.

UNESCO. (2003b). *Overcoming exclusion through inclusive approaches in education. A challenge and a vision.* Paris: UNESCO.

UNESCO. (2005). *Guidelines for inclusion: Ensuring access to education for all.* Paris: UNESCO.

UNICEF. (2013a). Educating teachers for children with disabilities. Mapping, scoping and best practices exercise in the context of developing inclusive education. *Rights, education and protection (REAP) project.* (UNICEF) Retrieved November 23, 2016, from https://dl.dropboxusercontent.com/u/8608264/UNICEF%20Educating%20Teachers%20for%20Children%20with%20Disabilities1a.pdf

UNICEF. (2013b). *The state of the world's children 2013. Children with disabilities, Report for United Nations Children's Fund.* New York: UNICEF.

UNESCO. (2001a). International Bureau of Education. The Development of Education. National Report of Ethiopia by Ethiopian National Agency for UNESCO (Final Version) March 2001. Retrieved on June 6, 2016, from http://www.ibe.unesco.org/International/ICE/natrap/Ethiopia.pdf

Üstün, T. B., et al. (Eds.). (2001). *Disability and culture. Universalism and culture. ICIDH-2 series. Published on behalf of the world health organisation.* Seattle: Hofgrefe & Huber.

Waldschmidt, A. (2005). Disability Studies: Individuelles, soziales und/oder kulturelles Modell von Behinderung? *Psychologie und Gesellschaftskritik, 1,* 9–31.

Warnock, H. M. (1978). *Special educational needs. Report of the committee of enquiry into the education of handicapped children and young people.* Report for English Parliament, Secretary of State for Education and Science, the Secretary of State for Scotland and the Secretary of State for Wales by command of her Majesty, London.

Wedell, K. (2005). Dilemmas in the quest for inclusion. *British Journal of Special Education, 32*(1), 3–11.

Wedell, K. (2008). Evolving dilemmas about categorisation. In L. Florian & M. J. Mc Laughlin (Eds.), *Disability classification in education. Issues and perspectives* (pp. 47–67). Thousand Oaks/London/New Delhi/Singapore: Sage.

Weisser, J. (2003). "Behinderung": Zur Politik des Begriffs. Eine funktionale Analyse. *Schweizerische Zeitschrift für Heilpädagogik, 9*(10), 15–22.

Weisser, J. (2005). *Behinderung, Ungleichheit und Bildung. Eine Theorie der Behinderung.* Bielefeld: Transcript.

WHO. (1980). *International classification of impairment, disability and handicap (ICIDH).* Geneva: World Health Organization.

WHO. (2001). *International classification of functioning, disability and health.* Geneva: World Health Organization.

WHO. (2011). *World report on disability.* Geneva: World Health Organization.

Zehle, J. (2008). *Dropout im Schuleingangsbereich an staatlichen Primarschulen Äthiopiens als ein Indikator für Lernschwierigkeiten. Eine wissenschaftliche Untersuchung im Rahmen der interkulturell und international vergleichenden Sonderpädagogik in der qualitativen Eentwicklungszusammenarbeit.* Berlin: Logos.

Chapter 4
Facts and Challenges Regarding Grounded Theory, the ICF and Ethical Issues

Abstract Regarding methodology and methods, grounded theory becomes the major tool. Thereby, Kathy Charmaz is the leading scholar I am referring to. As grounded theory is discussed on a very broad basis in the scientific community, also critical voices are included. However, it becomes clear that I am following the constructivist tradition and I am basing my research on these epistemological grounds. The interpretive character of the research method is also highlighted.

As a second aspect, I am describing and discussing the International Classification of Functioning, Disability and Health – Child and Youth Version (ICF-CY) in detail. The ICF-CY is presented, as it has been used as a research tool in the beginning of the study. At the same time, the classification is critically examined. This gives me the chance to introduce critical voices and open up the discussion referring to points that are relevant for the study (special emphasis is put on the environmental factors of the classification).

Finally, this qualitative study is based on interviews (children with disabilities, parents, teachers, experts). Thus, individual as well as focus group interviews were the main sources of information. This is the reason why the last part of this chapter is dealing with ethical concerns.

Grounded Theory

Attempts to close the gap between theory and research have concentrated principally on the improvement of methods for testing theory, and sociologists, as well as other social and behavioural scientists, have been quite successful in that endeavour. Attempts to close the gap from the 'theory side' have not been nearly so successful. In fact, 'grand theory' is still so influential and prevalent that for many researchers it is synonymous with 'theory' – and so they think of 'theory' as having little relevance to their research. (Glaser and Strauss 1967/2008, vii)

Glaser and Strauss wrote "The Discovery of Grounded Theory" in an effort to change this perspective of theory, which is not directly connected to research, to a theory that is directly related to research. *"The Discovery of Grounded Theory* (1967) provided a powerful argument that legitimized qualitative research as a cred-

M. Schiemer, *Education for Children with Disabilities in Addis Ababa,*
Ethiopia, Inclusive Learning and Educational Equity 4,
DOI 10.1007/978-3-319-60768-9_4

ible methodological approach in its own right rather than simply as a precursor for developing quantitative instruments" (Charmaz 2006, 6).

Grounded theory is often referred to as a methodology as well as a method. The correct use of terms would be to distinguish between grounded theory and grounded theory method. In this way, grounded theory methods are used to develop grounded theory (Bryant and Charmaz 2007). "As a heuristic device, it may be helpful to view objectivist and grounded theory as located on two ends of a continuum. […]. Using grounded theory is a process; the method itself is in process. Its fluidity and flexibility inhere in the method itself" (Charmaz 2009, 137). In the book at hand, grounded theory is referred to as the underlying methodology as well as a method to develop a theory.

The development of grounded theory is described in the Sage Dictionary of Social Research Methods as follows:

> Grounded theory is an approach to research that was developed in response to concerns over the predominance of quantitative methods in social sciences and the tendency for research to be undertaken to test existing grand theories. Glaser and Strauss (1967: p. vii cited in Harding 2006, 131) perceived that there was an 'embarrassing gap between theory and empirical research'. They proposed instead an inductive process in which theory is built and modified from the data collected. (Harding 2006, 131)

This statement reveals the efforts that have to be made for developing new theories inductively by using qualitative methods. Equally, by using grounded theory for answering the research question, the structure of this book will lead through the steps taken to develop a theory. Consequently, this book can also be seen as a small contribution to the discussion about possibilities of theory generation in general (Lamnek 2005, 101).

To illustrate the importance of new generations of theories, Glaser and Strauss describe in the preface of their first book "Awareness of dying" (1965) what they concentrated on in their research:

> If increasingly Americans are dying within medical establishments, surrounded more by nurses and physicians than by kinsmen, then how do these representatives of the wider society manage themselves and their patients while the latter are dying? How is the hospital's organization capitalized upon in this process? What forms of social action, transitory or more permanent, arise while handling the dying of people? What are the social consequences for the hospital and its staff, as well as for the patients and their families? (Glaser and Strauss 1965, viii)

Developing a theory regarding this issue was of great importance to the researchers. The attempt to develop theories on social processes and developments in today's world is challenging. Yet, it can lead to insights that are useful for the future because they make processes transparent. Hence, conflicts and problems might be more easily identified, approached, and eventually solved.

With the child with disability at the centre of my investigation, grounded theory helped to focus on the processes and activities that take place in his/her surroundings and that affect the child's situation in his/her educational environment. Furthermore, I could place emphasis on reactions, feelings, perceptions and behaviour of the people in the immediate surroundings. Such possibilities lead to a compact set of data that can be combined and compared and finally lead to statements that enable outsiders to understand actions, reactions, behavioural patterns, etc. Those statements are supported by the experiences of a bigger group of people from various perspectives.

As grounded theory does not provide a theory at the beginning of a research process in the sense of offering a theoretical background, this research won't fulfil expectations of deductively proving existing theoretical assumptions, perspectives and points of view.

At the beginning of a research, researchers should approach the field of interest without biases, without predefined categories or hypotheses. However, it cannot be avoided that every researcher has background knowledge and experiences (Lamnek 2005, 106).

Furthermore, the area of field research should be one where not much research can be found yet because "Not much can be gained from energy expended to investigate issues that have already been explored extensively" (Birks and Mills 2011, 17). Therefore "[a]ll researchers should be able to demonstrate that their proposed study will generate knowledge that is relevant and significant" (Birks and Mills 2011, 17).

Birks and Mills mention three points that indicate that grounded theory is the best approach to working on a research project:

- Little is known about the area of study.
- The generation of theory with explanatory power is a desired outcome.
- An inherent process is imbedded in the research situation that is likely to be explicated by grounded theory methods. (Birks and Mills 2011, 16)

In other words, "new knowledge in the form of theory" will be the output of the research (Birks and Mills 2011, 16). The intention of the research at hand was to develop a theory from the information that was provided by the research participants and my own experiences and observations. In fact, little is known about factors that influence participation and activity of children with disabilities in educational environments in Addis Ababa. Last but not least, by looking at children with disabilities in primary schools, there are processes of developing relationships, inclusion, exclusion, dynamics between different actors (children, parents, teachers), etc. to be studied. The resulting categories that will lead to a final theory reveal a certain pattern. According to Glaser this pattern reflects the concept that has been studied (2010).

Yet, this is not to be misunderstood as a simple description of a process. Moving "analytical processes beyond simple description through exploration" (Birks and Mills 2011, 18) will lead to new insights into the issue of education for children with disabilities in a so-called developing country or country of the majority world.

Some More Insight into the Structures of the ICF

In the field of special education, the approach to classification is extremely important because it reveals a great deal about dominant discourses and the underlying relationships of knowledge and power. From a social policy perspective, Kirp (1982) and others have noted that the way in which a social problem is described says a great deal about how it will be resolved. (Florian et al. 2006, 37)

The view of disability in the ICF and ICF-CY as a product of impairments of physical and mental structures and functions, activity limitations and participation restrictions in combination with environmental and personal factors seems promising for further developments within the research field of special needs education and inclusion. Unfortunately, the relation between the discourse on ICF/ICF-CY and the topical inclusive education is not very strong. However, the classification can be understood as a means that can be used in scientific as well as practice-relevant areas of special needs and inclusive education. Yet, Manser (2005) states that the ICF is neither meant to provide an additional instrument for analyses or observations nor does it offer a theory for inclusive or special needs education. Instead he describes the ICF as a technology that can be used to make the functional health of every person visible. Furthermore, he claims that the ICF has to be understood as a resource that can have different functions in different contexts (Manser 2005). Considering the ICF as a tool for multiple purposes, it can serve various approaches within special needs and inclusive education.

The ICF is split into two parts, each of which consists of further components. Part one deals with functioning and disability and includes body functions/body structures, activity and participation. The second part deals with context factors. This part comprises environmental factors and personal factors. The latter are not defined in detail in the classification (WHO and DIMDI 2005, 16). The different components of the classification stand in mutual dynamic relations that can influence the activity and participation of a person. Functioning and disability are thus constituted by the components body functions/body structures, activity and participation. Simultaneously, environmental and personal factors describe contextual aspects. In other words, functioning and disability are influenced by external environmental factors and internal personal factors. The environmental factors refer to two different levels: one concerning the individual (domestic area, school, workplace, social contacts) and one concerning society (structures and systems of the community) (WHO 2001, 2007). They influence all components of functioning and disability; they are arranged in the order of intensity of the relation between people and their environments, ranging from immediate to general environment (Hollenweger 2008; WHO 2001, 2007). In this research, Bronfenbrenner's bioecological model serves as a basis for describing and measuring the interplay between environment and human development at different stages. Environmental interactions may incorporate micro-, meso- and/or macro-systems in the course of an individual's lifespan (Bronfenbrenner 1980, 1999). This is integrated in the resulting models of this research. According to Simeonsson et al. (2008), environment as

Table 4.1 ICF (WHO 2001)

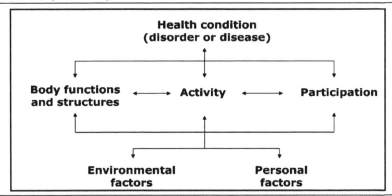

defined by Bronfenbrenner plays a key role in identifying possible supportive measures for children and adults. These might lead to enhanced participation within the school environment. According to the authors, an assessment of requirements within the school environment can contribute to an overall picture when using the coding system of the ICF/ICF-CY (see also Hollenweger 2008). Generally speaking, relations exist between all of these conceptual aspects. Hence, activity and participation can be supported or limited by the contextual factors (Table 4.1).

Hollenweger states that this approach opens new perspectives for special needs and inclusive education. She highlights that by using the ICF, foundations for new hypotheses and research questions have been established and dynamics between biological, psychological and social aspects of disability can be considered (2006, 51).

The ICF seems to provide a variety of possibilities to see disability in a context that includes environmental influences. Nevertheless, it can't be forgotten that there are still aspects within the classification that are not resolved satisfactorily. The chapter on environmental factors, for example, is relatively short compared to the other chapters and in need of further expansion. However, the awareness of the fact that the environment plays a decisive role regarding the construction of disability is of major importance. It has changed the interpretation of the questions of integration and inclusion fundamentally. Interventions can start by looking at the environment of a person with a disability rather than by looking at the person himself/herself first. Disability is not understood as a characteristic of a person but as the result of the interaction between a person and the environment (Schneidert et al. 2003, 588).

Conducting research in different cultural environments is very challenging as the various backgrounds have a tremendous influence on constructions of disability. Thus the question remains if disability can be approached systematically on a global level and hence if the ICF can really be applied on an international and intercultural level (Chapireau 2005; Schiemer 2010).

The ICF was used as a language for this research, although with constant awareness and reflection about possible insufficiencies regarding the culture and society studied. Therefore, the meanings of terms and phenomena have to be handled with utmost attention. The WHO states that the classification has to be seen in constant processes of development and that only research applying the instrument can eventually show its usability worldwide (Üstün et al. 2001; WHO 2001). The book at hand can be understood as a small contribution to this process as the ICF-CY has been used as a language and help for orientation to develop first research instruments for doing research in a foreign culture. In other words, the ICF-CY and the environmental factors of the classification have to be explored as a framework for this research in order to make the initial approach to the topic transparent.

Furthermore, the ICF-CY served as a framework for all three countries in the larger project. The chapter on environmental factors was used for developing guided interview guidelines and a questionnaire for the first phase of the field research. This indicates that the three-country project had been developed by using a mixed-method approach. However, in the book at hand, I only applied qualitative methods. Yet, it is important to mention that a quantitative questionnaire was used for further studies, as it led to special situations in the field like spontaneous group discussions that were very fruitful for the qualitative research.

The ICF-CY provides five chapters regarding the environment:

1. Products and technology
2. Natural environment and human-made changes to environment
3. Support and relationships
4. Attitudes
5. Services, systems and policies (WHO 2007)

These chapters constituted the first basis for developing research instruments for the first of three phases of the field research. In the part on activities and participation, Chap. 8 of the ICF-CY is on "major life areas". Education is defined as one of these major areas. Code d820 indicates that education should include:

> Gaining admission to school, education, engaging in all school-related responsibilities and privileges; learning the course material, subjects and other curriculum requirements in a primary or secondary education program, including attending school regularly; working cooperatively with other students, taking direction from teachers, organizing, studying and competing assigned tasks and projects, and advancing to other stages of education. (WHO 2007, 180)

However, in relation to educational areas and in combination with the participation of children, these points are defined quite vaguely (Biewer 2009a), making it necessary to elaborate an extension of the specific area of education and participation. Therefore, the study at hand goes beyond the use of the ICF-CY.

Against the background of the already mentioned discussions regarding international and intercultural concepts of disability, the ICF-CY has been used with reservation, as stated before. On the one hand, the gap in the definition related to education and participation of children (Biewer 2009b) makes it incomplete. On the other hand, the development of an international classification for disability generally poses certain challenges. One of the most important points in this context is the before-mentioned claim of international and intercultural applicability (Chapireau 2005; Üstün et al. 2001). The cautious position regarding the use of the ICF-CY is hence also to be understood as a critical objection towards this claim. At least, there are recognised differences regarding the interpretation of the phenomenon "disability" as such in different cultures (Ingstad and Whyte 1995) as well as cultural differences regarding the aspects that are involved in a definition of disability, as already indicated in the chapters above. Furthermore, even if similar aspects are involved, they might have different meanings and importance in different societies and hence have to be given respective weight or neglect. This is the reason why it is important to find out about the category or concept of disability and its meaning in a certain culture. Furthermore, it is important to consider which consequences certain perspectives and models of disabilities might imply before the system of the ICF-CY can be used. Such a procedure can indicate the usefulness or uselessness of applying parts of the classification in certain environments. For the research at hand, the environmental factors in the ICF-CY provided me with an optimal starting point in regard to the initial research question. This makes clear that it is advisable and even necessary to use only the parts of the classification that make sense for the respective case.

However, especially the area of education represents a sensitive zone regarding classification and labelling. A problematic issue could develop unintentionally from an overidentification of children belonging to marginal groups. This again could lead to lower expectations towards this group and forward a system of separation (Florian et al. 2006, 37). Classifying children in the educational system in order to satisfy political demands and to have a basis for the request of resources is a dangerous proceeding. Such an approach can have consequences for the lives of children that cannot be foreseen. Furthermore, […] a universal system of classification or categorization in education does not exist. In practice, various approaches are used, and these may be based on different assumptions about human difference and disability (Florian et al. 2006, 37). This again underscores the caution that has to be taken when using classification systems in general and the ICF-CY in particular when working in the area of education. It also explains why the ICF-CY could only be used as a starting point and was not employed as general instrument throughout the research.

An Example of the Limited Power of the ICF-CY

The use of the ICF-CY for developing the first research instruments was helpful as questions around thematic blocks could easily be created for interview guidelines and a pool of questions. It served as a functional basis to support me in covering the main aspects of educational environments for children with disabilities. At the end of the research, the question came up, how single aspects of "developing a sense of belonging" would be interpreted by the ICF-CY.

Considering the environmental factors of the ICF-CY, the codes that would probably be used for some of the main aspects of the results would be related to Chaps. 4 and 5 of the classification: "relationships and support" and "attitudes". Both of these chapters are not very extensive. The codes that are suggested to be used in these cases are equipped with a qualifier that indicates if the respective code is, e.g. no barrier or a complete facilitator for a person or situation, offering eight different nuances between the two poles of barrier and facilitator. Additionally there are "not specified" qualifiers (WHO 2007, 189f.). For example, the code "e310: Immediate family" could be coded as e310+3" meaning that the immediate family is a substantial facilitator for the child. This makes clear what kind of information can and cannot be communicated by using the ICF-CY in relation to environmental factors. It is not detailed or extensive information and can only be used in a very restricted way. Only being able to make statements about the intensity of family being a facilitator or barrier does not explain the reasons nor consequences of this fact and hence can only provide very limited information about the environment of a child. Consequently, the explanatory power about the special needs a child with a certain disability (or health condition, using the terminology of the ICF/ICF-CY) in his/her educational environment is also limited.

> In short, there are problems in defining and providing for the significant numbers of disabled children and youth many of whom are excluded from educational opportunities for primary and secondary schooling. The usefulness of categorical classifications of disability is being questioned in terms of their cost-effectiveness and their ability to identify needed services. Environmental factors play a significant role in disabling the vast majority of students. (Peters 2007, 120)

Regarding inclusive education, the ICF-CY is still not a language that can be internationally applied satisfactorily. Even though some scholars suggest that the classification can be used to provide people with an overall picture about certain requirements within a school environment (Hollenweger 2008; Simeonsson et al. 2008), restrictions become evident.

In this context it may be legitimate to ask in which ways the ICF can be relevant for the case of Ethiopia. It would be very revealing to learn which items are missing to be able to include all important functionings of a child who wants to participate and be involved in his/her community life in Ethiopia. The ICF was invented to offer a language for describing the functioning of a person. This language should serve for enabling scientists and other experts to exchange and use information on an interdisciplinary level. The challenge at this point is that a language has to be learnt before it can be used, which already poses serious problems, as projects involving the ICF in Italy can tell (De Polo et al. 2009).

It is indeed difficult to determine the relevance of the ICF in Ethiopia, as I couldn't find published, or otherwise accessible, examples of its use. This brings us back to the study of Üstün et al. (2001), who stated that the ICF *can* be used interculturally. However, I doubt that we always *should* use it. Is using the ICF really suitable for any cultural context? Isn't it possible that using such a classification undermines values in certain cultures and leaves black spots on important issues? For example, the chapter on environmental factors in the ICF is not as extensive as other chapters. In the case of the study at hand, in which the environment of family and community plays such an important role, it might just not cover enough aspects. Moreover, existing structures may be far better for enabling all people of a community to participate in an inclusive way.

My conclusion so far is that from an outside perspective, using the ICF may be helpful (for doing research or collecting data for estimating needs…). But inside an Ethiopian community itself, the ICF may exhibit many inadequacies and restrictions, thus failing to lead to the expected results. As a supporting tool, the capability approach could be a possibility to get closer to the real needs of the people.

Ethical Concerns

In recent years, a greater focus on cross-cultural research and on research undertaken by multidisciplinary national teams has raised significant challenges with regard to how educational research is conceptualised, conducted and disseminated in an ethical manner. (Robinson-Pant and Singal 2013, 417)

Issues that are usually discussed in research literature on ethics are aspects of consent, confidentiality, ownership and power relations. We should be aware also in the context of the ICF that certain power relations develop by simply using pre-defined codes to describe certain environments of a person (insufficiently, as described above). It seems that aspects of the power relation which develops between the researcher and interviewees mark the starting point of ethical considerations in research in general (Marshall and Batten 2004; Powell 2011). Since these points are crucial for the research at hand, this chapter aims at addressing major aspects that are perceived as important regarding ethical implications for this book; these are children, vulnerable groups, informed consent, cultural differences and power relations.

Many of the people involved in the study at hand did not have concepts of science or research and might not know about their rights to refuse an interview or withdraw their consent. However, I always pointed out the possibility to withdraw the given consent. Especially interviews with children had to be conducted with utmost empathy but, above all, with their informed consent (Carter 2009; Eder and Fingerson 2003; Grob-Paeprer and Podlesch 2000; Roberts 2008). This required explaining clearly what the purpose of the study, the possible impact, issues about anonymity, etc. were. In the research at hand, the informed consent to conducting interviews included consent on taking pictures and collecting any other material related to the children. In addition to the child's consent, the consent of the parents or caretakers was collected before the child was interviewed. It is natural that challenges arise when trying to explain the research aims and possible consequences to the different groups. This leads to ethical concerns for the researcher. Lewis (2002) identifies six areas of concern regarding interviews with children. These are access and gatekeepers to reach the children, the children's consent and assent for conducting the interview, confidentiality, anonymity and secrecy regarding the handling of gathered information, recognition and feedback, ownership and social responsibility regarding the usage of the data (Lewis 2002, 110f). All of these areas are of major importance when interviewing children and have to be regarded accordingly. Discussions about ethics in research also involve the terminology of vulnerability and vulnerable groups. According to Solomon (2013), there are two groups of vulnerable research participants: the ones who are cognitively and the ones who are economically vulnerable. For this research it is especially the group of cognitively vulnerable participants, who are not able to decide deliberately if they want to participate in the study or not. In this context, children can be defined as especially vulnerable, as their decisions might be influenced by adults. However, children should be given the possibility to speak for themselves if they wish to do so.

> Children have historically been marginalized in research with proxies used as appropriate sources of information about children's experiences, perceptions and understandings. In the context of research governance and ethical review, the default setting in many countries reflects a long history of framing children within a discourse of vulnerability and seeing research with (or on) children as inherently risky. This perspective inevitably positions researchers as '(potentially) dangerous' and requires reviewers to adopt a (super-) cautious approach to any research proposal involving children's participation. (Carter 2009, 858)

Even though some of the children showed that they decided for themselves by refraining from participating in this study, it can never be said if they really understood the whole context.[1] However, as Carter correctly indicates, "the discourse of child vulnerability competes with the discourse of child participation and involvement" (2009, 858). In the case of this study, it would have been paradox not to involve children, as the whole research framework dealt with inclusion, participation and activity of children with disabilities. Therefore, it was of utmost importance to involve the children, listen carefully to their needs and messages and react accordingly. In doing so, it was indispensable to involve an Ethiopian researcher, who had experience in interviewing children and showed empathy throughout the interviews.[2] There might be an additional concern about interviewing children with disabilities and in particular children with intellectual disabilities. A number of publications explore this issue (Aarons et al. 2004; Grob-Paeprer and Podlesch 2000; Lewis 2002, Odom et al. 2004).

As far as the parents are concerned, some – despite repeatedly explaining the opposite to them – continued to believe that I was sent by an NGO in order to support their child. This became clear during consecutive interviews in which they started to speak about support they expected from us. The parents therefore seemed

---

[1] Yet, this is also the case for any of the participants.

[2] It has to be considered that by involving an Ethiopian researcher, cultural and societal values and norms that possibly restrict free speech of children might also be imported to the interview situation. This would be the case if children are not seen as capable or mature enough to speak for themselves. Even though this perception can be found in the Ethiopian culture, the research team tried to encourage the children to speak freely. On the other hand, a person with a Western background (skin color, language, behaviour etc.) might also influence the course of the interviews to a certain extent. Hence, having a local and a non-local researcher in the team can be considered as a good precondition for overcoming those challenges by including emic as well as etic perspectives.

to belong to the group of the economically vulnerable, as they expected that support would be provided because of their participation. This shows that it can be very challenging to communicate research purposes and issues concerning the ongoing process of field research, etc. This was the case despite the fact that the research team included an Ethiopian researcher with an emic perspective. Aspects that have to be considered beyond informed consent while conducting research in different cultures are cultural and ethical differences.

> The implication for researchers rests in not adhering to any universal ethic in designing and conducting research, while simultaneously attempting to respect the particular and contextual ethical norms of a given social or ethnic group. Flexibility on the part of the researcher may be one way to deal with such cultural norm differences. (Marshall and Batten 2004)

This statement makes it clear that the field research was a balancing act for me, as I had to react flexibly to different situations. Correspondingly, the research activity was partially learning by doing, as many situations that arose could not be predicted, which made preparation difficult.

A last point that has to be mentioned regards the power relations which were mentioned at the beginning of this chapter. In this respect, it is important for me as a researcher to be aware of the power relations between me and the participants. Especially in the setting of this research study, where I am of European descent (but also female and without an obvious disability apart from reduced eyesight), it was essential to be aware of the impact and consequences that this circumstance might have on the interview situation in general and on the participants in particular. However, not only power relations on this level have to get attention. As the research was conducted with the participation of colleagues from Addis Ababa University, there were also dynamics that have to be taken into account on this level.

> When those in privileged positions and in wealthier countries consider undertaking collaborative research with colleagues in developing countries it is necessary to understand both their own framework of thinking, and the implications of very different mind-sets and environments in which research projects may be carried out in developing countries. (Benatar 2002, 1132)

Thus, understanding new frameworks and ways of thinking was one of the most important tasks for me at the beginning as well as throughout the research project. In this regard it was helpful to work very closely with the Ethiopian team and especially with my research assistant. I highly valued considerations and advice from the Ethiopian side, and – when possible – I tried to adapt the research activities accordingly. This shows that it is very important to consider the cultural environment in which research is conducted. This environment might have ethical issues that are different to the ones that I might consider when coming from a minority world background. Therefore, this chapter is concluded with the following statement:

> The ethical issues in the literature regarding research in the Majority world context clearly have significant ramifications for cross cultural research. Ethical issues have different resonances in different world contexts, and research planned and undertaken in Majority world countries challenges assumptions underlying Minority world ethical guidelines. (Powell 2011, 3)

References

Aarons, N. M., Powell, M. B., & Browne, J. (2004). Police perceptions of interviews involving children with intellectual disabilities: A qualitative inquiry. *Policing and Society, 14*(3), 269–278.

Benatar, S. R. (2002). Reflections and recommendations on research ethics in developing countries. *Social Science & Medicine, 54*(7), 1131–1141.

Biewer, G. (2009a). *Grundlagen der Heilpädagogik und Inklusiven Pädagogik*. Bad Heilbrunn: Klinkhardt.

Biewer, G. (2009b). Vom Verschwinden der Etiketten zum Verlust der Inhalte. Heilpädagogische Klassifizierung im internationalen Vergleich. In A. Bürli, U. Strasser, & A. D. Stein (Eds.), *Integration/Inklusion aus internationaler Sicht* (pp. 169–176). Bad Heilbrunn: Klinkhardt.

Birks, M., & Mills, J. (2011). *Grounded theory. A practical guide*. Los Angeles/London/New Delhi/Singapore/Washington, DC: Sage.

Bronfenbrenner, U. (1980). *The ecology of human development. Experiments by nature and design*. Cambridge: Harvard University.

Bronfenbrenner, U. (1999). Environments in developmental perspective: Theoretical and operational models. In S. L. Friedman & T. D. Wachs (Eds.), *Measuring environment across the life span. Emerging methods and concepts* (pp. 3–28). Washington, DC: American Psychological Association.

Bryant, A., & Charmaz, K. (2007). Introduction. Grounded theory research: Methods and practices. In A. Bryant & K. Charmaz (Eds.), *The sage handbook of grounded theory* (pp. 1–28). Los Angeles/London/New Dehli/Singapore: Sage.

Carter, B. (2009). Tick box for child? The ethical positioning of children as vulnerable, researchers as barbarians and reviewers as overly cautious. *International Journal of Nursing Studies, 46*(6), 858–864.

Chapireau, F. (2005). The environment in the international classification of functioning, disability and health. *Journal of Applied Research in Intellectual Disabilities, 18*, 305–311.

Charmaz, K. (2006). *Constructing grounded theory: A practical guide through qualitative analysis*. London/Thousand Oaks/New Delhi: Sage.

Charmaz, K. (2009). Shifting the grounds: Constructivist grounded theory methods. In J. M. Morse (Ed.), *Developing grounded theory. The second generation* (pp. 127–154). Walnut Creek: Left Coast Press.

De Polo, G., et al. (2009). Children with disability at school: The application of ICF-CY in the Veneto region. *Disability and Rehabilitation, 31*(S1), 67–73.

Eder, D., & Fingerson, L. (2003). Interviewing children and adolescents. In J. A. Holstein & J. F. Gubrium (Eds.), *Inside interviewing* (pp. 33–53). Thousand Oaks et al.: Sage.

Florian, L., et al. (2006). Cross-cultural perspectives on the classification of children with disabilities: Part I. Issues in the classification of children with disabilities. *Journal of Special Education, 40*(1), 36–45.

Glaser, B. (2010). *Grounded theory is the study of a concept*. (Youtube, Glaser, B.). Retrieved November 23, 2016, from http://www.youtube.com/watch?NR=1&v=OcpxaLQDnLk&feature=endscreen

Glaser, B., & Strauss, A. (1965). *Awareness of dying*. Chicago: Aldine Transaction.

Glaser, B. G., & Strauss, A. L. (1967/2008). *The discovery of grounded theory: Strategies for qualitative research*. New Brunswick: Aldine Transaction.

Grob-Paeprer, B., & Podlesch, W. (2000). Forschen bei Kindern mit geistiger Behinderung und Kindern mit schwerer Mehrfachbehinderung. In F. Heinzel (Ed.), *Methoden der Kindheitsforschung. Ein Überblick über Forschungszugänge zur kindlichen Perspektive* (pp. 265–278). Weinheim/München: Juventa.

Harding, J. (2006). Grounded theory. In V. Jupp (Ed.), *The sage dictionary of social research methods* (pp. 131–132). London/Thoudand Oaks/New Delhi: Sage.

Hollenweger, J. (2006). Der Beitrag der Weltgesundheitsorganisation zur Klärung konzeptueller Grundlagen einer inklusiven Pädagogik. In M. Dederich, H. Greving, & P. Rödler (Eds.), *Inklusion statt Integration? Heilpädagogik als Kulturtechnik* (pp. 45–61). Gießen: Psychosozial.

Hollenweger, J. (2008). Cross-national comparisons of special education classification systems. In L. Florian & M. J. McLaughlin (Eds.), *Disability classification in education. Issues and perspectives* (pp. 11–30). Thousand Oaks: Corwin Press.

Ingstad, B., & Whyte, S. R. (Eds.). (1995). *Disability and culture.* Berkeley/Los Angeles/London: University of California Press.

Kirp, D. (1982). Professionalism as policy choice: British special education in comparative perspective. *World Politics, 34,* 137–174.

Lamnek, S. (2005). *Qualitative Sozialforschung. Lehrbuch.* Weinheim: Beltz.

Lewis, A. (2002). Accessing, through research interviews, the views of children with difficulties in learning. *Support for Learning, 17*(3), 110–116. Library of Congress *Glossary Ethiopia.* Retrieved March 8, 2014, from http://lcweb2.loc.gov/frd/cs/ethiopia/et_glos.html. (not available anymore).

Manser, R. (2005). ICF und ihre Anwendung in der Heilpädagogik. Ein kritischer Diskurs. In H. Dohrenbusch (Ed.), *Differentielle Heilpädagogik* (pp. 25–54). Luzern: Edition SZH/CSPS.

Marshall, A., & Batten, S. (2004). Researching across cultures: Issues of ethics and power. *Forum Qualitative Sozialforschung/Forum: Qualitative Social Research.* Retrieved November 23, 2016, from http://www.qualitative-research.net/index.php/fqs/article/view/572/1241

Odom, S. L., et al. (2004). Investigating inclusion: A review of research mehods for individuals with intellectual disability. In E. Emerson et al. (Eds.), *The international handbook of applied research in intellectual disabilities* (pp. 281–295). Chichester: Wiley.

Peters, S. (2007). Inclusion as a strategy for achieving education for all. In L. Florian (Ed.), *The sage handbook of special education* (pp. 117–130). London/Thousand Oaks/New Delhi: Sage.

Powell, M. A. (2011). *International literature review: Ethical issues in undertaking research with children and young people* (literature review for the childwatch international research network). In Lismore/Dunedin, Southern Cross University, Centre for Children and Young People/University of Otago, Centre for Research on Children and Families.

Roberts, H. (2008). Listening to children: And hearing them. In P. Christensen & A. James (Eds.), *Research with children. Perspectives and practices* (Vol. 2, pp. 260–275). Oxon/New York: Routledge.

Robinson-Pant, A., & Singal, N. (2013). Researching ethically across cultures: Issues of knowledge, power and voice. *Compare: A Journal of Comparative and International Education, 43*(4), 417–421.

Schiemer, M. (2010). ICF – Instrument für eine interkulturell vergleichende Heilpädagogik? In U. Schildmann (Ed.), *Umgang mit Verschiedenheit in der Lebensspanne.* Bad Heilbrunn: Klinkhardt.

Schneidert, M., et al. (2003). The role of environment in the international classification of functioning, disability and health. *Disability and Rehabilitation, 25*(11–12), 588–595.

Simeonsson, R. J., et al. (2008). International classification of functioning, disability and health for children and youth. A common language for special education. In L. Florian & M. J. McLaughlin (Eds.), *Disability classification in education. Issues and perspectives* (pp. 207–226). Thousand Oaks: Corwin Press.

Solomon, S. R. (2013). Protecting and respecting the vulnerable: Existing regulations or further protections? *Theoretical Medicine and Bioethics, 34*(1), 17–28.

Üstün, T. B., et al. (Eds.). (2001). *Disability and culture. Universalism and culture. ICIDH-2 series. Published on behalf of the world health organisation.* Seattle: Hofgrefe & Huber.

WHO. (2001). *International classification of functioning, disability and health*. Geneva: World Health Organization.

WHO. (2007). *International classification of functioning and health. Children & youth version*. Geneva: World Health Organization.

WHO & DIMDI. (2005). *Internationale Klassifikation der Funktionsfähigkeit, Behinderung und Gesundheit*. Genf: Deutsches Institut für Medizinische Dokumentation und Information (DIMDI).

Chapter 5
Reality Bites: Listening to Children, Parents, Teachers and Other Experts

Abstract This is one of the central parts of this book. It elaborates the emergence of different categories related to the groups of participants of the study (children with disabilities, parents, teachers) as well as it includes the additional perspective of experts. This means that four perspectives on the situation of children with disabilities in schools in Addis Ababa are presented. By referring to the categories that developed from analysing the interviews of children, parents, teachers and other experts, the mentioned perspectives are discussed. Having elaborated the categories for each perspective, each part is concluded with a summary that focuses on the meaning of education for each of the participating groups. This is then linked to a discussion in relation to educational equity.

At the beginning, the big question was how to find participants in Addis Ababa who would be willing to tell me their stories, which – very often – started with painful memories of the moment when parents learnt that their child had a disability. These times were coined by uncertainties, grief, guilt and not knowing how to cope with the situation in a life which was already difficult because of poverty. Talking to the children, I just asked them about their daily life in school and at home and about their experiences and impressions. In most cases, they were very excited to tell me about their thoughts, dreams and desires. Lastly, the teachers were sometimes suspicious because they did not know where all the questions would lead to. In the end, finding participants was not a problem. All of the participants were very happy about the fact that someone had come to listen to them.

Looking at the research situation, we have to see that the child with a disability is identified as such by persons that surround him/her. People who have a relation with the child, people who talk about the child, people who construct environments around the child and consequently the child him/herself define what is special about him/her and why.

© The Author(s) 2017   87
M. Schiemer, *Education for Children with Disabilities in Addis Ababa,*
Ethiopia, Inclusive Learning and Educational Equity 4,
DOI 10.1007/978-3-319-60768-9_5

I chose to speak to children, parents, teachers and other experts as sources of information because I thought that those people would be able to give information about the situation of children with disabilities at school. Additionally, observations in the classes and in the school compounds provided me with information that the interviewees might not have been able to give. All these perspectives opened a compact set of views on a certain aspect. That means that the child with a disability was constructed within these views and additionally through my interpretation of these views.

Throughout the process of analysing the data, it became clear to me that emerging topics have to be analysed based on the different perspectives, meaning from the parents', teachers' and children's points of view, rather than looking at each "case" (child–parent–teacher), as categories developed (and were constructed) in relation to one or the other group.

I considered it as essential to analyse how the disability of the child affected each of the participants and vice versa. By analysing emotions, issues that were raised, actions and reactions in the data, it was possible to get an impression of what disability meant to the people and hence of how the parents, teachers, experts and children constructed and maybe also deconstructed disability in relation to the field of education. I followed Charmaz' way of analysing the data: "I pieced together what people said and did and looked for their implied meanings. In this way, a constructivist goes beneath the surface and enters the liminal world of meaning" (Charmaz 2009, 144).

The goal of this approach to analysis was to obtain an answer to the question of which environmental factors were identified by the participants as influencing education for children with disabilities. In this regard, the participants exhibited different roles: children on a "trying to find my place" level, parents on a "caring about the child" level, teachers on a "being responsible for education" level and experts on a "having to know what the problem is" level.

In this part, I will explain how I moved towards the final core category of *feeling like a family*. I attempt to do this by using the different perspectives of the interviewed children, parents and teachers as well as experts. My specific aim was to discover the "implicit meanings" (Charmaz 2003, 314) of the participants' experiences. The analysis of the interviews led towards the development of categories[1] that reflect the participants' actions. I will guide you to the main topics which emerged from my interviews and became categories. As a support, I will use some network views to better visualise the connections between these topics (categories).

However, it was not considered as productive to strain your attention by adding too many detailed network views. Instead, detailed reflection of the analytic process and condensed versions of network views will clarify the construction of categories.

---

[1] In the following chapters, titles of categories are written in italics.

In the research at hand, the focus was placed on spelling out the characteristics of each category to enable you to grasp the meaning of the categories. Therefore, at the end of each chapter on a category, you will find the condensed network views of the most significant properties (in bold in the text) and further influences of that category.[2]

> Diagrams can enable you to see the relative power, scope, and direction of the categories in your analysis as well as the connections among them. You may find that diagrams can serve useful and diverse purposes at all stages of analysis. You might revise an early quick clustering about a category into a more exacting form as a diagram illustrating the properties of a category. You might develop a conceptual map that locates your concepts and directs movement between them. (Charmaz 2006, 118)

For these reasons, throughout the following part of the book, diagrams are used to support the analysis as well as to make the process of the analysis transparent.

Listening to the Children

When asking children what was necessary to become what they were dreaming of, many of them mentioned having to be a good student (an important detail at this point may be the fact that all the interviews were conducted at school). This credo was repeated by parents and teachers alike. The children were convinced that by studying hard they could reach what they aspired in their future. One of these aspirations was to support and help their families and overcome poverty:

Y[3]:   *What do you want to be in the future? What is your ambition?*
E: I want to support my mother and father. I want to provide them with everything they need. That's all. (Embaye, child)

Their other aspiration was to become a full member of society, to be successful and to make a meaningful contribution to the community: "In order to lead a good social life with the community, I want to help people like me. Besides, I want to help my mother and father" (Embaye, child).

---

[2] "Properties of categories and subcategories should be considered in terms of their dimensions or the range of variance that the property demonstrates" (Birks and Mills 2011, 98). The authors furthermore give an example of this analytic process: the category "walking the dog" can have properties like time, enjoyment and energy. These properties again can have dimensions like "spending a short amount of time" because it is raining (Birks and Mills 2011, 98). In this work, dimensions of properties are not elaborated specifically, as not all of the properties have dimensions. It was regarded as more useful to deeply analyse and describe the properties themselves not referring to dimensions in particular. However, in some cases, dimensions of categories were listed (e.g. for the category *parental support*), and consequences were added to the network views if considered important.

[3] Y stands for Yeshitla Mulat, the interpreter.

The categories *developing a positive self-concept* and *question of belonging* emerged from the children's interviews. To add a more exact description of the categories, keywords (e.g. necessary basis) to characterise the categories in the process of children receiving education are attached to each category (this is done also for the categories which emerged from the other interviews).

Developing a Positive Self-Concept: Necessary Basis (For Development/Change)

School attendance meant an increase in the positive perception of self for the children that I interviewed.

New possibilities seem to open for them and lead to new perspectives in their lives. A major part of this category is the influence of family, friends and surrounding regarding support. Children who are supported to reach their goals are also more included in the community than children who are not supported. Furthermore, the goals of supporting the family and becoming a valued member in society become more achievable through education, as children get the feeling of being able to reach those goals.

Y: *What are those things that entertain you?*
E: For me, the best sport is education. (Embaye, child)

The *development of a positive self-concept* of the children as related to getting access to school became clear to me only during the second phase of the field research. The children told me that attending a school gave them the possibility of becoming full members of the community as well as of their families. Consequently, their self-esteem and self-perception were positively influenced by receiving education.

One important element of this development is the ability to support and help the family. Even though the category itself developed only later, the aspect of help and children wanting to help and be able to help appeared already in the very early stages of the analysis. The children reported that they needed education to be able to help their parents as well as people in need, especially people with disabilities. There was a high awareness of general problems for disadvantaged people, like homeless or ill people, living in Addis Ababa.

E: I think about the society. There are many beggars. I want this problem to be eliminated.
Y: *Do you sympathize with them?*
E: I wish something to happen. If I get a house, I will bring them together. I will treat those who are sick. I would do this if there are people who assist me. (Embaye, child)

Embaye here speaks about his wish to help but also mentions that he would need support for this. **Being able to help** can be identified as a property of *devel-*

oping a positive self-concept. It is related to the children being given meaningful tasks or the feeling that they are needed. Above all, the children felt that they were needed if they could act as supporters of their family. Thus, having tasks at home gave them a feeling of being needed and valued. "On Saturday, I usually wash my school uniform and let it dry. After that I clean everything, and then I clean my house. If my Mom is at home, I will arrange everything so that she can make coffee[4]" (Yirgashew, child). In this quotation, Yirgashew fulfilled tasks that supported his mother, which gave him a function in the family and raised his self-esteem.

As mentioned above, the aspect of studying hard was strongly emphasised during the interviews. **Studying hard** is related to the children's striving to be successful in their education. Their positive self-concept is supported because the children can actively contribute to reaching their goals. Furthermore, the positive effects are enhanced if predefined goals are achieved. In this context, possibilities to study hard depending on their own capacities,[5] time and space at home as well as support from their home or friends have to receive attention. Sometimes the children spoke about not having a desk or room to study at home. This aspect is closely related to the parents' category *parental support* and the aspect of support in general. In other words, support in this context may be a key element contributing to the development of a positive self-concept by enabling the children to study hard and consequently opening up further possibilities. One of these possibilities can be that of being able to help people in need after having finished education and working in an appropriate profession. This adds to their feeling of being able to **become a valued member of society**, which is clearly linked to aspects of the capability approach (reaching valuable beings). Therefore, the possibility to contribute to and be part of social life already leads to a positive self-image.

Becoming a valued member of society is related to knowing what is valued in society. Health was repeatedly mentioned by the parents as an important value. They considered disability as something that is not healthy, even though they did not put it on the same level as illness. Having a disability was seen as the opposite of being normal. This is why, very often, being healthy was considered to be one of the conditions for being able to support the family and contribute to the community. Looking at it from this perspective, disability automatically excludes children from participating in family and community life as a full member. Therefore, it is even more important for children to be able to counteract stigma and exclusion

---

[4] Making coffee is a traditional event in Ethiopian culture.

[5] A question that might arise here is to what extent children with "intellectual disabilities" can study hard. Studying hard is not necessarily only related to academic subjects but also includes things that are of importance to the children. For instance, the children were proud to be able to sing a song for us or demonstrate other achievements like counting or writing their names. All these things can also be studied at home.

by being educated "like normal children". Through education disability seems to lose some of the negative connotations, as children with disabilities are not expected to be able to learn. Proving the opposite by receiving education provides an argument against such prejudices and supports the development of a positive self-perception. This leads to statements like, "we are able to act like other children if given the possibilities".

In some cases, the children were able to speak out for themselves and to **bring about change** at school. Such an experience counteracts a feeling of helplessness and promotes the feeling of being able to change conditions and circumstances. "One teacher got transferred; he didn't know sign language. He taught us only by speaking. We complained about his way of teaching; as a result they changed him" (Berhanu, child). Here, the children experienced that their opinion was valued. This is a very important step towards strengthening their self-esteem.

Consciousness of support is another important factor that sustains the development of a positive self-concept. Many of the children knew that they were supported by either their parents or their teachers or both.

> Y: *The last card is about family. Tell me about your family.*
> Yo: If you have a family, you will get support. (Yirgashew, child)

This quotation indicates a strong conviction of and trust in the system of "family". Additionally, friends[6] played an important role in regard to having people who help and support them in reaching their goals. These goals were often related to supporting the family or aspiring professions like teacher or doctor that serve people and the community. Besides, groups of people who were there to support the child to be able to succeed indicate the children's degree of involvement and acceptance at school, in the community, etc. In other words, they were visible, and their needs were noticed and respected by the environment.[7]

Furthermore, the expectations which parents and teachers had of the child played a significant role. "Our parents expect us to learn like other children, be successful and help them" (Embel, child). It seems interesting to look at the expression "like other children" in this quotation: education seems to make the children more "normal". The children strived to satisfy their parent's expectations and felt valued by being expected to achieve certain things, as this indicates that they are thought to be able to accomplish specific tasks. This is why receiving education gave the children the possibilities to **fulfil the expectations** of their parents and teachers. It became clear that expectations were communicated to children directly or indirectly. Moreover, as soon as children with disabilities attended a school, the expectations of them changed and grew in some cases. "[…] [my parents] want me to become a medical doctor" (Serawit, child). This indicates that the parents had higher expecta-

---

[6] Having friends is an interesting topic within the field of research; however, no category developed in relation to it. Therefore, friends are not a major aspect in the book at hand. However, it might be worth exploring the friendship aspect in another paper.

[7] Not to be understood in terms of a pity-based charity model of disability.

tions of their children when they received education. Hence, the parents attributed a lot of power to education.

To subsume, the category *developing a positive self-concept* exhibits different properties. It is defined by a child's ability to help, especially regarding the family, by their permanent effort to study hard, by the feeling of having the possibility to become a valued member of society, by using possibilities to bring about change, by knowing that they are supported by the people surrounding them, and by trying to fulfil – sometimes challenging – expectations of parents and teachers. By listing the most significant properties of this category, it becomes clear that *developing a positive self-concept* depends very much on the possibilities that the children can identify in their lives and especially in relation to the community. This again can be seen against the background of turning capabilities into functionings, i.e. having/getting the possibilities to reach valuable states of being. Additionally, the degree of involvement plays an important role. The degree of involvement is defined through possibilities of participation and interaction within the school community. The more possibilities can be identified and the more the degree of involvement increases, the more positive the self-concept becomes. Thus, having possibilities to participate at school, in the family life and in the community and having friends and supporters strengthen the children. It supports feelings of equity and equality and adds to their quality of life. Accordingly, the category *developing a positive self-concept* has consequences (CONS) in terms of new possibilities that open up as illustrated below next to listing the most significant properties.

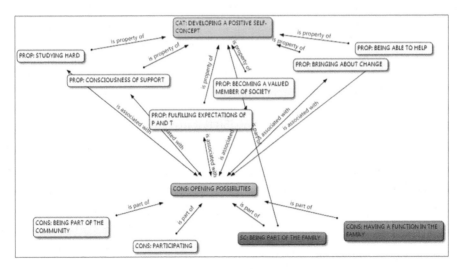

Network View 5.1 Properties of *developing a positive self-concept*

This network view gives an overview of the category and its most relevant properties and shows the significance of the family in this context (in pink). The consequence of having certain functions in the family has to be considered as essential, as it was identified as one of the most important aspects by the children. The most meaningful task in this context was to be able to support the parents and family now and in the future as an adult. Another consequence was the aspect of participation. Through the development of a positive self-perception, the children exhibited a feeling of being able to participate in school and maybe later also as a valued member of society. All these aspects resulted in the children's conviction of being able to become a valued part of the community and the family.

Question of Belonging: Struggle

The question of belonging describes the children's struggle regarding a feeling of belonging. It includes negative aspects that are not included in the former category. However, it also contains positive aspects. It is a moving back and forth between possibilities and restrictions, between rejection and acceptance, between exclusion and inclusion. The children's environment provides them with conflicting input they have to deal with in the process of trying to find their place in society.

The category *question of belonging* emerged from code families and subcategories that were related to aspects like discrimination, restrictions and concern about the future, as well as different emotions expressed by the children (happiness and satisfaction as well as sadness, worries and anxiety). Furthermore, it included the way in which the children were involved in daily activities at school (morning ceremony, classroom activities, breaktime) but also punishment and teachers' advice, which defined the children's "belonging to school", the role they played in the school community and how they were integrated. In this context, being punished like other children or not is also an important aspect of equal treatment and, ultimately, equality.

The *question of belonging* refers to the children's position in their society (in the school community, in the community at home, in society in general, etc.) and the difficulties that arise when given the possibilities that education seems to open for the children. On the one hand, they experienced discrimination, exclusion, injustice, restrictions and negative reactions related to their disability. This led to a feeling of inferiority and of not belonging, whether at school, in the community or at home. The negative identification with the disability hampered a positive outlook for the future. However, on the other hand, the positive self-concept of the children proved that an optimistic attitude predominated when talking about education. Nevertheless, the children were aware of the problems that existed and with which they would be confronted (like finding a school or university that was accessible for them, restrictions in choosing certain professions, etc.).

> What is very important for me is that it is only in this school that people have a positive attitude towards us. There are many clubs in this school. We also visit various schools. And when the people who are there see us, they wonder why we came to their school. When we go to the town, mini-bus drivers do not welcome us. But in our school, we participate in many activities. I have no words to express everything. (Erevu, child)

These positive and negative aspects that children with disabilities are confronted with stress the significance of the question "Where do I belong?". The possibilities that education seems to open for them are always clouded by the additional challenges they have to face. Thus, they don't really belong to the school community, as their participation in activities is restricted. However, the children's self-esteem grows as their "attending a school" usually leads to a revaluation of their person in their closer environment and in their families. Consequently, a feeling of belonging to the family and being of value for them starts to evolve and supports the positive attitudes that the children generally have towards their future.

All in all the children were satisfied with their schools. They liked their teachers and they liked to study. However, when asking children about the change they would like to see in their schools, the most common answer was in regard to the cleanliness and neatness of their schools – or the lack of it. They complained about broken doors and windows, wished for classrooms to be painted, etc. "When we were in [the old buildings of] school F, the school was old, the classrooms were old, and the doors were broken. But here, the school is in a new building. So, it is pleasant" (Elisa, child). The children were very critical about these issues. They wanted their schools to be painted, broken doors and windows to be repaired, and toilets to be cleaned. Hence, the possibility of getting education was not satisfying for them in a "no matter how" way. They expressed a strong wish of attending a clean, neat and beautiful school. It therefore became evident that the learning environment was of major importance for the children and their feeling of well-being, which also influenced the teaching–learning process.

The last subcategory that has to be mentioned here is language. Considering the richness of languages in the Ethiopian culture, it has to get special attention. The subcategory started to develop because there were lots of families who had moved to Addis Ababa from the countryside. Therefore, some of the participating families spoke languages other than Amharic, which is used as language of instruction in the lower grades at the schools of the capital. However, none of the participants spoke about problems regarding language. Some explained that they spoke their mother tongue at home, but Amharic in general. Yet, there was one exemption: sign language. Sign language was the most prevalent topic regarding the subcategory "language". It became obvious that this was an important issue because questions of belonging are usually also defined by language affiliations. In other words, one characteristic of groups and communities is their way of communicating. It seems that people who use sign language have a double challenge regarding their place of belonging and integration in society: first, negative attitudes towards their disability and, second, problems of communication.[8] No other challenges regarding language were communicated in the interviews of this research.

To recapitulate, the category *question of belonging* is connected to the children's feelings of **excludedness and includedness**, to their **possibilities of participation** and the **restrictions** they had to face. This was related especially to the school community but has also to be understood in relation to their position in their families. The attitudes of the people surrounding them played a major role. Discrimination and exclusion are attached to people's negative attitudes towards people with disabilities. But attitudes can change, as will be demonstrated when looking at the parents' perspectives.

By describing how much they liked their teachers, the school and receiving education in general, the children communicated a **very positive image of their school environment**. Their well-being was influenced by all those aspects (e.g. having friends, playing with friends during breaktime, liking teachers). At the same time, the children were **critical towards the school environment**. They criticised the school appearance, the teachers and other aspects (e.g. transport to school). "Everything is good in this school. But our parents are tired of bringing us to school and back home. Therefore, it is better if we get transportation services" (Melat, child).

Here again **conflicting positions** can be identified. On the one hand, the children felt comfortable and were very happy attending their school. They wanted to belong to that school. On the other hand, there were many aspects they would like to change. Furthermore, by not being fully integrated, the feeling of belonging was limited. The following network view illustrates the elaborated properties of the category *question of belonging*.

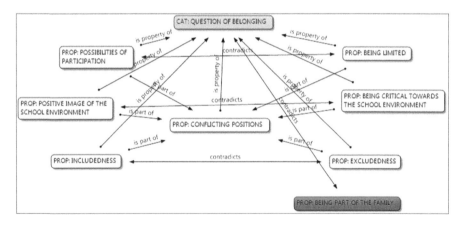

Network View 5.2 Properties of *question of belonging*

---

[8] The use of sign language and the challenges that people experience in relation to it are worth being analysed in depth. As this is not possible within this framework, it has to be postponed.

The central property in this network view is the "conflicting positions". However, being part of the family does not have a counterpart here (not feeling as a part of the family), as it was not part of the discussions with children. This does not mean that the feeling of not being part of the family does not exist. It just was not addressed by any of the statements made by the children. This can be interpreted in the way that it might be hard to talk about or that it really did not exist as such amongst the participating children. In any case, this question cannot be answered here. It has to be added that in the cases where children had left their closer families, their family was replaced by their extended family or the like.

Throughout the discussion, the significance of education to the children was apparent. Therefore, the following chapter summarises the listed categories and concludes with the meaning of education for the children.

Summary and the Meaning of Education for Children

The predefined groups of disabilities (physical, visual, hearing and intellectual) do not play an essential role regarding the categories that emerged, with the exemption of the subcategory language,[9] which is related to the category *developing a positive self-concept*. The reason why the different types of disabilities did not receive special attention individually might be because the interviews were analysed in groups of participants and not following the individual cases (child–parent–teacher), which would have been more according to the different types of disabilities because the individual child would have been at the centre. However, in the present case, the categories *developing a positive self-concept* and *question of belonging* are reflected in one way or the other in all the interviews.[10]

It is in fact not astonishing that the children interviewed exhibited a positive self-perception related to issues of education. Knowing about the background and the meaning which parents, teachers and the society in general gave to education, it became evident that the possibility to attend a school had a positive effect on the children's self-perception. This was especially important as it gave the participating children a feeling of being integrated in society. Simultaneously, the significance of knowledge and learning skills became manifest. The positive self-image can only persist if enough knowledge and skills are acquired to be able to undergo further education, get a good job, support the family or what other wishes the children expressed. This also includes knowledge and skills that allow a person to be as independent as possible and is especially relevant for children with intellectual disabilities. Finally, this leads to the category *question of belonging*, as the children did have the possibilities to attend a school, obtain skills and knowledge and develop feelings

---

[9] Children with other disabilities (especially PI and II) sometimes also exhibited speech problems. This can lead to challenges similar to those faced by children who use sign language.

[10] This should be further explored in another research to identify differences by analysing cases, not groups, of participants.

of belonging. Yet, they were still not treated equally in society and experienced restrictions, discrimination and exclusion. Therefore, this category is based on the question "Where do I belong?". In other words, the possibility of receiving education did not automatically lead to a change in societal attitudes towards children with disabilities, which would be essential for successful inclusion. However, the same was not true for the families of most of the children. Attending a school often led to a revaluation of the child in his/her family.[11] Education therefore led to a different perception of the child as a member of the family. This seemed to be true also for the children themselves. Their perception of their possibilities and their values changed by receiving education. The change of attitudes in the society seems to take a comparatively longer time. Nevertheless, a slight change in attitudes and awareness was already visible. This became clear in particular in the parents' interviews.

Regarding societal and cultural aspects, it can be stated that the view that education leads to a better future reflects the attitude of the Ethiopian society as a whole. Education is generally perceived as one of the main aspects for an improvement of life conditions.

Speaking about education thereby is not reflecting quality education or educational equity. It is simply the fact that the children went to a school, like all the other children. They participated more or less in the classrooms and received more or less education. Hence, education in this context is related to the possibility of going to a school and sitting in a classroom. This clearly shows that future developments have to concentrate on inclusive schooling and quality in education (education as a capability) in order to offer children with disabilities equity in education and equal possibilities to participate in society (reaching functionings that people have reason to value).

Listening to Parents and Caregivers

It became evident very soon that a lot of emphasis was placed on aspects of communication by the parents[12] and teachers. Communication played an important role for the parents after finding out about the disability of their child. The information that the parents got from doctors, friends, the community and their families was a first basis for them to position themselves and react to the situation. This continued when a school had to be found for the children.

The category related to communication and information finally resulted in the category *establishment of knowledge about the child and education*. The parents' knowledge about their child as well as about education grew through communica-

---

[11] There were cases where children were orphans or had moved from the countryside to the city without their parents. In those cases, usually grandparents, aunts or other relatives took care of them and substituted their family.

[12] In the following, the term "parents" is used for parents and caregivers alike, as they play similar roles in this context.

tion and information. Furthermore, this category contains a lot of information about the relation between the parents and their children.

Once at school, the parents' attitudes and expectations usually changed. The category *the walk of shame* reflects this process. "But all in all, we can say that culturally, parents have a negative attitude towards handicapped children. As far as I am concerned, there seems to be a problem in this respect" (Mekoya, teacher). This perception expressed by a teacher might not be applicable for parents in general; however, lots of parents reported a change in their attitudes towards their children, as will be explicated below.

The parents mostly did not have a good education themselves or none at all and did not think they could make any contribution at all to the education of their child. Hence, it became the teachers' responsibility to educate the child and to convince the parents of their abilities and possibilities to support their children regarding education. This is elaborated in detail in the chapter on *parental support*.

Establishing Knowledge About the Child and Education: Developing Trust

The key terms in this category are communication and information. Through communication and interaction with the surrounding, parents gain information about their child and the possibilities that education can offer. Additionally, some parents start to discover new potential in their children. Having this knowledge enables parents to develop trust in their child, and it establishes the foundation for future perspectives and support for the children. However, in order to start the process of establishing knowledge, first and foremost parents have to show interest in and care for their child.

> In fact, I really don't know what he does in his school. (Semira, mother)

The first impression was that the parents seemed to have little information about their child. However, the information which I asked for in the interviews was largely related to school. The majority of the parents did not know very much about issues related to school. However, they had a lot of knowledge about their children in many other areas. These include the child's personality, relation to God, worries, preferences, feelings, physical condition, desires, abilities, behaviour, problems, disadvantages, etc. Yet, after being informed or having learnt about the child's disability, the parents had to deal with a completely new aspect in their life.

> [T]he principal doctor said that my daughter was recovering. She was in the hospital for two days. She received medical treatment and she was well again [...] He explained that she is retarded and that she needs proper care. He went on saying that she walks slowly and eats slowly. He insisted that she should be well taken care of. It was only then that I knew what was wrong with her. I did not know anything about her before she was eight months old. (Mesret, mother)

Visiting hospitals and doctors became a new occupation for parents if they could afford it. Most of the parents also invested a lot of time and energy in religious and traditional beliefs, according to which disabilities can be healed through holy water and other practices. Only later the aspect of education received more attention. Finding a school for the child was very difficult for most of the parents. **Information about schools** that accepted children with disabilities was often not accessible for parents, especially if they were illiterate. This information usually depended on people in the surrounding who made the parents aware that there were schools for children with disabilities and that their child was able to learn.

> People informed me that there is such a school. They suggested that I should take her to this school, where she can learn something. They told me that there is some hope for her there as she will be engaged in some activities. They said that if I keep her in the house, her condition will worsen due to lack of activity. They also felt that she will be prone to other diseases if she remained in that condition. Because of this then, I brought her to this school. It is now three years since she joined this school. (Mesret, mother)

Teachers often also inform their surroundings about the possibilities of education for children with disabilities. Other informants are NGOs or community-based rehabilitation workers. "There was an organization which […] takes care of the orphans due to HIV/AIDS. When they saw her on their way they told me that possibly she can get into a special school" (Almaz, mother). All this information is accessible for the parents as it is communicated verbally.

The way in which the parents got information at schools differed from case to case. At school some had good relationships with the teachers, particularly in the special units and special schools, and communication was facilitated in a familial atmosphere. Others relied on the communication with the child, and some had hardly any communication at all about school with teachers, principals or their children. Hence, when the latter was the case, knowledge about the school hardly existed. This again was related to the parents' belief that they were not of use for their child in school-related issues, as they were not educated themselves. Regarding exchange with other parents, it was interesting to find out that in every school there was a parent–teacher association (PTA). However, many parents did not attend the meetings for different reasons like lack of time, not knowing about the PTA, etc. Therefore, exchange between the parents of children with disabilities did not take place usually. Additionally, in most cases, the school was not located in the vicinity of the families, and the parents did not know other parents from their community who sent their children to the same school. Yet, the parents of children attending special schools seemed to have more **communication** with each other than other parents. This could be related to the size of those schools. Special schools are quite small compared to regular governmental schools, which leads to the situation that people usually know each other. Similarly, the special units in regular schools provide parents with better possibilities to communicate with parents and teachers. Here, the already mentioned **familiarity** plays an essential role regarding information and communication between schools and parents.

Having sent their child to a school, the parents were often surprised about the changes that could be observed in their children. "Previously, he would run, disturb and damage things. But now, although I wonder whether it is caused by mental development, he has changed tremendously" (Rahel, mother). Many of the parents started to **discover the potential of their children**, which is connected to the category *the walk of shame*. Establishing knowledge, however, has further important properties. The parents' **interest and engagement**, for example, as well as their **caring about the child**, are essential preconditions for exchange of information and knowledge.

This network view shows the most essential properties of the category *establishing knowledge about the child and education*. Additionally, first connections are drawn to categories and subcategories of the children's perspective. As the establishment of knowledge is related to caring, interest and engagement on the parents' part, it is related to the child that is perceived as part of the family that has to be taken care of. The aspect of being part of the family is a property of the children's *question of belonging*. I will further explain connections and relations between different categories during the development of the theory.

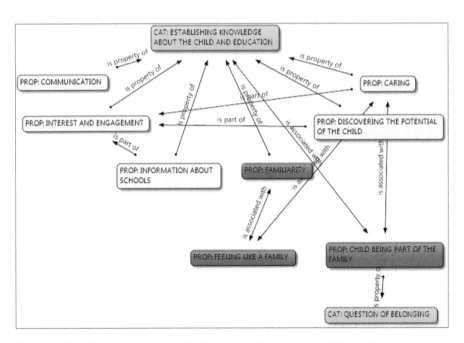

Network View 5.3 Properties of *establishing knowledge about the child and education*

"The Walk of Shame" – Towards a Change in Attitudes: Breaking Free

The basis for this category is viewing disability as a curse by God. It involves feelings of shame and burdens children as well as parents. Education seems to offer a way out of this dilemma and changes the perception of disability. Hence, parents discover the significance of education and possibilities that are opening up. Consequently, they might feel an "atmosphere of departure". They walk the *walk of shame* when they break free from old convictions and take on new perspectives regarding disability in general and their child with a disability in particular.

> I don't believe that disability is a hindrance. I don't think that she will fail to do what others have done. I should bear in mind that there are other people who are in a worse condition than herself. As far as I am concerned, I don't feel bad about her disability now although I used to in the past. (Wongel, mother)

This category contains a more complex process than the ones before. It was therefore considered as helpful to visualise a simplified version of the process in a network view (CAT = category, SC = subcategory).

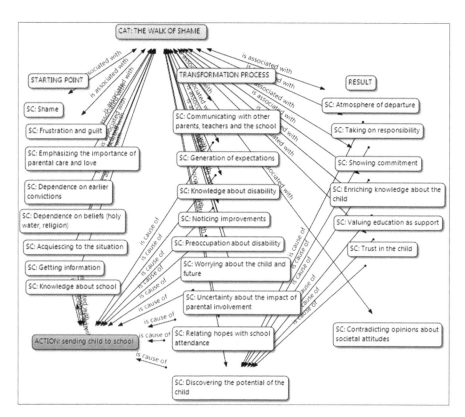

Network View 5.4 The different stages of *the walk of shame*

Different stages can be observed in *the walk of shame*. The three most important ones can be grouped as <u>STARTING POINT</u>, <u>TRANSFORMATION PROCESS</u> and <u>RESULT</u>. The <u>STARTING POINT</u> describes the parents' situation and attitudes before the child was sent to school. Very often the expectations of parents of children with disabilities were not fulfilled, and they had to deal with disappointments and issues which they had not expected (e.g. various perceived restrictions like communication, support at home, school access). The parents usually considered their children not to be able to learn. The disability of a child can provoke a feeling of shame and guilt in the parents' life. Therefore, especially mothers took on a role of being guilty and tried to change the "fate" of having a child with a disability by, e.g. going to holy waters to heal their child. "When I think about it now, I had a great impact on her. If I had accepted all the problems gracefully when I was pregnant, she might not have become a retarded child" (Tigist, mother).

If parents express grief because of a child's disability, the community might feel pity or try to support the family. On the other hand, as disability is understood as a curse, the community often believes that there is a reason for a child's disability and hence locates the responsibility for it in the parents. This can also lead to a feeling of shame. The reasons for shame are usually created by the society itself. There were contradicting statements about societal attitudes. On the one hand, the society and communities seemed to be supportive and helpful for the families. "Society's attitude towards disabled people is now positive. It is positive here in Addis" (Almaz, mother). On the other hand, there are experiences of insult and scolding: "Mostly I quarrel with men; I told them not to touch him. I lost one of my eyes because of him. I always quarrel with my neighbours again because of him. My neighbours insulted me saying I have this kind of child due to my evil deeds and curse" (Adanesh, mother). Seeing disability as a consequence of parents being cursed or having done something wrong has negative implications. From such a perspective, the disability uncovers a weakness that parents seem to have. This again can lead to loss of reputation and negative emotions attached to the child with a disability or the disability as such. However, these feelings did not seem to persist in the parents. "I didn't expect he was able to learn; just like my eldest daughter. Later on when I realised this I was very happy" (Mersha, father). Additionally, beliefs and convictions prevent parents from being able to see the potential of their children with a disability. It seemed that especially the education for their children led to a change in these attitudes.

The <u>TRANSFORMATION PROCESS</u> already began at the end of the first stage by acquiescing to the situation and getting information about education and schools, which is related to the former category *establishing knowledge about the child and education*. However, the main part of the transformation process happened when the child was already at school. On the one hand, the communication with other parents and teachers led to a change in attitudes. On the other hand, improvements that were observed by the parents contributed to a positive attitude towards education and the child with a disability. Throughout this process, certain expectations developed on the parents' part. Education gave the parents hope for the future of their children. The initial feeling of shame and guilt turned into hope and higher expectations. Children performed well at school, or they improved in other aspects related to daily life.

"Some time ago, my son got lost. People found him because he was able to tell the school where he learnt. Education is useful" (Tigist, mother). Hence, the parents started to discover potential in their children which they had not expected. This led to the last stage, the RESULT, which started with a new feeling for the parents: the atmosphere of departure. In other words, the disability of their child was suddenly not only debilitating or producing suffering. There was a way to go, a solution, a new goal to reach that led to a benefit for the children as well as for the whole family. Therefore, the parents started to take on responsibility and show commitment regarding the education for their child with a disability, whereas before uncertainty about the impact of their involvement in educational issues had prevailed. They supported the child and distanced themselves from old beliefs of guilt and shame. As a consequence, their knowledge about the child was enriched, and education was valued as support and constructive input. This is also related to the category *establishing knowledge about the child and education*. Viewed in this context and from the perspective of the capability approach, education can be interpreted as a capability that can lead to certain functionings in life (independence, jobs, etc.). It seems that the parents experienced the possibility of education for their children as such a capability. However, this capability only exists because it was enabled through a first step towards educational equity. This means that equity in education starts with equal possibilities to receive education, i.e. access to schools. The basic capability for education is the ability to learn. Being able to learn, getting the possibility to access school and receive (quality) education finally leads towards more possibilities in life and hence functionings that are valued by the individual as well as society. This improves the children's as well as the parents' well-being and quality of life.

The parents trusted that their children were able to learn and that they might even be able to support the family in the future; in other words, that they were growing up to become a valued member in the community. Hence, the category *the walk of shame* describes the process of change in the parents' attitudes from being ashamed and burdened with their child's disability towards being proud and having future prospects for the child and his or her family. There is a close relation with the category *parental support* as well as with the children's category *question of belonging*. The parents' acceptance of the child and the value which the children gained through education strengthened a feeling of belonging to the family. Furthermore, it supported the children's category of *developing a positive self-concept*.

Communication with CBR workers, teachers, other parents, etc. about the problems that the parents experienced led to more information and knowledge about disability in general.

Most of the parents believed that there was still a reason why their child had a disability and that it was the will of God that put them in this situation. However, it was no longer perceived as a burdensome situation. Parents who sent their children to school developed certain new attitudes and spoke about disability as "nothing", meaning that their child could be a part of society and contribute to the community. In this way, disability did not mean anything. As soon as their child attended a school, the parents were convinced that the child was able to learn. The possibility of education for a child with a disability alone changed the attitudes of his or her parents. In this context, the fact that teachers and principals accepted their child played a major role. Before, negative attitudes on the part of the society and the surrounding community had often influenced the feelings and thoughts of parents regarding disability to a great extent.

The most important properties of the category *the walk of shame* are first and foremost the **possibility and readiness to change** an attitude. Especially in a society where attitudes towards people with disabilities are mostly charged with feelings of pity, shame and guilt, it is not easy to take on a different position. This is true in particular in cases where the community has a big influence on the lives of the people. "I usually cry saying why God gave me this thing. The people also comment 'what did they do', so I just keep crying. But thanks to the Almighty God, he spends his time at school" (Liya, mother). Nevertheless, the parents seemed to distance themselves more and more from such comments and develop different viewpoints: "People used to say that the evil thing they did is why they have dumb and deaf children. However, parents have handicapped children not because they are cursed" (Agnes, mother). **Access to information** and **environments for discussion** can be regarded as further properties of the category as well as the **feasibility of combining the new attitude** with old convictions (from e.g. religious or other traditional backgrounds). **Breaking free from assigned accountability** for a disability requires support. This support can be attained through discussions, exchange and information but also by experiencing change through education.

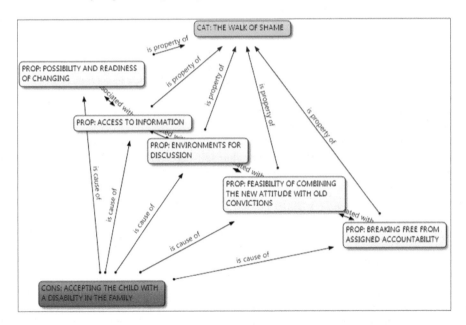

Network View 5.5 Properties of *the Walk of Shame* (This network view only contains properties that have not been listed as a subcategory before. The level of abstraction has grown compared with the other categories at this stage of analysis. Only the category *question of belonging* has reached similar levels of abstraction. The researcher attempts to reflect the process of developing a theory as it actually took place. This includes depicting the stages of each category individually. Hence, the aim to unify these stages exists only up to a certain level to make it convenient for the reader. The reason for the different levels of abstraction is related to the process that the researcher went through in the course of the analysis)

Most of the parents exhibited a certain "walk of shame". For some, it was harder than for others, and it might have taken more time. However, parents who did not feel ashamed of their children with disabilities usually had more information about disability in general before they learnt about the disability of their child. Another important factor was the communication with the child and the possibility to communicate. Hearing-impaired children were often considered as "dumb", as the possibility of communication was usually limited. This connects the topical category to the category *establishing knowledge about the child and education*, as mentioned above. Hence, communication and information becomes a factor for counteracting shame and guilt.

Parental Support: Departure

The most important aspect in this category is the aspect of responsibility that has to be taken on by the parents. Furthermore, parental support is influenced by fears and worries, awareness, possibilities and efforts on the parents' part. All these aspects lead to the different areas of support that parents do or do not give to their children. However, the possibilities that open up through the help of parents for the children add to the atmosphere of departure that is evoked by the parents' *walk of shame.* If parents support their children in education, they contribute to their departure towards their new possibilities.

> I prepare his uniform in the evening. In the morning, he says that he does not want to go to school. He has other brothers, whom I have to see off to school. Then, it is already 9 a.m. when I have to beg him to go to school. I have a hard time with him, but I can't help it because I feel that nothing else is more important to me than my son. (Felekech, mother)

As already indicated in the chapter on children's perspectives, parental support has a lot of influence on the child and his/her self-perception. The relation between the two categories *developing a positive self-concept* and *parental support* is further explicated later.

The category *parental support* started to develop as a code family including codes on **worries and fears** that were grounded in the parent's interviews. Hence, the category was elaborated by exploring the different worries that parents had and how these worries and anxieties were reflected in the support that parents did or did not give to their children. An example of this process is reflected in my following memo:

> There are different types of parental support.
> A very important one is the support that parents (caregivers) give to their children when it comes to the way to school. Children say 'she protects me' (Semret, mother) and most parents talk about how to support their child so he/she gets save to school. Some parents go with their children, stay at school and go home with their children; some only take them and pick them up again; some send them with friends or siblings, so they don't have to go alone.

The fears that the parents are telling us about are first of all related to the transport and traffic. This is due to the problems that the children exhibit because of their low vision, hearing or other restrictions in body functions. It is not really clear if parents would be as worried about their children who don't have a disability. (Memo 22/11/2012)

In addition to worries and fears, parental support is determined by other aspects. These include beliefs and convictions, attitudes, possibilities, the surrounding environment, etc.

However, in a first step, it has to be clarified that "parental support" is everything that parents define as support. In other words, it means getting active for the child and investing time and other resources. Support can be understood as everything that parents believe helps and supports their child, regardless of the effect it has.

The category *parental support* can be divided into six **different types of support**:

- Health and disability: visiting doctors and holy waters
- Independence in daily life: teaching cleanliness, house chores, etc.
- Studying environment: finding a school, supporting studies at home, transport
- Studying at school: getting involved, attending PTA meetings, communicating with the school and teachers
- Encouraging the child: giving self-confidence, being proud, having hopes and expectations, changing attitudes, believing in the child
- (Not being able to support the child: feeling helpless, not having time, illiteracy)

These types of support can also be observed in a process that is similar to the change of attitudes in the category *the walk of shame*. First support is related to expectations of healing and to dealing with the situation, and only later it is related to education.

Regarding the chronological development, the aspect "health and disability" stands first. Visiting doctors and going to holy waters for healing were usually the first measures reported by parents in order to support their child, as many parents took on responsibility for the disability. Furthermore, they tried to support their children in becoming independent. As many of the parents were illiterate, the first aspect in this regard was independence in the daily life. Formal education did not play a role at this stage. Only later, parents also started supporting the child in regard to education, as it promised further independence for the child. This already included the decision to send the child to school. Finding a school for their child and organising transport were the two aspects that were identified where parents **invested** the highest **efforts** to support their children. The parents were very worried about their children getting lost on their way. This problem was connected to the fact that schools that accepted the child with a disability were usually not in the neighbourhood of the communities in which the families lived.[13] This resulted in ways to school which were by and large longer than they are for children without disabilities. Consequently, some parents stayed in the school – as mentioned in the memo above – or in the surrounding of the school until school ended, as going to school twice a day to take and pick up the child was in some cases not affordable due to the

---

[13] This circumstance led to further complications: the parents usually did not know other parents at school from the community, they did not benefit from getting involved in educational matters in the community by sending their child to the neighbouring school, etc.

transportation cost. Further support was identified in relation to education at school. Parents got involved in school related issues only on a very low level. However, a difference could be observed between literate and illiterate parents. Literate parents considered themselves more able to support their child in school related issues. The dread of some (especially illiterate) parents to get involved in such issues could be overcome by communicating with teachers but also with children. Thereby, the parent–teacher association (PTA) of each school played an important role. In regard to the parent–child communication, it was interesting to see that if parents were called, sometimes children insisted that they really came to school. This kind of communication also shows that at times children have the power to influence their parents.

> If the school sends a note to me asking me to come, but I fail to report, she refuses to go to school. She says to me, 'You have been asked to come, not my sister.' And then, she starts crying. But when I react to that saying, 'What will you eat if I don't work?' She replies to me, 'I won't eat. I only want you to come to school.' Even today, she said to me, 'Berhane [the teacher] wants to see you.' I came today because she insisted. When she saw me here, she happily went to class. (Wongel, mother)

This reveals that in some cases children took on the responsibility for their education and familial support. By having children in such a position, also illiterate parents who were not involved in educational matters at school could be informed step by step about their **possibilities to support the child in education**. Others were keen to support their child in any way they could from the outset and considered it as a right that they had. "What does the school expect me to do? If there is anything, I have the right to participate using my potential" (Abraham, father). Whether parents supported their child or not was furthermore closely related to their possibilities and time resources. The explanations of parents who did not come to school often and did not get involved very much in school-related issues were related to time constraints because of having to earn the daily bread or being involved in other daily activities at home,[14] etc. "I know nothing about education. If I had some knowledge about education, I could ask about the performance of my son. I should also do this but I am so busy to get my daily bread" (Semira, mother). Another factor related to time was the parents' fear of what would become of their child when they died. "Besides, I also help him as much as possible. If he gets support from the school, it is my obligation to help him at home. But my fear is that I might die soon before he achieves success. I don't think I will stay long in this world because I usually get sick" (Fatima, mother).

The support that the children received in terms of education also included encouragement. This point might be one of the most important ones for some children. Most parents were happy about the achievements of their children. However, there was also disappointment in cases where the expectations were higher than the achieved results. In these cases the parents had mostly hoped for improvements regarding the child's disability. This was especially visible in relation to the children identified as having an intellectual disability.

---

[14]Concerning this point especially, the financial compensation for the interviews was very important.

Y   *Were you following her up before that?*
Me   I was. The teachers are right. She has gradually gone worse. I am disappointed. All
       my efforts are in vain. (Mesret, mother)

Parents usually had great hopes as soon as their child attended a school. These hopes turned into expectations and were as such easily disappointed. "Others say that they have not seen any change. If we don't see any improvement in spite of all the time that we have invested, we get disappointed" (Rahel, 2E-II-D-8-GIP). Yet, lots of parents were proud of the achievements of their children. They believed in their children and developed positive attitudes towards education in cases where they had not already known about the child's abilities related to educational achievements before. Furthermore, education seemed to develop to be one of the most important aspects for the parents in regard to the future of their child with a disability. It was the key for escaping poverty and having the chance to live a better life. "I don't let him stop schooling. I know how difficult it is not to be educated" (Semira, mother). This shows that the parents' **awareness of the importance** and possibilities **of education** was sometimes already there before the child was sent to school. However, mostly it developed with the child attending school.

The last type of support was "not being able to support" the child. This constitutes the counterpart to the aforementioned types of support. Here, the feeling of helplessness because of illiteracy, lack of money and other means was as hindering as time constraints.

Within the category of *parental support*, three dimensions[15] could be singled out:

– Time
– Energy
– Money

The first two dimensions were applicable for most of the parental support. The third dimension "money" was not always needed in relation to caring for the child. This would indicate that poverty is not decisive regarding parental support. However, the dimension of "time" could be identified as the most significant one in relation to the parents supporting their children. And this again is connected to the dimension of "money". Most of the parents reported that they were too busy to support their children adequately as they needed to earn their income. Furthermore, the parents felt guilty for not being able to help their children more: "If they ask me to leave my job even for one day, I can't do it. What I have to do is that I have to work everywhere; when he returns home from school I have to feed him properly. Other than this I'm afraid I can't help him" (Semira, mother). Hence, the dimension of "time" determines the extent of support which the parents could give to their children.

The following network view gives an overview of the category including its most important properties.

---

[15] Dimensions are always measurable extents or quantities. The researcher mentioned in the earlier footnote number 46 that dimensions cannot be applied to all of the categories. However, in the case of *parental support*, different dimensions could be identified clearly.

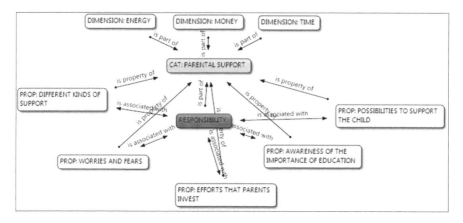

Network View 5.6 Properties of *parental support*

The analysis showed that the category of "parental support" is strongly related to responsibility. Responsibility can be understood as taking on responsibility for the child's disability, being responsible for the child or being overburdened by taking on responsibility. Furthermore, without any feeling of responsibility there would not by any kind of parental support. In this way, responsibility was the motor for the parents supporting their child. In this context, one exception has to be mentioned. Religious beliefs were sometimes also a reason for supporting the child. One parent stated that she was afraid to be punished by God if she would not support the child properly. This indicates that it is also the will of God that parents care for their children with disabilities. However, responsibility as a motor for support can have positive effects (enhancing support) as well as negative effects (not feeling responsible and hence not supporting the child).

Summary and the Meaning of Education for the Parents

The three categories *establishing knowledge about the child and education, the walk of shame* and *parental support* share one essential aspect: responsibility. This aspect became relevant in all three categories. It was a prerequisite for establishing knowledge as well as for changing attitudes and for supporting the child. Without a feeling of responsibility (and possibilities) for influencing and improving the future life of their children, the parents would not go through the mentioned processes. Thus, communication and information shaped the parents' views of their children and influenced the development of responsibility as regards education.

> My son encountered hearing problems when he was two years old. Before that he could hear; his problem is the result of meningitis. I have never thought of getting educational opportunities for him. When he grew up, people informed me that he could learn in a school

where disabled children attend. The moment I heard about this I was really happy. My worry was what would happen if he was deaf and illiterate and stayed at home for the rest of his life. (Mersha, father)

The parents' worries were usually about the children's future. In this context education played a significant role. However, in the focus group discussion in school C during the second phase of interviews, it became clear that the school was considered much more than just a place for education. The parents expressed their worries when their children were in the village. They spoke about them being insulted, beaten and not respected. In the school, the parents felt that their children were safe and could not get on the wrong track. In other words, they were looked after and would not develop bad habits. Hence, school assumed the role of supporting the parents. The parents believed that education established a strong foundation for the future lives of their children. Furthermore, education enabled the children to care for their family.

Regarding societal and cultural aspects within these categories, the aspect of caring for the family can certainly be mentioned. On the one hand, it was a relief for the parents to be able to see their children attending a school like other children. In this way, the children were integrated at school to a certain extent and new possibilities started to open for them. Consequently the parents discovered future perspectives for their children. On the other hand, education served children with disabilities to be able to support the family in the future. In other words, education led to a better integration of the children and hence to relief for their parents and provided the children with future perspectives and capabilities that might serve their family and also disburden their parents. Education therefore can be understood as support for the parents and family as it takes a lot of worries and pressure from them.

An important cultural aspect was the one of religion. The people in the interviews turned out to be very religious and give a lot of meaning to their beliefs. Even though there are several religions, Christianity and Islam are the predominant ones in Ethiopia. The participants were all either Muslims or Orthodox Christians. God was always referred to as the one who decides, as the one who gives and takes and as God the Almighty. Lots of parents thought there must be a reason why God decided to give them a child with a disability. In some of these interviews, obvious contradictions could be observed. Belief was not coherent with the later explanations of parents that disability was not related to God or religion at all. This indicates that even if parents learnt about and explained the reasons for disabilities, the belief in a deeper meaning of the child's disability was very strong. The coexistence of both convictions did not seem to cause problems. This point is also strongly related to the property "feasibility of combining the new attitude with old convictions" of the category *the walk of shame*.

The question of equity and justice was raised in relation to two aspects: First, parents discussed and also questioned the belief of divine justice in relation to having a child with disability. Second, most families aspired equity for their child with disability through the possibility of receiving education and educational equity. The latter again is referring to achievement, fairness and opportunity in education.

Listening to the Teachers

For this chapter, it is important to recapitulate that the schools of the sample can be divided into those with a special setting[16] and those with an integrative setting. Special setting refers to a special school or a special unit (classroom(s)) within a regular school. In the following, they will be called schools with a special setting. In this setting, the children in the classes usually have the "same kind of disability" (categorised by teachers or doctors). In schools with integrative classrooms,[17] between one and three children with different disabilities attend a regular classroom together with children without disabilities. In the following, they will be called schools with an integrative setting.

As mentioned in the previous chapter, the communication between teachers and parents was often identified as a problematic aspect in the teachers' interviews. This led to the development of different code families and subcategories that were related to the way of exchanging information between parents and teachers and communication in general. The category that emerged from this analysis is called *establishing relationships*. Another category that was identified is related to teacher education. Lots of problems raised by teachers were grounded in the need of teacher education. This in turn is related to the second category *quality of education* in the schools. Last but not least, *commitment and motivation* was discovered as the most important category related to the teachers' interviews; it was the most important because compared with other categories it reflected more various aspects that were considered as essential regarding the education for children with disabilities. In other words, it was the "richest" category related to teachers.

Establishing Relationships: Investing in Working Atmosphere

This category is about building a basis for teachers to cooperate with parents in a way to be able to support the children. Conflict and trust between parents and teachers both play important roles in this context. Teachers often complain about parents who do not cooperate in the way they would expect it. Establishing relationships therefore can be seen as an investment by teachers to improve their working atmosphere with the children. An important aspect is the *feeling like a family* that refers to special relations between teachers and parents mainly in special settings.

> [...] [I]f the teacher discusses with the student or parents, he can solve the student's problem. Moreover, if parents inform teachers about the problem of their child, his problem can be solved [...] in the school. Similarly, if the problems of the school are communicated to parents, parents may solve the problems of their children to improve their behaviour. Therefore, to make students clever in schools, I believe that parents and teachers should get together regularly and have a good relationship. (Kadhi, teacher)

---

[16] Four schools of the sample (C, D, F, G).

[17] Three schools of the sample (A, B, E).

The category of *establishing relationships* is mainly related to the communication with parents, even though communication with children also played a role in the interviews. However, the subcategories that developed in relation to communication involved parents only. One observation in the teachers' interviews showed that in schools, the communication between parents and teachers was not really enough. "We need information from parents more often. We want to know their [children's] improvements daily. What we do here, in this school only, is not enough. All of us if we don't cooperate and work together, we do not bring any change" (Abkale, teacher). Furthermore, **the teachers complained** about parents not coming to school when they were called; the teachers did not usually call the parents except when there were problems which they could not solve by themselves. But since mobile phones had reached such a high degree of distribution also amongst the poor population, the possibility to call parents or text them on their mobile phones **facilitated the communication** between parents and teachers tremendously.[18] The teachers also expected the parents to support their children. "We would like parents to encourage their children to engage in vocational work. But we don't expect any support from them regarding our teaching profession. We want them to be self-reliant and not to expect anything from the government and the school" (Abeba, teacher). This is a clear statement indicating that teachers did not see the parents' responsibility in any teaching related issue. Besides, the teachers saw problems related to their own responsibility: "In reality, there is a **weakness** on our part too. It would have been good to know how she [a student] studies at home and how she lives. But I never asked such questions" (Biniyam, teacher). The parents in turn were generally very content with teachers and also with the level and frequency of communication with them. Hence, a **differing perception** of the situation regarding exchange could be observed between parents and teachers. This might lead to conflicts. The teachers also identified **potential areas of conflict**:

> If students who join grade one often come from a poor family, it will be difficult for parents to fulfil the needs of their children. This, in turn, can create conflict between the teachers and the students. The students don't have exercise books and pens. Besides, they fail to take good care of the materials they need for school. And if we insist that this has to be done, conflict might arise between the children and their parents. (Yemenushal, teacher)

In this case, the teacher was also aware of the **risk of creating conflict** between family members. Without sufficient communication, such problems could lead to difficult situations. An interesting point that arose within the topic of communication was the **attribution of "family"**. This was used more by teachers from special settings but also by the ones in inclusive settings. The teachers repeatedly described their communication with parents in family-related terms.

Y: *How do you work with parents?*
A: With parents? We are just families and they proved this on different meetings we had. We know each other with every family. When their students misbehave they come

---

[18] "Similar to industrial, newly developing and other so-called developing countries, the use of ICT devices in Ethiopia, such as mobile phones, computers, etc., has risen substantially within the last 15 years" (Schiemer and Proyer 2013, 102).

straight to us and tell us everything such as if they [the children] come very late at night, and when they steal their money, everything. [sic] (Temesgen, expert and teacher[19])

Additionally, teachers who did not communicate very much with parents in some cases talked about the child with a disability as a family member. This mostly happened in the integrative settings and hence in bigger groups and classes: "By the way, I don't want to call parents to school. I take my own measure. First I warn him and if it is worse I beat him myself.[20] This is because I consider my students as my own children" (Kadhi, teacher). The attribution of family meant on the one hand **taking on responsibilities** like in a family, which obviously includes taking disciplinary measures. On the other hand, it implied a familial atmosphere and **trust** between parents and teachers. In this way, family meant supporting and helping each other as well as mutual understanding. Beating a child was also considered as supportive for the child by the teacher, as it seemed to lead to an improvement in behaviour from the teacher's perspective. However, it is important to mention that children did not talk about the school in such a way. When talking about their family, they never included teachers or school staff. It is clear that children put the focus on supporting their families in the future, which did not include teachers. In the children's interviews, aspects mentioned in relation to school were always education, studying, friends and ideas about their future occupation.

Teachers with commitment wanted to support the students and their families. To be able to do so, information and communication were an essential basis. In some cases, however, it was not easy to get the information needed.

Some other parents do not tell us their problems. Some say that they did not come to school because of shortage of transportation. Some others say that they come from a distance of 30 to 40 kilometres, that is, from Sebeta. Some come late to school despite the fact that they live in the vicinity. All sorts of reasons are given. (Belte, teacher)

The communication within the school differed mostly depending on the setting. The smaller schools and classes (usually special settings) showed closer relations amongst teaching staff and principals. However, this could also be observed in one integrative setting in school E, where the principal showed a lot of commitment and the teachers felt supported.

Communication establishes relationships, which can lead to solutions for various problems. Yet, the teachers had a **two-sided attitude** towards the necessity of communication regarding the parents. On the one hand, they complained about parents who did not go to school even when they were called. On the other hand, they preferred to solve problems by themselves. Hence, the **degree of involvement** that was expected of parents was not always defined clearly by the teachers. The following network view gives an overview of important properties of the category.

---

[19] The expression "expert and teacher" is used for differenciating special needs experts in schools and headmasters from teachers without such an additional role.

[20] Physical punishment is not allowed anymore in Ethiopian schools. Nevertheless, some teachers still use it as a disciplinary measure.

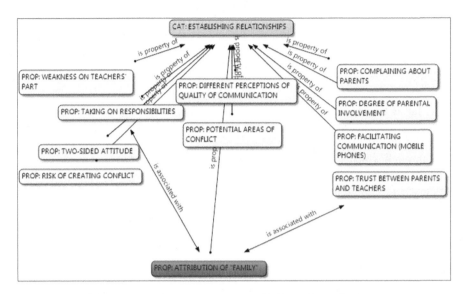

Network View 5.7 Properties of *communication (establishing relationships)*

The left-hand side of the network view is only about teachers, whereas the right-hand side is about the teachers' relationship with the parents. The part in the centre is about parents and teachers. This illustration shows that the relationships between teachers and parents were very unsteady. On the one hand, there were feelings of family in some cases; on the other hand, parental involvement was considered not to be enough. And again in other cases, the teachers preferred not to involve parents too much in school-related issues. It did not become clear which degree of parental involvement was considered to be the best for the children and their education.

However, establishing relationships in general can be seen as a resource that serves the education for children with disabilities. Hence, also relationships and communication between teachers but also between teacher and child are essential resources for the teaching–learning process. Resources also play an important role in the next chapter.

Quality of Education: Needing Support

The category *quality of education* refers above all to the support that teachers need in order to be able to improve the situation for children with disabilities (as well as for children in general) at school. It deals with teacher education in terms of teachers' frustration due to a lack of teaching methods and material as well as with the resources that teachers themselves use when teaching children with disabilities.

> I am trained in a special needs college. But it doesn't give me full capacity to help such students [with disabilities]. A teacher who specialises in one area can't manage everything. The course which I took in special needs is another thing. If I don't include my creativity, it wouldn't help me in all aspects to handle problems. Students with such problems must not be trained in such a school which has not enough facilities. All of their teachers must be well trained and well equipped. (Emayu, teacher)

As far as the aspect of teacher training regarding the management of inclusive classrooms is concerned, all the teachers asked for more training. The Ethiopian government initiated a mandatory special needs course in the teacher training colleges through which all teachers received an introduction into special needs education (Alemu Aberra,[21] expert). This course is not very extensive, and the interviews with teachers showed that it gives insights into causes of disability and focuses on a medical model rather than providing teachers with tools for classroom management and teaching methods and adding the perspective of different models of disability (e.g. the social model). The problem of quality in teacher education was also addressed in the interviews with experts from outside the schools including the interviews with the Minister (see in the chapter on experts). However, the category *quality of education* refers to the education for children with disabilities, which is strongly related to the quality of teacher education. In this regard, the parents did not see a problem related to the qualification of teachers. In most cases, they were very happy about the teachers' skills, and they even argued that the teachers had more potential in dealing with their children than they themselves. Hence, teachers **are highly valued by parents.** However, in general teachers do not have a high **value in society,** and their payment is low. Additionally, the teachers themselves felt overwhelmed by many challenges that they had to face. Here it could be argued that from a capability approach perspective, the capabilities of the teacher to teach well are not supported to reach the functionings to really teach well. In other words, the conversion factors that would turn the capability to teach into a functioning are not applied enough. A conversion factor in this context would be, e.g. teacher training.

However, a lack of teaching resources, the high number of students and a lack of knowledge often led to **frustration** amongst the teachers. Additionally, they realised that they would need more training in some aspects like methods of teaching and integrating children with disabilities.

> There are many things I feel I lack. For example, I would appreciate if somebody like you, who is an expert in special needs, observes how I teach and tells me that I have to develop this skill or that. But I face reality by myself. I apply the methods I was taught. Earlier, there used to be a foreigner from whom we learnt many things. So, we try to apply that. I strive to do as best as I can. (Abkale, teacher)

Then again, the interviews revealed many **resources** that can be attributed to the teachers and that were used for solving most of their problems. Amongst them were communication with others, becoming active, having confidence, having additional knowledge, having positive attitudes, etc. "Yeah, in here ah, just we shared ahm, there is an experience sharing, we share experiences with each other. [*I: Between teachers?*] Yeah, teachers with teachers or, that's good for, for us, for new teachers

---

[21] Head of the special needs department at Kotebe College of Teacher Education in Addis Ababa.

especially [...]" (Mamite, teacher). Other resources included the teacher's awareness of the child's problem, seeing the child as an individual and discovering
resources in the child. These resources often became visible through the child's
improvements, development and positive impressions that the teachers had of the
children. In other words, the teacher's knowledge about the child can unveil hidden
resources. Of course, the quality of education is closely related to the teacher's
competencies. However, children's and parents' resources can also contribute to a
good quality in education and support the teaching–learning process.

A surprising aspect was the fact that many of the teachers reported that it was not
their first choice to become a teacher. The following quotation is a special one as the
interviewed teacher was blind. She was one of the teachers who had a disability and
was interviewed in the course of this research. Other teachers with disabilities were
only found in schools for hearing impaired students. There most of the teachers had
a hearing impairment.[22]

> No, if I were not blind, I would not have become a teacher; you see our destiny is quite limited,
> not like you the seeing; we have few alternatives including sociology, law or teaching; I think
> I will change [my profession] in the future. At the moment, what is available is a diploma
> programme in teaching; yet in the future I have plans to change my field. (Belte, teacher)

This blind teacher clearly stated that it was not her choice to become a teacher but
that it was due to few alternatives. Further reasons were given by other teachers:
"Generally, this [becoming a teacher] was an option in the place where I was living.
Since I didn't have a job for a year, I hate being jobless. At that time there was a
vacancy announcement looking for teachers whereupon I applied there even though
my interest was to be a nurse" (Alem, teacher). These quotations show that a lack of
possibilities restricted these teachers in choosing the profession they wanted. This can
also have consequences on the quality of the teaching–learning process. Nevertheless,
some teachers liked certain aspects of teaching despite not having chosen it in the first
place. "The salary is low. I never thought I would be a teacher. In addition, I don't
know what I will be in the future. It gives you pleasure to see the children changeas
you teach them. But I don't like it as a profession" (Biniyam, teacher).

The teachers also talked about the challenges of being a teacher: "We also teach
them slowly since they lack knowledge of the subjects they learn. We also use various teaching aids to enhance their understanding of what is taught. We try hard to
help them. So, teaching is a demanding job" (Yemenushal, teacher). This demanding job needs support in lots of aspects, especially in cases where a lack of material
and teacher education complicates the situation. Therefore, the teachers talked
about **different areas where they needed support**:

- Cooperation at school (with other teachers and administration)
- Solutions regarding restricted time (workload) and number of students
- Material (regular textbooks as well as special material for teaching children with
  disabilities)

---

[22] It would be interesting to analyse how the statements of teachers with and without disabilities
differ from each other and to what extent. However, this would go beyond the scope of this book
and is recommended for a separate study.

– Knowledge and information about children from parents about disabilities (reasons of the disability, possibilities of rehabilitation, etc.), and about special needs education (including Braille and sign language)
– Motivational support (in cases of feeling frustrated and overburdened)

> B: We haven't got any training in special needs.
> Y: *So, how can you help her?*
> B: There isn't any special support that I can give. In a classroom where there are sixty students it is rather difficult to properly follow up what students are doing. So, the way things stand, it is impossible to give special assistance to an individual student. We teach twenty-four periods per week. Perhaps, we have only two free periods. Being as it is, it will be difficult to give individual attention to a student. (Biniyam, teacher)

Hence, the quality of education for children in general and for children with disabilities in particular depended on various factors. From the teachers' perspective, there was a clear need for support regarding special needs education. In other words, they needed tools to be able to manage classrooms with integrative settings as well as with special settings. Therefore, they needed special training, information from the parents (communication) and support material. Furthermore, most classes were too big in terms of the number of children. All of these aspects limited the quality of education for the children with disabilities. Last but not least, motivational issues and teachers' commitment played an essential role. This will be discussed in the next chapter. The following network view gives an overview of the most essential properties and essential aspects of the category *quality of education*.

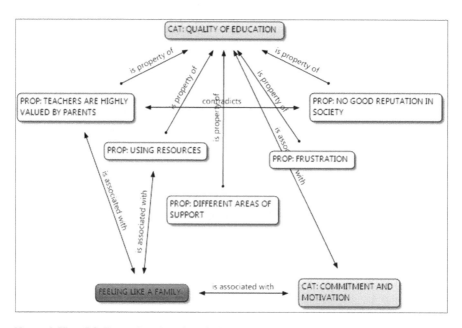

Network View 5.8 Properties of *quality of education*

It seemed that the high value that parents usually attributed to the teachers did not give them enough motivation. The low reputation in society rather added to feelings of frustration and low motivation. However, also referring to the previous chapter on establishing relationships, it can be stated that the communication with parents had an important influence on the quality of education. At this point, the item "feeling like a family" comes into play. The analysis showed that the commitment of the teachers was higher when a familial atmosphere existed between teachers and parents. A high degree of commitment enhances the quality of education, as can also be seen in the next chapter.

Commitment and Motivation: Being on the Road

This category is based on teachers' well-being in the school community (including teaching staff, children and parents). Working with and supporting children with disabilities requires commitment and motivation. Hence, "being on the road" refers to the teachers' situation in the process of supporting children with disabilities in receiving education. The more teachers like their working environment, the more commitment and motivation can be identified. Additionally, it is essential what teachers think about their profession, that is, if it makes sense for them and what they gain from it themselves (reassurance, satisfaction or frustration, excessive demand, etc.). In this way, it is linked closely to the category *quality of education*. However, it differs from the latter regarding the surrounding that is involved. Quality of education refers more to teachers' macro-systems (teacher education in general, different resources and society), whereas commitment and motivation refer to the teachers' micro-systems inside school (Bronfenbrenner 1980).

> You would be happy if you see the changes of these children. One boy came to this school almost a month ago. He couldn't even walk; they brought him to our school carrying him on their back. Within one month he started to walk carrying his own bag. When we see this kind of improvement, we feel very happy for ourselves. We thank also our Almighty God. Once I convinced myself this is my profession, I like it. Especially I am observing improvements on the children. This makes me happy. I will not be offended by people's misconduct. But the profession needs commitment. The education itself brings behavioural change. That is to say it also changes your behaviour. (Abkale, teacher)

Many of the issues and actions which the teachers talked about were related to commitment. In this context, commitment can be identified as becoming active to support the child, using own resources, showing empathy for the child and caring for the child. Furthermore, the teachers talked about the goals that they wanted to reach by supporting the parents and children. Hence, they took on responsibility for educating and supporting the children. This also became visible in the teachers' knowledge about the needs of the children, including health issues. Last but not least, the degree of satisfaction with their profession had an influence on the teachers' commitment. Within the category *commitment and motivation*, I found out that in relation to children, commitment was shown more in cases where the teacher felt like family concerning the child. "I have little brothers, and I consider my students as if they are my children or my little brothers. Unless I consider them as my own family there is no way of improving their character. Thus, this needs commitment" (Kadhi, teacher). Considering students as family also means taking on responsibility for their education and issues beyond education. Hence, the teachers partly took on the responsibilities of the parents. This goes along with the aspect of 'taking on responsibility' of the category *establishing relationships*. Consequently, the aspect of family was a key element for improving the student's achievements and well-being.

The biggest challenge regarding the teachers in this context were motivational issues. Motivational issues include a set of feelings and circumstances that were expressed by the teachers. They reached from "not wanting to become a teacher" in the first place to lack of material and teacher training amongst others.

Hence, **factors that discouraged** the teachers in schools in general were the low payment and the low reputation which the job has in society. Most teachers – especially in governmental schools – seem to be frustrated or feel a lack of support in their efforts to find solutions to their problems. "You know, many teachers are quitting the job. Others go home as soon as they have finished teaching. No one wants to spend more time at school" (Biniyam, teacher). However, there were teachers who still had goals and visions for the children. Furthermore, I identified differences in teacher motivation and attitudes between schools with special settings and integrative settings in governmental schools on the other hand. This is not surprising, as special units and special schools tend to organise themselves in different ways. As the focus in these settings lies on disability, almost everybody in the special unit or school is informed about and also experienced in the challenges teachers and children with disability are facing. This means that a higher level of awareness prevails.

In addition to that, I observed a **high teacher turnover** in governmental schools. The same did not seem to happen as frequently in special units or special schools. This also suggests a stronger bond between the teachers in the special settings. Hence, their **identification with the job** was higher and their commitment led to more motivation in the job. This might also result from a feeling of community and belonging in the special settings. This sense of community might have been missing for some of the teachers of our sample especially in governmental schools and therefore have added to frustration and dissatisfaction. For teachers in special settings, the sense of belonging seemed to exist to a very high extent. This could be identified by statements like: "We feel like a family here."

In regular classrooms in governmental schools, the teachers did not seem to have many **possibilities of exchange** or discussion about disability issues in relation with education. An interesting aspect in this context was that many of the teachers in special units that were integrated in regular schools did not feel supported by their colleagues from the regular classrooms.

> Yes, all the teachers should take training. They [regular teachers] consider everything as our [teachers in special unit] own job. They do not give any attention at all. Even if disabled children disturb in the other sections, they order us to come and take them. They don't even

think of helping us with their potential. Last time one boy was missing and we were worried too much, finally he was found. The boy was autistic; even if seeing him they don't bother about him. Even if we go to our home, they phone us if there is any problem. (Abkale, teacher)

This indicates that the separation of the classes separates the teachers in this system. This again leads to a lack of cooperation between the teachers. Therefore **solidarity** or **good working climate through exchange and mutual understanding** were major factors for teacher motivation when having to deal with special needs and inclusion. These situations might also lead to a positive feeling of community or a familial atmosphere in the school.

The teachers in the special settings mostly received better training than regular teachers. This was due to the fact that those teachers were usually special needs teachers from teacher training institutions that had a focus on special needs. Nevertheless, special needs teachers also claimed that they needed more training, tools, etc. for teaching children with special needs.

I observed that the conditions for children with disabilities in special settings seemed to be better in relation to the teachers' knowledge and training as regards class management, disability issues in general and teaching methods. As disability was an everyday reality for those teachers, their level of awareness and engagement was usually higher. The colleagues and the school administration in special schools seemed to be much more involved also in disability-specific topics, which contributed to a positive attitude concerning the inclusion of children with disabilities. This was an important aspect for teacher motivation.

Looking back on the discussion, a first reasoning would be that a feeling of togetherness and belonging becomes crucial for teacher motivation. Referring to the different settings of the sample, the positive climate, teacher motivation, commitment and the "feeling of being a family", a kind of "community feeling", dominated in the special settings. This might also be related to the size of the schools and classrooms in those settings.

This community feeling seemed to increase the teachers' mutual respect, their feeling of responsibility and belonging to the school. Hence, **approaching school itself as a community** can be very fruitful especially regarding the Ethiopian context. The special societal and cultural meaning of community in Ethiopia (Schiemer 2013) seems to have an essential impact on teachers' commitment and motivation. The following network view lists the properties of the category *commitment and motivation.*

Almost all of the teachers were aware of the problems and challenges that people and especially children with disabilities faced. The tendency showed that the teachers in special units were more committed to addressing these problems than the teachers in integrative settings, who seemed to be detached and more frustrated.

What is described here points at conditions for the teachers' commitment and motivation. In other words, with a lack of certain circumstances, the teachers lost or did not develop commitment in their profession. Teaching in an environment where support, solidarity and a familial atmosphere did not exist, teacher motivation was more likely to turn into frustration. However, there were teachers who were very committed to their profession.

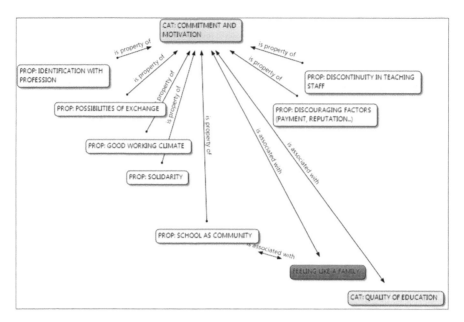

Network View 5.9 Properties of *commitment and motivation*

M	*Why did you want to teach these children? What is the reason?*
A	The reason?
Y	*Yes.*
A	Shall I tell you the real reason? Well, that is because of an internal yearning. While I was teaching regular students, special needs students would come to the school. Since neither the teachers nor the administration have any idea about special needs, they would be told to go back home. Then, I began to think. I said to myself, 'What would I do if these are my children since I myself have children'. I would think about this the whole night. There were one beautiful girl and two boys. They were deaf. They were in my friend's class. Their parents were called and were told to take back their children. They did that with tears. Three days later, a girl with behaviour disorder was dismissed. Then, while sleeping at night, I began to think of something. I said to myself, 'Why shouldn't I take these students to my class, sit them in the front row and control them?' I then started with two of my students and these students. I desired to see change in them. I didn't know sign language. There was also a blind student. They were altogether five disabled students. I sat them in the front seats. I would write for them. I began to teach them in this way. (Adanesh, teacher)

Summary and the Meaning of Education for Teachers

The main aspect that was part of all categories that developed from the teachers' interviews was taking on responsibility. This was also the main aspect in the parents' interviews. *Establishing relationships*, *quality of education* and *commitment and motivation* are categories that are mainly related to the interaction between parents, children and teachers and the responsibilities that were shared, distributed or included in this interaction. Furthermore, all of the categories are connected to the quality of the educational environment for children with disabilities. Hence, they have an influence on the quality of education. Even though the children were not given much emphasis in this part, the teachers were aware of their challenges.

> The other thing is that it is difficult to teach both disabled students and normal students together. Especially for the teachers it is difficult to manage. For instance, those who are mentally retarded cannot cope with other students. It is difficult to teach them equally. The way they understand the lesson is different. The normal students can understand quickly, whereas the mentally retarded children need quite a long time to understand. Those disabled children who have got a problem physically, since they don't have mental problems, can understand any subject like normal students. But, there is a problem when they do sport activities. It is not possible to train them in a comfortable manner. (Kadhi, teacher)

It became evident that it was almost impossible to focus on an individual child due to the high number of children and the workload that the teachers faced. In other words, if they were given the required support, they would not have a feeling of being overburdened. Nevertheless, it was clear to the teachers how important education for children with disabilities is. Hence, also here the aspect of responsibility got special attention. Teachers who took on responsibility for the children that they were teaching showed a high level of commitment but at the same time seemed to be more exposed to potential frustration. They reached their limits more often, as their striving to support the children often went beyond their possibilities. Therefore, teachers who did not take on so much responsibility, who did not show as much commitment to quality of education for all children as other teachers, were not exposed to this kind of problems. However, the teachers' possibilities were very important in this context. They depended on their personal skills, their education and their experience. Sometimes a lack of interest also led to lower quality in the teaching–learning process. This lack of interest and low motivation usually resulted from limiting factors (lack of material, lack of teacher training, etc.). Finally, even though the tendency was such that in special settings the teachers were more able to support the children, in school E the teachers seemed to be very well trained and supported in managing the integrative setting there.

> They are lucky when they come to this school. When they leave the school completing grade eight after national examination, they will face problems when they go to government schools. They do not support them like us; they do not protect them. As you see here the compound is small, we do have only fifty students in a class; because of this they are privileged. In school E I do not think they have problems. (Aster, teacher)

This teacher emphasised the problematic situation in governmental schools compared to school E where he was working. Hence, it is clear that the quality of education that the children received differed from school to school. This fact is also addressed in the OECD report "Equity and Equality in Education" (OECD 2012). "Low performing disadvantaged schools often lack the internal capacity or support to improve, as school leaders and teachers and the environments of schools, classrooms and neighbourhoods frequently fail to offer a quality learning experience for the most disadvantaged" (OECD 2012, 4).

Defining Conflicts and Relating Categories

This part of the book is about developing theoretical concepts that explain the relations between the categories that were discussed above.

The following table gives an overview of the categories. The core category (*feeling like a family*) is left aside as it will be considered on a different level of the analysis.

In each of the groups (children, parents, teachers), there seems to be a category that marks a starting point (necessary basis, developing trust, investing in working atmosphere) and a stage of dispute (struggle, breaking free, needing support). Furthermore, it stands out that only in regard to parents and teachers, categories have developed which reach the phase of the already discussed "atmosphere of departure" (breaking free, departure, being on the road). It cannot be neglected that also in the children's interviews clear goals were set and ways towards reaching these goals were defined. Hence, also for children, education means an opening door for their future. In the words of the capability approach, the children's capability of "education" can lead to the functioning of "developing a sense of belonging" (to society). To be more specific, the functioning is precisely the reality of belonging to society by being a valued member (doing valuable acts).

Yet, it is also evident that children are still in the midst of the **struggle of where they belong**. Regarding the parents, the *walk of shame* is a category that clearly illustrates the parents' **struggle towards a change in attitude**. As far as the teachers are concerned, the struggle that could be identified takes place in the areas of commitment and motivation, support and teacher education, possibilities and frustration. This can be subsumed under **taking on responsibility** for the children and education.

Hence, one consequence of education for children with disabilities is a struggle about belongingness. Thereby, the disability and consequently exclusion and restrictions form the basis. For parents a struggle of changing their attitude is the main conflict. The situation of sometimes being perceived in their communities as cursed by being parents of children with disabilities and also their own attitudes form the starting point of their conflict. As far as the teachers are concerned, a struggle of taking on responsibility in their profession receives the most attention. Regarding this conflict, the low reputation of their profession in society can be seen as one indicator. However, different interests (e.g. wanting to change professions) also

Table 5.1 Overview of categories

Children	Parents	Teachers
Developing a positive self-concept (*necessary basis*)	Establishing knowledge about the child and education (*developing trust*)	Establishing relationships (*investing in working atmosphere*)
Question of belonging (*struggle*)	"The walk of shame" (*breaking free*)	Quality of education (*needing support*)
	Parental support (*departure*)	Commitment and motivation (*being on the road*)

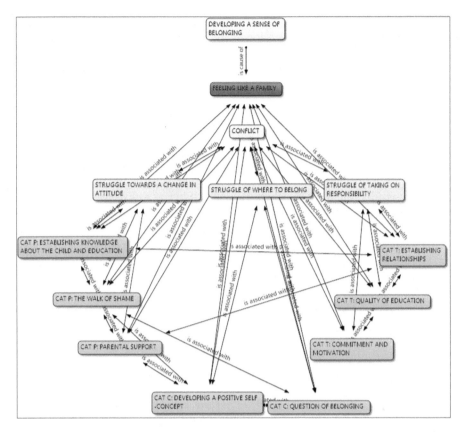

Network View 5.10 Conflicts related to categories

come into play. It becomes clear that conflicts do exist for all participants. These conflicts hamper the capability for education in order to reach the functioning of belonging in the children. *Feeling like a family* is the main vector to pull the conflicts towards solutions.

The following network view illustrates the conflicts and relations between the categories, including the core category *feeling like a family*.

The core category *feeling like a family* constitutes a concept for managing difficult situations as it solves the identified conflicts on a certain level by leading towards "developing a sense of belonging". Looking at "developing a sense of belonging" as a functioning that develops through certain capabilities, one barrier, but also motor, to develop such functionings is – next to *feeling like a family* – poverty, as will be explained at the end of this chapter. However, it must be pointed out that the core category can also be identified as a functioning on a different level (e.g. when looking at it on the meso-level, where only the school community is contemplated, not society in general).

For children one major reason for striving to reach their goals of being educated and independent is being able to support the family. This supports *developing a positive self-concept.* By reaching this point, they would integrate themselves in society and define their place of belonging, hence answering the *question of belonging.* For parents, having a child with a disability puts them in the situation of being special and excluded in a certain way. *Establishing knowledge about the child and education* together with walking the *walk of shame* changes their attitudes and opens up the possibility to belong to the school community, which in some cases gives them a feeling of family and hence also a sense of belonging. Those who do not exhibit such a feeling do not develop a sense of belonging in the same way to school, which influences parental involvement and in consequence *parental support* for children with disabilities. Teachers treating children as well as parents "like family" members have a different approach towards their profession and their responsibility. Hence, *feeling like a family* seems to strengthen the people who share this feeling. However, the children depend on the parents' change in attitudes and teachers' taking on responsibilities to reach their goals (and functionings). By supporting the child in the mentioned ways, parents and teachers provide the necessary environment for children with disabilities to develop a *positive self-concept* and furthermore a sense of belonging. This means that the core category *feeling like a family* related to teachers and parents finally supports the children in reaching their goals. Hence, the school environment regarding relations and attitudes is prepared for the child to depart towards a valued, equal, accepted and respected life. The "only" aspect left open is the society, who has to accept and realise that people with disabilities can be of value for society like any other member.

Parents and teachers benefit already in the environment of the school, as *feeling like a family* is there to support them. They gain their values of respect and acceptance already at that point. For children, it is different as they gain positive energy from their access to school, but their goal to support their family and be of value to the society also by other means can only come into effect in the future. *Feeling like a family* related to children (e.g. being able to support the family) therefore constitutes only a possibility without guarantee. However, what can already happen at this point is the development of a positive self-concept.

On the other hand, parents who cannot be related to the core category still struggle with certain aspects of the situation of their child being at school. Here, it cannot be forgotten that poverty plays a major role. If it is poverty that prevents parents from going to schools and develop a closer relationship with teachers and invest time in getting involved, it can be identified as a major barrier to "developing a sense of belonging". Teachers who do not have a close relationship with parents *(establishing relationships)* and/or children usually seem to exhibit less commitment *(commitment and motivation)* and show less satisfaction regarding their profession. This has consequences for the *quality of education* for children with disabilities (as well as for children without disabilities).

Listening to Other Experts

Most[23] of the experts were interviewed following theoretical sampling strategies. This means that emerging topics and categories were further elaborated. In other words, in this chapter, the categories and topics are confirmed and enriched by including the experts' perspective.[24] Furthermore it adds supplementary information and important issues that were not given attention before. I collected the data (experts from inside and outside the schools) in addition to the cases (children, parents, teachers). During the analysis of these interviews, the category *atmosphere of departure (positive developments)* developed from the discussion that will be elaborated in the following.

The atmosphere of departure describes a development towards a change in attitude in society regarding people with disabilities. This change is supported by certain developments but also hampered by some aspects. Experts generally have the impression that positive developments regarding attitudes towards persons with disabilities can be observed in the Ethiopian society.

After analysing the children's, teachers' and parents' interviews, the analysis of the experts' interviews provided me with a fourth perspective on education for children with disabilities. In these interviews, different problems were identified as number one problem concerning education for children with disabilities. The most prominent one was attitudes. Furthermore, the aspects of religion and belief, which were regarded as a major factor influencing attitudes, were examined referring to a representative of the Orthodox Church[25] and its doctrines. Another point that was discussed in the experts' interviews was the aspect of community. It was referred to either as the source of negative attitudes towards disability or as a supporting entity for families who had children with disabilities. Not surprisingly, emphasis was also put on teacher education. In this respect, the issue of commitment was raised on several occasions. The aspect of parental involvement also got special attention in some of the interviews. Last but not least, the implementation of legislation was discussed from the experts' perspectives.

---

[23] Some of the experts were also interviewed at the beginning of the research phase, where theoretical sampling was not applied. These interviews gave an overview of the situation for children with disabilities and were more open than interviews with experts at a later stage, which were geared to previously collected data.

[24] The whole second and third phases of the field research were also dedicated to enriching and supporting previously developed preliminary categories.

[25] As already mentioned, it was not possible to contact representatives from the Muslim mosque. Hence, this perspective could only be derived from the interview with a representative from the Orthodox Church.

Attitudes and Awareness

This chapter complements in particular the parents' category *the walk of shame*. However, not only the parents were addressed here. Therefore, new elements were discussed that are related to this category.

The attitudinal problem was raised as problem number one by the Finnish expert in the ministry, by the special needs expert Yeshitla Mulat[26] and by the programme officers of LIGHT FOR THE WORLD. "[…] when it comes to the disability issue, when it comes to the inclusion issue, when it comes to the mainstreaming of, you know, disability and social services and development services, there is a real lack of awareness of the topic as well from the top officials down to the low level institutions" (Abraham, LIGHT FOR THE WORLD). At the same time, the experts observed changes in attitudes. "I can clearly, clearly, clearly see that attitudes are changing and ah, this inclusive education approach is also sort of taking place among professionals" (Finnish special needs expert in the Ministry of Education). It seems that also here an **atmosphere of departure amongst higher levels** prevails. This atmosphere was already observed in the parents' category *the walk of shame*. There, it was related to the hopes that the parents developed as soon as their child attended a school. However, in this case "departure" refers to the change of general attitudes towards disability in society. Both can be related, as on the one hand schools – as public institutions – are more likely to start to accept children with disabilities through a societal change of attitudes and, on the other hand, parents are also a part of society and their change of attitudes also influences society. Jana Zehle, at that time special needs expert at Addis Ababa University (AAU), comes to the same conclusion regarding the parents. Even though the parents were sometimes not aware that their child with a disability could attend a school or they were afraid of being discriminated, a clear change in attitudes and awareness could be observed in Addis Ababa. Uncertainty sometimes still emerges when parents and children are confronted with unexpected barriers: "I think it starts with the attitude, […] but when the parents are convinced […] and they or the child are confronted with barriers, a relapse [in attitudes] can easily happen" (Jana Zehle, AAU). All in all, the experts observed a development in Addis Ababa where not only **parents** of children with disabilities **seem to be more interested in education** in general.

An atmosphere of departure regarding education was also suggested by the vast construction of new school buildings all over the country. However, a lack of awareness seemed to cumber accessibility for children with disabilities. "The schools, all the schools that have been constructed in Ethiopia, could have been made accessible. Especially the ones that have been constructed recently over the past five/six years could have been made accessible […]" (Abraham, LIGHT FOR THE

---

[26] "I have been working in the Ministry of Education, and I have been the head of the teacher education programme, and I was facilitating, at a federal level, the education programme, the general education programme, including the special needs education at a federal level to be delivered in schools, as well as the special teacher training in the universities and colleges" (Yeshitla Mulat, special needs expert).

WORLD). All new schools were built according to the same scheme. They were five floors high, with stairs that the children had to climb. Hence, especially for children with physical disabilities, it might be a problem to reach their classrooms. Changes of attitudes seem to have taken place to some extent in society.

> Now there is a positive attitude and work by the society and the government. Let's take leprosy. In the old days, it was considered as contagious, it transmitted from one person to another and they were stigmatized, now due to media awareness they aren't considered as before, that it came by the curse of parents. Generally we are changing our old attitude towards disabled people. (Geta, expert and teacher)

The experts also believed that the teachers' awareness of disabilities in general was good. This change in attitude can partly be explained by the environment, as one expert described. He also used examples of leprosy, amputation because of mines, former combatants who were injured be the Derg[27] regime (Melese, expert and teacher). Hence, the visibility of people with disabilities who were obviously injured seemed to influence many people's attitudes towards disability.

The higher awareness and **positive attitude resulted in** teachers and other people taking **more initiatives**. These initiatives to raise awareness in the schools, and the use of different media, led to a change in attitudes. Principals spoke about different programmes that they were implementing in an effort to raise awareness. Amongst them were sign language training for hearing students as well as for parents, measures to raise awareness during the morning ceremonies, using mini-media,[28] etc. It became clear that **children were perceived to be the best multipliers** for distributing information on disability-related topics to the families and communities.

> [The disability clubs in the schools, including teachers and students] are the ones to regularly on daily basis from Monday to Friday raise awareness through different mechanisms *[mini-media]* yes they use mini-media, school mini-media. Through poems, through drama all different… they really teach the whole school community, teachers and students on daily basis and the… they are, you know the children they are really the means and the tools who are now talking and teaching to their parents, to their neighbours, to their family members, to the relatives, who are really changing the awareness level and the attitudes of the people at this moment. (Getachew, LIGHT FOR THE WORLD)

What can be observed in this case is that children are also seen as capable of taking on responsibility for the task of changing attitudes in the communities. In regard to the community as such, most of the experts felt a change in attitudes. The Minister of Education came to the conclusion that the communities around the schools had a major influence on the schools: "So more or less the schools are led [...] by the community. This is our achievement" (Demeke Mekonnen, Minister of Education). He pointed out that the surrounding communities were highly involved and participated in discussions with the school board. This might also be related to a changing attitude towards education. The Minister of Education sees the Ethiopian society trans-

---

[27] See Chap. 2 "Understanding the context…"

[28] Mini-media is a kind of radio station in the schools that is used by children and teachers to distribute all kinds of information.

form into a **knowledge-based society**. This statement underscores the importance of knowledge. The aspects mentioned here are not so much related to disability directly as to education in general. The representative of the Orthodox Church, for example, was convinced that the Ethiopian people had changed their attitudes towards disability in general. "Another example, my teacher was blind; we went to different places by mini-bus. When we entered in the mini-bus, everybody would rise up. This is because the attitude of the people towards disability has changed. Therefore, they treat them; they also contribute money" (Administrative Head of the Ethiopian Orthodox Tewahedo Church). What can be observed in this context is that a **charity model** of disability often prevails in the society. The change in attitudes seemed to take place above all in terms of refraining from the convictions that people with disabilities were cursed (e.g. Geta, expert and teacher). Another important aspect regarding the change in attitudes involves community-based rehabilitation workers (**CBR workers**). As CBR workers work at the grass root level, they reach the people in the communities and at home. In this way, it is possible to raise awareness within the communities, to support parents by accompanying them to school for a first interview, etc. (Jana Zehle, AAU). The experts thus identified different ways of creating awareness and changing attitudes regarding people with disabilities at different levels of the Ethiopian society. Yet, attitudes are influenced to a great extent by the people's beliefs and religion.

Religion

This chapter explores aspects that can be related to the parents' *walk of shame*. The parents referred a lot to their belief and to God in general during the interviews. However, it seemed that there were differences between what people believed and what the Church wanted to communicate, especially regarding disability.

> At one time God teaches his disciples that a lame person was cured. At that time people asked Jesus Christ, why was he born handicapped? Was it because of his sins, his mother's sins, or his family's sins that he became handicapped? Jesus Christ answered it was not because of his sins or his family's sins; it was because God wanted to show a miracle to the world. (Administrative Head of the Ethiopian Orthodox Tewahedo Church)

Hence, there are clear **misunderstandings** between what the Church teaches and what people think about the role of God. The expert interview showed that the text in the Bible could be interpreted in different ways. According to the interviewee, one miracle is Christ's resurrection. Another point referred to God's wisdom and knowledge. He wanted people to learn from each other. The argument in this aspect was that people could not learn from each other if they were all the same.

> Therefore, since there are rich people, there will be poor people. If there are normal people, there will be disabled people. If there are evil people, there will be children of God. If there are happy people, there will be sad people. If there is light, there will be dark. If there are kind people, there will be mean people. In order to show God's wisdom, there are children

who are born normal, and there are children who are born with disabilities. (Administrative Head of the Ethiopian Orthodox Tewahedo Church)

It was clearly stated that the **Church does not believe that disability comes from sin**. Additionally, in this case, the Church employed people with disabilities and in this way integrated them in their institution. Furthermore, according to the interviewee, the Church teaches not to discriminate people with disabilities. Accordingly, there is a clear gap between people's beliefs and what the Church teaches. "If disabled people are rehabilitated and supported, they can actively work like normal people. As a human being: rich, poor; black, white; normal, disabled; before God everybody is equal. This is what the Church preaches" (Administrative Head of the Ethiopian Orthodox Tewahedo Church). The question if God cursed people who might have done something wrong, and if disability could be seen as a punishment for that, was answered negatively in the first quotation. Nevertheless, this belief is widespread. The majority of the people who were interviewed were very religious. Their belief influenced their everyday life to a great extent. Consequently, the importance of the Church and respect for the Almighty God could be observed in many of the interviews. Even though the Orthodox Church seemed not to disseminate the belief in disability as a curse, it remained in the heads of its followers. Traditional beliefs could play a role here too.

Teacher Training

Demeke Mekonnen, the Ethiopian Minister of Education, identified quality assurance as the number one challenge regarding education in Ethiopia. In this respect, good teacher education was essential for quality in education. Teachers had to be equipped with tools in order to be able to manage their classrooms in a way that ensured the greatest possible benefit for the children. Regarding inclusive education, this point has to get even more attention, as the teacher is confronted with even more diversity[29] of special needs that the children in his/her classroom exhibit. Hence, quality teacher education is indispensable for making inclusive classrooms possible. This chapter therefore supports the category *quality of education*.

> Ma: *What are the three major changes you think that have to take place in the very near future to make inclusive education a reality?*
> SF: In the near future [...] well I would say, that teacher training, teacher training and teacher training [...] yeah, when teachers they have to be trained I mean properly to manage inclusive classrooms. (Finnish special needs expert at the Ministry of Education)

However, most of the teachers could not be made responsible for not knowing how to manage an inclusive classroom. Yetnebersh Nigussie from ECDD (Ethiopian

---

[29] The researcher believes that diversity and special needs can also be found in regular classrooms without children with disabilities.

Centre for Disability and Development) stated that it was the lack of experience rather than the lack of commitment on the teachers' part. She saw a clear need to support teachers at the classroom level. Consequently, the focus should be put on **practical skills**. In this context, Jana Zehle identified a problem in teacher training regarding the intensity of the mandatory special needs course which could already be observed in the teachers' interviews. She claimed that this course provided the teachers with insights into the topic of disability but did not seem to equip them properly with tools for handling an inclusive classroom. Furthermore, she observed differences in the quality of integration (as it was not yet real inclusion) in different schools that might be due to a higher or lower degree of **engagement** of the teachers. Hence, **teachers' engagement** once more becomes a major aspect of functioning inclusion. However, Jana Zehle (AAU) stated that very often it was not easy to keep the enthusiasm of some teachers as they were often overburdened or lost motivation because of a lack of material, lack of special teacher education, and general lack of support, etc.

Another aspect that seemed to be a challenge for teachers according to Yeshitla Mulat was the fact that they were evaluated according to how far they had proceeded with their textbooks during the school year. The inclusion of children with disabilities might slow down the completion of the textbook, as teachers did not know about teaching methods that supported all students similarly according to their needs. Therefore, children with disabilities were usually treated differently from the rest of the class, which took more time and might be of less quality. This might be the case because the teachers did not have enough time and maybe energy in classrooms of 60 children. As the teachers were also not equipped with the practical skills to handle these challenges, they faced severe problems (Yeshitla Mulat, special needs expert). **Teachers' preparedness** will be addressed again at a later point. It is also rated as more important than the availability of material when it comes to inclusion. In this context, one problematic aspect that was raised especially by school principals was the scarcity of trained staff. However, the schools had started to be equipped with one **special needs expert**. These experts support teachers and students.

> My task is to teach how to handle disabled students. I also teach students study skills. I instruct people about the best sitting arrangement in the classroom. I see to it that teachers do not write in very small characters on the board. I also inform them that they should not be too fast when they teach the students. (Melese, expert and teacher)

It became clear that already this kind of advice might be of major importance for teachers and consequently for children with disabilities. It is the first step towards identifying the needs of the children and reacting to them.

Not surprisingly, the experts defined a clear need for teacher training. Practical skills for classroom management were needed most. As could be demonstrated, the statements of the experts corresponded with the outcomes of the analysis and hence supported and enriched the relevant categories. Teacher training cannot lead to quality education without teachers' commitment. The next chapter focuses on this aspect.

Teachers' Commitment

This chapter supports the category *commitment and motivation.* The impression of some experts was that teachers did not like to spend more time at school than necessary. Hence, sometimes negative perceptions of teachers' commitment and their willingness to invest resources prevailed (e.g. Melses, expert and teacher). However, there were many principals and other experts who praised teachers' dedication to their profession. In some schools, teachers even supported children with disabilities **beyond issues of education** (e.g. financially) (see, e.g. Geta, expert and teacher; Melese, expert and teacher). Other experts spoke about the **teachers' creativity,** which was often used to create teaching material with things that were available to them (Jana Zehle, AAU). Hence, from the experts' perspectives, there were teachers who showed a lot of commitment and engagement. Still there was a need for even more commitment: "I mean, we do have to do more and commit ourselves more with further strength and awareness and knowledge, as to what we are expected to do, what we are supposed to do" (Temesgen, expert and teacher).

Parental Involvement

In this chapter, the category *parental support* will be enriched. The experts also mentioned that it was the parents' energy or time that was not available for them to support their children at school. In this context, poor families were mentioned explicitly (Jana Zehle, AAU; Melese, expert and teacher). In other words, poor families had less time for supporting their children at school, as they had to ensure their daily income. One expert made a clear distinction between two categories of parents:

> I have already said that there are two categories of parents. Educated parents come to inquire about their children. They want to know how their child is doing. We tell them. Uneducated, poor parents don't mind so much. They don't even come when we call them. Only 10 or 15 out of 60 such parents come. When they are asked why they failed to come, they give many excuses. They give priority to social commitment. They only come when we celebrate holidays, which makes them happy. They even help us a lot then. Educated parents buy the artifacts produced by their children. Hence, they cooperate in this way. (Bruck, expert and teacher)

From the experts' perspective, this statement underscores the perception of a clear difference between poor families and families that were well-off. To them, poverty and not being educated were related in this way. In other words, poor parents were usually more likely to be illiterate and consequently also less involved in school-related aspects. Accordingly, the **aspect of poverty** played a major role regarding parental involvement. Furthermore, parental involvement was often related to the frequency with which parents came and asked about their children or how often they could come when they were called by the teachers. In general, the experts, who demonstrated awareness of the parents' problems, had the explanations for a lower degree of parental involvement. They knew about time restrictions and problems of generating income.

> The big problem is poverty. Since most of them are daily labourers, they are unable to come. There are also many parents who can't come because of transportation problems. There are some families who bring their children here and stay the whole day in the school because they don't have money for transportation. These kinds of problems force them not to come. (Bruck, expert and teacher)

This shows the influence that poverty can have on the children's education regarding parental involvement. Consequently, it might also influence the children's self-perception, as less involvement also means less support.

Implementation of Legislation

One of the main aspects that were discussed in the experts' interviews was the implementation of inclusive education. Again, the teachers' category *commitment and motivation* was most prominent here. The main problem that was addressed was the **infeasibility of the environment for inclusive education**. In this context, the already discussed lack of teacher training and lack of sufficient staff constituted the major barriers. One problem that was seen as a result of this was the teachers' **loss of motivation** (Geta, expert and teacher). Hence, two mutually increasing challenges can be identified at this point: on the one hand, more commitment amongst teachers is needed for inclusive education, and on the other hand, the attempt to implement inclusive education without appropriate preparation can lead to demotivation. However, there was no doubt amongst the experts that the law and regulations for implementing inclusive education existed in Ethiopia. "Drafting or enacting a law doesn't create any change unless it is properly applied, I can't judge if we applied all the laws that were made by the government. The problem arises from issues of application. Otherwise we have extraordinary laws" (Habtamu, expert and teacher). Doubts arose only related to control mechanisms. For example, who controls whether a school accepts students with disabilities and what are the consequences if it fails to do so? Principals of the schools also identified problems in this regard:

> For example, there are blind students who learn here, but they don't get any support. They don't have books. It is written that they have equal opportunities, but this is not implemented. It is easy to write it on paper, but it is difficult to put it into effect. Higher authorities do not follow up the implementation. (Adanesh, expert and teacher)

Ethiopia is not the only country where the law is in place while its implementation is lagging behind. Nevertheless, the negative effects that this has on the motivation of not only teachers but also children and parents must not be underestimated. Without the instruments (teacher training, material, information, awareness, support, etc.), it will be impossible to implement inclusive education on a broader basis. Putting motivated teachers in such a situation can have **negative consequences** for teacher motivation and therefore **for the education of children with disabilities**.

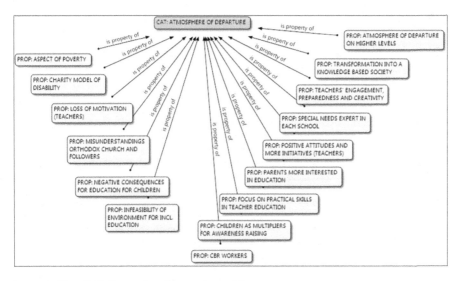

Network View 5.11 Properties of *atmosphere of departure*

Summary

The analysis and description of data collected from further informants led to additional aspects and enriched some of the existing categories, namely, *the walk of shame, quality of education, commitment and motivation, parental support* and *question of belonging.*[30] I called the category which developed from this discussion *atmosphere of departure,* which will be explained below. To continue in a consistent way, the following network view shows the properties of the category.

The left-hand side of the network view contains hindering aspects of an *atmosphere of departure*, whereas the right-hand side lists the supporting aspects. This explains that the atmosphere of departure is also sometimes confined by various aspects. However, as the supporting aspects predominate over the hindering aspects, it becomes clear that all in all the analysis of the experts' interviews showed a positive picture regarding the change of environments (including attitudes, physical environment, relationships, etc.) for education for children with disabilities. Further thoughts on this process are presented later in the development of the theory.

---

[30] The three categories that are not mentioned here were referred to in the discussion, as most of the categories are interrelated.

References

Birks, M., & Mills, J. (2011). *Grounded theory. A practical guide*. Los Angeles/London/New Delhi/Singapore/Washington, DC: Sage.

Bronfenbrenner, U. (1980). *The ecology of human development. Experiments by nature and design*. Cambridge: Harvard University.

Charmaz, K. (2003). Qualitative interviewing and grounded theory analysis. In J. A. Holstein & J. F. Gubrium (Eds.), *Inside interviewing: New lenses, new concerns*. Thousand Oaks: Sage.

Charmaz, K. (2006). *Constructing grounded theory: A practical guide through qualitative analysis*. London/Thousand Oaks/New Delhi: Sage.

Charmaz, K. (2009). Shifting the grounds: Constructivist grounded theory methods. In J. M. Morse (Ed.), *Developing grounded theory. The second generation* (pp. 127–154). Walnut Creek: Left Coast Press.

OECD. (2012). *Equity and quality in education. Supporting disadvantaged students and schools*. OECD.

Schiemer, M. (2013). Zur Bedeutung von Individuum und Gemeinschaft in einer fremden Kultur am Beispiel Bildung für Kinder mit Behinderung. In P. Sehrbrock, A. Erdélyi, & S. Gand (Eds.), *Internationale und vergleichende Heil- und Sonderpädagogik und Inklusion* (pp. 184–191). Bad Heilbrunn: Klinkhardt.

Schiemer, M., & Proyer, M. (2013). Teaching children with disabilities: ICTs in Bangkok and Addis Ababa. *Multicultural Education & Technology Journal, 7*(2/3), 99–112.

Chapter 6
The Core Category: Feeling Like a Family

Abstract Presenting the core category "feeling like a family", one could say this chapter is the heart of the study. It is used to go into depth regarding the core category by explaining the characteristics and the meaning of family and the phenomenon of "feeling like a family" as such. The properties of this category are elaborated and connected with the earlier developed categories. This enables the author to link the different parts and indicate relations and connections between the categories and their properties. Like this, the whole picture that resulted from the analysis is made comprehensible. Furthermore, the logic of why "feeling like a family" emerged as the core category can be demonstrated.

The core category is the only category that is not related to only one of the interview groups (children, parents, teachers). It developed from the whole body of interviews with children, parents and teachers. *Feeling like a family* describes a process in which the participants develop a sense of belonging. This indicates that especially aspects of the children's category "question of belonging" are reflected in the core category. The expressions "feeling like a family", "being part of the family", "familiarity" or "accepting the child with a disability in the family" are mentioned in the chapters above (highlighted in pink in the network views), sometimes as a property or consequence of a certain category. This was part of the process that finally identified *feeling like a family* and raised it to the level of a core category. Furthermore, it shows that this process developed to be the core category, as it is related not only to the *question of belonging* but to all other categories as well. In this way, the developed categories become subcategories for the latter:

Subcategories (SC)	Core category
Developing a positive self-concept	
Question of belonging	
Establishing knowledge about the child and education	
"The walk of shame"	*Feeling like a family*
Parental support	
Establishing relationships	
Quality of education	
Commitment and motivation	

© The Author(s) 2017
M. Schiemer, *Education for Children with Disabilities in Addis Ababa, Ethiopia*, Inclusive Learning and Educational Equity 4,
DOI 10.1007/978-3-319-60768-9_6

Types of "Feeling Like a Family"

There are important differences in *feeling like a family* comparing parents and teachers on the one hand and children on the other. These differences are exemplified in the following.

Feeling Like a Family *Within the Closer Family*

The children's *feeling like a family* is usually related to their closer family, to receiving support and supporting. It is about the matter of course that children **take care of their aging parents** in Ethiopia. Hence, it is also about **duties and responsibilities** within a family and about "being part of the family".[1] Related to school, it could be observed that children seemed to benefit from the school in more ways than expected (e.g. getting education, being able to participate, gaining more self-esteem). The values that they gained from attending a school were more than that. In the interviews it became clear that the majority of the children preferred to be at school than to be at home. This was related to friends, possibilities to play and space to play. Further arguments were that it was boring at home. However, the respective statements of the children were not related to feeling like a family. It was rather the parents who made such statements: "Any way she is called teacher B. She is her second mother" (Almaz, mother).

The different types of *feeling like a family* led to different types of "developing a sense of belonging". For the children developing a sense of belonging was related to their place in society, the community and their family. Hence, it was also related to a more profound process in which identity and concept of self were influenced to a big extent. This is relevant especially regarding the already discussed aspects of "being able to help" (support the family) and thereby "becoming a valued member of society". This is a clear link to the capability approach, as capabilities are described as "a person's real freedoms or opportunities to achieve functionings" (Robeyns 2011) and functionings as "beings and doings" of a person (Robeyns 2011). Being able to help is one of the functionings that can be achieved by having the freedom and opportunity to receive quality education.

Feeling Like a Family *Within the School Community*

For the parents, the core category "feeling like a family" was related mainly to the teachers and the school. It gave them a feeling of being understood and valued especially after they had to deal with guilt and shame regarding the disability of their child.

---

[1] Children who do not live with their parents and orphans often substitute the missing parents with caregivers, siblings or the extended family.

Y: *Do you have anything else to say, let's say, about the teachers? Can you talk about the*
    relations with the teachers?
B: We are like brothers and sisters with the teachers. I am very close with them. (Beyene,
    mother)

It was something very valuable for the parents to feel like a family in relation with the school; for them it meant **getting** back **respect**, and additionally they "got back" their child as one to be proud of.

From the teachers' perspective, the feeling like a family was connected to communication and **support** in relation to parents and children. In cases where this feeling prevailed, responsibilities were taken on with more commitment.

> When I say it's the special nature of the school, it's only because of the support, only because of dependence of the children and the families on the school. This is what the situation has created. And because of this also, we don't consider ourselves – I think I've cited this somewhere in the course of our interview – that we feel like a family, not only as a teacher. It doesn't mean every teacher is a family, or feels like a father or mother, but in our case, we have that feeling. There are children who do not have mother and father; there are children who do not have a father, in most cases. So, this is what they are lacking. And for their education to be fruitful some of us have to feel as if we were trying to fill that gap. (Temesgen expert and teacher)

In this particular case, the teachers were very close to the families and they took on a lot of responsibility. However, also the children that were interviewed at this school did not speak about teachers in such terms. This makes it clear again that the *feeling like a family* in schools was one-sided regarding teachers and children and mutual only between parents and teachers. Yet, it can be assumed that it was also mutual between parents and children if it exists within the family, though this was not an issue in the interviews. The following figure illustrates through which relations *feeling like a family* comes into effect (Fig. 6.1).

Here too, it can be stated that education is the main capability for reaching states of beings and doings that are valued by the participants. In this case it would be

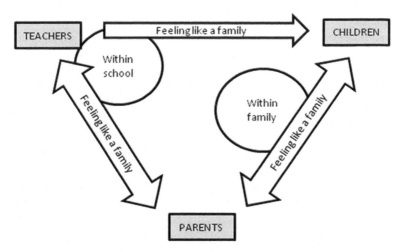

Fig. 6.1 Relations within the core category *feeling like a family*

"feeling like a family" as a general category. To be more precise, the functioning that could be reached could be described as gaining respect, being accepted, being taken seriously regarding one's problems and, finally, being part of a community and leaving stigma and prejudice behind.

The Meaning of Family

Feeling like a family was related to aspects of value, responsibility, reliability and mutual understanding. It provided the people involved with a **feeling of belonging**. Furthermore, family can be defined as something that is **deep-seated** within societal and cultural structures in Ethiopia. It is a reliable entity which supports the people who are part of it. In regard to children with disabilities, the entity of the family is challenged, as disability is not accepted in society as something "normal". The **challenge** lies in the family unit, which is highly valued by society, and that has to integrate a socially stigmatised child. Here the conflict to which especially parents are exposed at the beginning becomes clear.

> After concluding the collection of data, we met up with our Ethiopian colleagues from the language department at AAU, who were translating our interviews. It was very interesting and they told us that they really liked the research because it was so exciting to read the interviews. They were impressed by how much some parents cared about their children and then again by how sad and depressed some of the parents were. (Researcher's research diary, phase 3)

For children it means they have to work towards being accepted in society. The entity of the family is especially meaningful in this regard, as it is in the family where children can **prove** best that they are **valuable members of society** by being able to support their parents, which is of great importance for the society in general.

For the teachers, their feeling of being a family with parents and students meant **receiving them with open arms** in contrast to the prevailing attitudes in society. Teachers are free[2] to decide whether or not to welcome parents and their children with disabilities, even after they are accepted at school. In other words, the teacher has to accept the child with a disability in his/her classroom if the principal decides to accept them. However, teachers cannot be forced to give them special attention and support. This means that it is an even more meaningful step from the societal point of view if teachers welcome children with disabilities and their parents as parts of their family because there is no family relation that forces them to. Both types of *feeling like a family*, in the families themselves and in the "school-families", require effort on the part of the people involved. Usually these efforts involve **demonstrating a change in attitude** towards disability. The following network view shows the properties of the core category as well as the items that are listed in earlier network views and are related to the core category.

---

[2] Governmental schools in Ethiopia have to accept every child in their school according to the law. However, in practice principals usually decide whether to accept a child with a disability or not.

Properties of "Feeling Like a Family"

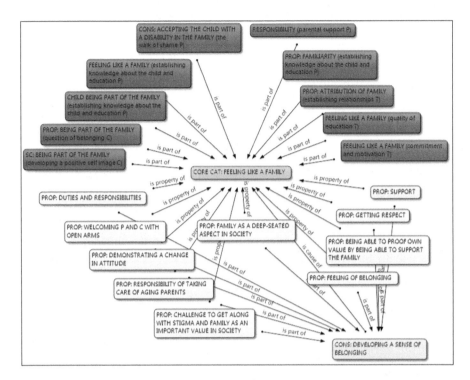

Network View 6.1 Properties of *feeling like a family*

This network view shows the most essential properties of the core category *feeling like a family* (grey items). The items in pink are the ones that are listed in the other network views of the earlier categories (in brackets). Their characteristic in relation to the respective category is indicated at the beginning (PROP = property, CONS = consequence, SC = subcategory, etc.). If there is no relation indicated, it was added to the category without a defined characteristic.

Regarding the properties of the core category, the left-hand side shows the efforts on the part of the participants that are necessary for establishing a *feeling like a family*. The right-hand side of the network view shows aspects that were gained by the participants through living the *feeling like a family*. The property that is placed between the two sides emphasises the significance which "family" has for the participants and for society as whole. Finally, all the properties of the core category can be identified as being part of the consequence "developing a sense of belonging".

The fact that *feeling like a family* was more likely in special settings than in integrative settings can be related to the difficult conditions in the integrative settings. These were found in governmental schools that had to struggle much more with aspects like resources and class size than schools supported by the church (like school E, which had an integrative setting but showed evidence of *feeling like a family* amongst the participants). However, special settings that were attached to governmental schools also had problems related to material, teacher-to-student ratio and further support. Yet, the teachers developed more commitment as they had a clear task and focus on children with disabilities in their work. Furthermore, the size of the special settings (in this case special classes) was smaller compared to the rest of the school (though still too big), and consequently the feeling of being a community was developed more easily, as the people were more likely to know each other. In this context, the following quotation is very interesting, as it is of a mother of a boy with an intellectual disability who was integrated in a regular class after being in the special unit for some years: "In fact, we had a good relationship when he was in the special unit. They called me and we discussed as a family. The others also call me but it is not like the others. There we had a good relationship" (Bamlak, mother). This case describes the difference regarding a feeling of belonging between special setting and integrative setting.

It is interesting that during the first steps of analysing the data, "developing a sense of belonging" seemed to become relevant only for the children. It became evident only by further engaging with the categories that this was also an issue for the other interview groups.

The Process

I mentioned before that the core category *feeling like a family* describes a process that eventually leads to developing a sense of belonging. This process has certain stages that enable the people involved to develop a *feeling like a family*. In this respect, it has to be considered that this process is different for every person. However, there were certain similarities within the individual groups. The group of parents, the group of teachers and the group of children each had similar issues. The categories that developed during the process of analysis contain certain aspects that indicate individual steps within the process towards *feeling like a family* and the consequent development of a sense of belonging. This means that the parents first of all had to *establish knowledge about their child and education* in general; this again accelerated the *walk of shame* that led to a change in attitude. It was only then that parents got actively involved in issues related to their child and education, and *parental support* started to come into effect (even though parental support, which is not related to education, can already be found before the child's access to school). Without a change in attitude and parental involvement, the *feeling like a family* at school cannot develop and neither can a sense of belonging. This means that the parents cannot establish a relationship with, and interest in, the school and the teachers and thus a *feeling like a family* with them, if they do not have a positive attitude towards their child with a disability and interest in his/her education. By going through the process of changing attitudes, the parents supported their children on their way towards being educated. At the same time, the parents developed a sense of belonging towards the teachers and the school.

From the teachers' perspective, the situation was different in many aspects. As mentioned earlier, in many cases the teachers were unmotivated or frustrated because they had not chosen to become a teacher in the first place or because the circumstances were counteracting their efforts to provide quality education for the children. Teachers who developed a *feeling like a family* in the schools were much more motivated and committed to their profession. Therefore, the sense of belonging that resulted from this process can be interpreted as a feeling of belonging to their profession. Hence, by *establishing relationships*, for example, with the parents, a first approach towards more commitment and engagement was made by the teachers, thus creating a *feeling like a family*. Furthermore, *quality education* illustrates problematic aspects that were tried to be solved by communicating with people from within the school as an institution, including parents. In this respect, a *feeling like a family* supports the process of finding solutions. It encourages the teachers to strive for the goal of giving quality education to the children. This becomes especially visible through the category of *commitment and motivation.* In other words, engagement on the teachers' part in cooperating with the families but also with colleagues can lead to a positive basis that might give them motivation and a feeling of belonging to their profession. Where this was the case, it supported the education for children with disabilities.

As regards children, the process that they went through started with the attribution of a disability. Being identified as a child with a disability, education was usually not one of the first considerations of the parents. Instead, the opinion that children with disabilities were not able to learn predominated. Furthermore, in many cases, access to school was denied by the schools or not possible due to various environmental factors (distance, physical accessibility, etc.). Therefore, the mere possibility of attending a school supported the *development of a positive self-concept*, as it constituted one step towards being integrated in society. However, the *question of belonging* is not answered by that. The children with disabilities had to find their place in society as they experienced exclusion in many areas of their life. For them, the *feeling like a family* constituted a possibility to become a valued member in society through education. With the vision in mind that education would enable them to support their families later, *feeling like a family* was a motor to reach their goal of being able to support their families and consequently develop a sense of belonging by defining their place in society. Thereby, other visions like becoming teachers and doctors also gained meaning, as those are professions that help and support people and hence society. Even though teachers are not highly valued in society, the children assigned the profession a deeper meaning. This is not surprising, as they saw the solution for their situation of exclusion in receiving education. Yet, the process which was started by *feeling like a family* for the children did not stop at school, as it did for parents and teachers.

In summary, three processes can be observed: the children's, the parents' and the teachers' process towards developing a sense of belonging. Additionally this sense of belonging had different meanings. For the parents it seemed to be very important to have this contact in order to feel respected and accepted. For the teachers it was important regarding their profession. And for the children it was about their future life. This means that the parents and teachers were able to put more effort towards supporting the children with disabilities from their respective positions, as they were strengthened by the *feeling like a family.*

Having exemplified the main aspects of the core category, the following chapter organises the elaborated content and structures it towards a comprehensive theory of "developing a sense of belonging".

Reference

Robeyns, I. (2011). The capability approach. *Stanford encyclopedia of philosophy*. Retrieved November 23, 2016, from http://plato.stanford.edu/entries/capability-approach/#FunCap

Chapter 7
Generation of Theory

Abstract This chapter starts by recapitulating the research process, to facilitate the understanding of the contexts. Consequently, the development from categories towards theory is described in detail. This is done by first giving short descriptions of the already developed categories, by defining conflicts that are related to the categories and by interconnecting the single categories with each other. The last part of this chapter finally is illustrating the development of the theory by showing single parts from the resulting graphic. This leads the reader step by step to the complex illustration of the theory. The final part of this section refers to the meaning of education. It hence reflects the perspectives of children, parents, teachers and experts on education for children with disabilities. To complete this chapter, the author discusses the meaning of educational equity in relation to the developed theory.

"A grounded theory generally provides a comprehensive explanation of a process or scheme apparent in relation to particular phenomena" (Birks and Mills 2011, 12). Accordingly, the following generation of the theory is a very complex explanation of the process that was investigated. Hence, it was considered as helpful to use diagrams for supporting the elaboration of the theory.

The core category *feeling like a family* can be identified as facilitator for "developing a sense of belonging" through education. Thus, both types, *feeling like a family* from the teachers' and parents' perspectives and from the children's perspectives, are supportive. Similarly, the conflicts that have been identified for each group can be regarded as barriers. They are barriers to developing a sense of belonging not only for the children – which is most obvious as their conflict is about developing a sense of belonging – but for all participants. In other words, there is no belonging together or *feeling like a family* between teachers and parents if the attitudes of parents haven't changed or responsibility for their profession has not been taken on by teachers. *Feeling like a family* allows the participants to (re-)gain respect in the environment of the school. This can be considered as special as the environment of the school develops to be a new kind of community next to other communities (like the neighbourhood.) where parents can develop a feeling of belonging. The cultural and societal aspects that come into play here are first of all the value that the Ethiopian society attributes to the family and community in a broader sense

(Schiemer 2013). Without such significance, *feeling like a family* would not have the meaning it has received during this study. Furthermore, the fact that disability is connected with guilt and shame as well as with pity plays an important role especially regarding the conflicts that parents struggle with. Last but not least, religion is a major variable in this picture. As God and belief play important roles in the lives of the participants, this influence cannot be denied. Starting from believing in disability as a curse towards believing that God is responsible for the good things and bad things that happen, all the participants are influenced by their belief in one way or another.

The following figure illustrates the simplified model of the theory of "developing a sense of belonging". It takes the already defined relations of *feeling like a family* amongst the participants as basis (Fig. 7.1).

What becomes visible in this figure is that "developing a sense of belonging" has different points of reference regarding children, parents and teachers: society, school as a community and the teaching profession. Hence, according to this model, children resolve their issue of exclusion by striving for a place in society. Parents strive to be included in a new community, to be accepted there. Last but not least, teachers adopt a clear commitment to their profession and get respect from parents.

Furthermore, there is one aspect that teachers, parents and children with disabilities share: their reputation in society is usually low from a traditional cultural and/or societal perspective. The *feeling like a family* helps in all three cases to find a way out of this dilemma, although it does not resolve it. This is true especially for teachers but also for parents, as their status in society does not improve through their *feeling like a family*. Instead, it seems as if parents and teachers integrate themselves into a new community in an effort to gain respect and understanding and improve their well-being. Only children aim at being accepted in the society as such (in this model) by going through the process of receiving education and developing a new concept of self.[1]

The next step is a very complex one regarding the visual illustration of the theory. Therefore it was regarded as helpful to split the figure into parts representing the children's, parents' and teachers' perspectives and only later merge the three dimensions.

The whole picture shows how *feeling like a family* leads towards solving the conflicts of children, parents and teachers by developing a sense of belonging. In this respect a differentiation is made between the basic conflict, which lies in the society (low reputation), and the main conflicts resulting from a closer look at the education for children with disabilities. In other words, the basic conflict is there already without the environment of the school (of course, teachers play a special role here, as they are seen as teachers only related to the school surrounding). However, the solutions for the main conflicts for the participants related to the area of research are connected to school with the exception of children, as their conflict is the same before receiving education and after having been accepted at school.

---

[1] Of course, also parents and teachers aim at a change of their reputation in society. However, this is not of relevance at this point.

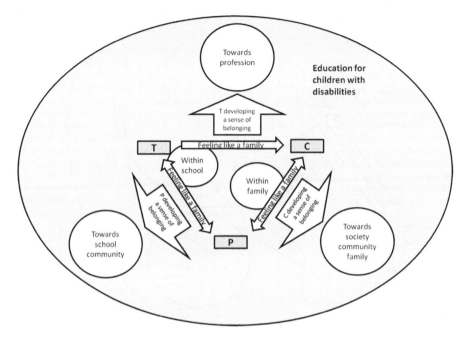

Fig. 7.1 "Developing a sense of belonging" basic. T teachers, C children with disabilities, P parents of children with disabilities

Hence, the low reputation in society of all three groups of interviewees has different consequences within the environment of the school and education respectively (Fig. 7.2).

For children (C), their low reputation, discrimination and feelings of pity on the part of the society lead to the need to develop a new self-concept by receiving education to find their place in society (Fig. 7.3).

The parents' (P) image of being cursed because of having a child with a disability leads to the need to change the attitude to disability in order to be able to obtain value and respect from the "new" community at school (Fig. 7.4).

The teachers' (T) low reputation in society leads to the need of taking on responsibility and show commitment to be able to feel devoted to the profession and be valued accordingly by the parents. This indicates that the problem of a low societal reputation is not solved in the general society but in the school community only.

The following figure merges the three perspectives to make the interconnections between "feeling like a family" of the three participating groups clear (Fig. 7.5).

It is crucial to assert that in the cases of parents and teachers, solving the conflicts leads to a certain kind of well-being in the school environment, as they gain respect and understanding. For children it is about developing a whole new self-concept, which is a comparably bigger step and hence more meaningful for their life. To complete the picture of the theory of "developing a sense of belonging", it is necessary to integrate the developed categories with their assigned keywords (in the black

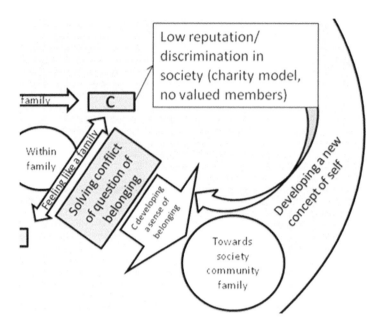

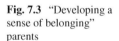

Fig. 7.2 "Developing a sense of belonging" children

Fig. 7.3 "Developing a
sense of belonging"
parents

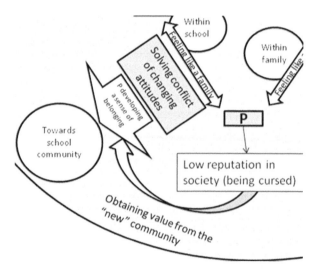

boxes). Especially the keywords of the categories make the processes visible that
lead to a sense of belonging (Fig. 7.6).

   This last figure of "developing a sense of belonging" through *feeling like a family*
shows the whole picture of the influence of education for children with disabilities
in relation to the three groups of participants.

Fig. 7.4 "Developing a sense of belonging" teachers

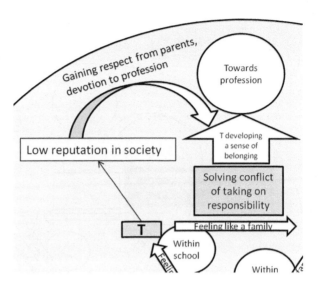

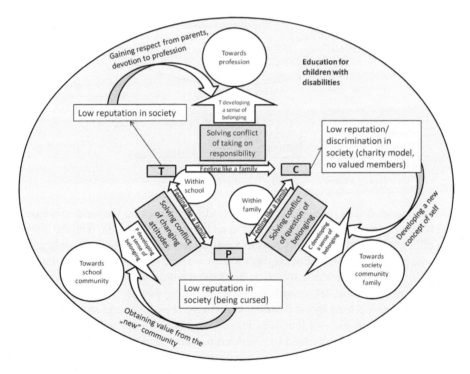

Fig. 7.5 "Developing a sense of belonging" merged

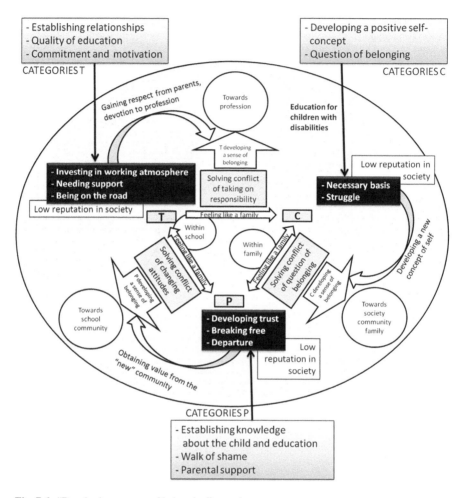

Fig. 7.6 "Developing a sense of belonging" complex

This[2] means that by receiving education children get input for the necessary basis that is developing a *positive* self-concept. In addition to their struggle with the question of belonging, this can finally lead to a *new* concept of self which possibly supports the growth of a sense of belonging towards society. The problem of developing a sense of belonging towards society is not solved within the school environment. However, positive attitudes towards the future are strengthened.

Parents develop trust by establishing knowledge about the child and education; they break free from old convictions by leaving negative attitudes and shame behind. These developments finally lead to enhanced parental support and involvement in school-related issues. Thereby parents obtain value and support from teachers (the

---

[2] In the following explanation of the figure, categories, and other items etc. are not, like in the text, in italics or quotation marks so as to enable fluent reading.

new community) and consequently develop a sense of belonging towards the school community. The conflict of having negative attitudes towards the child with a disability and not seeing their potential is solved. The problem of a low reputation in society, which is due to the widespread understanding of disability as a curse, can only be solved temporarily and as a substitution within the school community.

By developing relationships, teachers invest in their working atmosphere. They communicate aspects where they need support to improve the quality of education. The commitment and motivation that were enhanced by the feeling like a family lead towards "being on the road", which indicates that teachers are committed and motivated to invest in the education of the children. Thus, they are on the road of educationally supporting children with disabilities. The problem of a low reputation in society in general is not solved. However, parents of children with disabilities (as a part of society) highly value the teachers. The conflict of taking on responsibility in their teaching profession, meaning the responsibility to provide children with disabilities with quality education, was solved by developing a sense of belonging towards the teaching profession, supported by the feeling like a family.

What is still missing in this picture is the perspective of the experts. In the chapter on the input of the experts, it became clear that an *atmosphere of departure* regarding developments towards inclusive education and changes in societal attitudes towards people with disabilities seems to prevail amongst most of them. An atmosphere of departure could already be observed in the interviews of parents and teachers on a different level, because for parents it signifies the opening up of possibilities for their child through education and for teachers it indicates a different attitude towards their profession and hence more engagement. Experts take up a more distanced stance from outside the school. Hence, the *atmosphere of departure* means a general change in society (e.g. attitudes). However, also these changes in society are related to possibilities for children with disabilities (e.g. inclusive education). The differences between these "atmospheres of departure" are due to their points of reference towards the participants' micro-systems on the one hand (parents, teachers → children/school) and macro-systems on the other hand (experts → society). It is interesting that this atmosphere could be observed in the children's micro- as well as macro-systems. It appears as if the positive developments regarding attitudes and other relevant aspects towards children with disabilities dominate. Yet it has to be stated that these developments could only be observed to a relatively small extent compared to the still often negative attitudes towards people with disabilities in general.

The atmosphere of departure did not receive a place in the latest picture of the model of "developing a sense of belonging". It only becomes visible through the keywords "departure" related to the parents' category *parental support* and "being on the road" related to the teachers' category *commitment and motivation.* Looking at the *atmosphere of departure* from the experts' perspectives, it becomes clear that there are more barriers and facilitators which influence the situation of children with disabilities. However, in the interviews, positive developments are highlighted more often. In other words, from the experts' perspectives, changes in attitudes and other positive developments towards an environment that is conducive for children with disabilities were observed. Additionally, hopes were also expressed concerning a change in society.

> And, then, the time will come when they are not pushed aside because of their disability. Because these people are really confident, you know. Even regarding formation, these children with disability – most are the best among the school, the best performing students – so why not at the workplace? Why not in the community where they live and work? So this is the world which I would look forward to seeing. And I'm sure it will come. (Temesgen, expert and teacher)

It is evident that this situation – an inclusive society with equal chances for everyone – does not exist yet and hence still is one to work towards. In general, it can be concluded that the *atmosphere of departure* is an additional category that mainly facilitates the education of children with disabilities. On the other hand, if the *atmosphere of departure* is confined, it means stagnation of the process of inclusion which consists mainly in changing attitudes and raising awareness. The following illustration concentrates in particular on the situation of children in this context (Fig. 7.7).

This figure shows that developments within the school community like *feeling like a family* are not enough to support children with disabilities in reaching their goal of defining their place in society. Instead, processes taking place in society as a whole have to be regarded as well. This means that not only developments in the children's micro-system but also in their macro-system need to receive attention, as the final goal of "developing a sense of belonging" for the children is positioned there. Hence, the children's process of "developing a sense of belonging" has its starting point within the school community as it is there where education takes place to create more opportunities for children with disabilities in the future.

> When we talk about social exclusion of the disabled persons we are acknowledging that there is inequality in opportunities within society between those who are active participants and those who are forced towards the fringes (participation/exclusion). We are also affirming that, both for the persons concerned and society itself, this is a process of change and not a set of fixed and static situations. (Michailakis 1997, 18)

The process of "developing a sense of belonging" can only succeed in the wider society depending on variables like societal attitudes and awareness, which are addressed in the *atmosphere of departure*. Within this picture, education for children with disabilities serves as a facilitator that can achieve equal opportunities for all up to a certain level.

The Meaning of Education and Educational Equity

Related to the *atmosphere of departure*, *feeling like a family*, change of attitudes and further major aspects that have already been examined, education of children with disabilities is the main aspect of this book. The meaning of education was already discussed for each group of interviewees in the chapters on the categories. These serve as a basis for the following elaboration, as with this part I aim to combine the different aspects and discuss them in relation to the theory of "developing a sense of

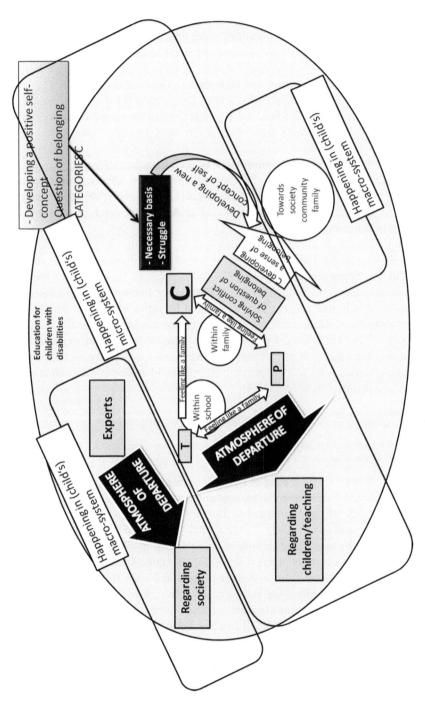

Fig. 7.7 Atmosphere of departure in relation to "developing a sense of belonging"

belonging". Furthermore, it explores in which ways education for children with disabilities can be seen as a facilitator or, more interestingly, can have negative consequences. Additionally, it reflects questions about educational equity.

Education seems to provide an encouraging impulse for children regarding the development of a positive self-concept as well as their future perspectives. In this way, a **revaluation** of their person can take place in their surroundings.

Parents of children with disabilities feel that education for their children takes away some of their worries and burdens. It reliefs them of their hopelessness regarding the future of their child with a disability and provides them with **new perspectives**.

Teachers are also aware of the importance of education for children with disabilities and their future. In the study, in cases where children with disabilities were outstanding students, the teachers highlighted their achievements. Very few teachers also addressed unsatisfactory performance of students with disabilities and their difficulties in following the lesson.

"Since Embaye is disabled, what I think is difficult for him might be participating actively during the sport period. When I teach him physical exercise during sport period, he might not do it like others" (Kadhi, teacher). However, they seemed to understand that education opens up **possibilities** (e.g. finding a job) on a theoretical basis, but that in real life, children will face **difficulties** in making use of them (e.g. regarding the problematic situation on the labour market in general).

Throughout the interviews, I perceived that a lot of **hopes and expectations** were put into the education of children with disabilities, especially by the parents and children themselves. Future expectations could be identified of children in good positions as a result of their education.

> I plan many things for the future. I want to check if she is passing the grades appropriately. If that is so she can reach a very nice position. (Meseret, mother)

> I ask Bizuie [a teacher], I ask her to promise me to make him a real person. I ask Ato T. [a teacher] if he can read and write. (Fatima, mother)

Education is not only promising in terms of influencing the future of the children in a positive way; it is also expected to convert the child with a disability into "a real person" in the view of this grandmother. In other words, education is perceived as **supporting integration in society**. Being a "real" person can be interpreted as "fitting" into society by being able to contribute to this community.

Although education takes place at school, it also contributes to the well-being of the children with disabilities and their parents at home. It eases worries and supports a positive attitude towards the child's future. When it comes to reaping the benefits, however, **disappointments** are most likely to arise. The high rate of unemployment in Ethiopia, especially in the urban areas (Federal Democratic Republic of Ethiopia Ministry of Labour and Social Affairs 2013, 21f, Serneels 2004), also worsens the situation of persons with disabilities. "The marginalisation and powerlessness experienced by disabled people living in isolated rural areas and urban slums across Africa, Asia and Latin America are often overlooked. Here, as everywhere, disabled people are disproportionately unemployed, underemployed and underpaid" (Barnes and Sheldon 2010, 775). When we see this in the light of "developing a sense of belonging" through *feeling like a family* (being able to support the family), it becomes clear that it might be a precarious process for the children to develop a positive self-concept and a sense of belonging. This is the case when the time comes for them to leave school and they find themselves labelled as disabled in the context of higher education or on the labour market. Positive experiences and success stories certainly exist. Nevertheless, it is known that the quality of education in governmental schools is relatively low compared to private and public schools, and accordingly low is the students' knowledge. Furthermore, the high dropout rates in primary schools must be considered (Zehle 2008). Especially children with disabilities in many cases do not reach higher grades due to a lack of support.

In relation to *feeling like a family* and the property "duties and responsibilities", it might be disillusioning and create a feeling of **having failed** when a child is eventually not able to support the family despite all his/her efforts at school. The question is if there is a better or different way than education to reach this goal.[3] The following figure illustrates the meaning of education for "developing a sense of belonging" (Fig. 7.8).

The figure illustrates that education opens up possibilities for positive developments as well as for negative developments regarding the child's development of a sense of belonging and consequently also the formation of a positive concept of self. This is the case because perceived success and failure have an impact on the child's self-concept and sense of belonging. Therefore, the items can be identified as either barriers or facilitators for "developing a sense of belonging". Looking at education from such an angle, it turns out to be an environmental factor by itself that influences the children's life.

As an environmental factor, education has the role of opening up possibilities for children with disabilities. In the light of the capability approach, education is a capability that provides equal opportunities for every child. As a capability, education has the power to lead to certain functionings that are valued by an individual. The important aspect here, according to Amartya Sen, is that equal opportunities should exist, no matter to which functionings they will lead eventually. In other

---

[3] "Education is frequently presented as a means of overcoming poverty and a necessary route to social inclusion. It also has a role to play in promoting the ideals of peace, freedom and justice (UNESCO 1996; ii). Yet the export of Western type schooling and skills often prove exclusionary or less than relevant to local needs (Miles 1996). The emphasis on specific skills such as literacy and numeracy, for example, may lead to the labelling of some children as 'educationally backward' or with 'learning difficulties' resulting in their marginalisation even in contexts where these skills are not vital to an individual's life chances (Ingstad 2001)." (Barnes & Sheldon 2010, 775) Tekeste Negash advocates non-formal education as a better solution than formal education for many Ethiopians, as it focuses on practical skills that are relevant for the majority population rather than skills achieved by formal education. "I argue that the current and planned expansion of the formal education sector cannot be defended either on moral or on developmental grounds. Inevitably, the expansion of formal education would mean the use of scarce resources (collected from the rural areas) for the benefit of school children in the urban areas. The great majority of school children and adults would fall outside the sphere of the Ministry of Education, since most of the expansion of formal education is bound to take place in the urban and semiurban areas of the country (Fig. 7.8)" (Tekeste 1996, 6).

The meaning of education

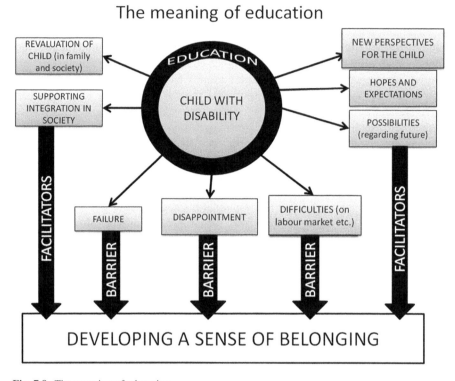

Fig. 7.8 The meaning of education

words, it is about "whether the wider freedoms that people have are enhanced" (Walker 2010, 161).

This indicates that educational equity and quality education are the most important aspects if we want to reach a level where children with disabilities have equal chances and possibilities in their lives like their peers. From this perspective, inclusive education is the best possibility for improving educational equity. When implemented in its classical form, inclusive education should support the different and diverse needs of *all* the students in the classroom. The Salamanca Framework of Action states:

> The fundamental principle of the inclusive school is that all children should learn together, wherever possible, regardless of any difficulties or differences they may have. Inclusive schools must recognize and respond to the diverse needs of their students, accommodating both different styles and rates of learning and ensuring quality education to all through appropriate curricula, organizational arrangements, teaching strategies, resource use and partnerships with their communities. There should be a continuum of support and services to match the continuum of special needs encountered in every school. (UNESCO 1994, 11f.)

It is thus essential that inclusive education should not be used to "integrate" special needs students in regular school settings but to serve *all* learners by embracing and benefitting from their diversity (see Ainscow 2007).

It is of major importance to mention that inclusive education will not work according to one general plan in all cultural environments. There are mechanisms that have different effects in different milieus; tensions emerge because of political decisions regarding education that encourage competition rather than supporting inclusion. All this factors have to be looked at on the background of the particular culture and society. Additionally, especially in the context of this book, the aspect of poverty and other exclusionary burdens plays a central role. Looking at the inclusive (or integrative) practices that could be observed in the schools as well as the concept of "developing a sense of belonging", it becomes clear that inclusive education represents a unique possibility as well as a strategy for moving towards equity in education. Approaching human diversity as something normal and given in any context, inclusive schools are able to offer a "sense of belonging" and comparable future possibilities to every child. Speaking about equity in education in the context of social justice, the capability approach offers valuable reference points. "In evaluating justice and education we would ask if all students enjoy an expansion in the capabilities that they value. Are they all equally free to achieve?" (Walker 2010, 161). The above-mentioned difference between achieved functionings and real opportunities is highlighted again: "This distinction between capability and functioning is important because it asks us to look beneath outcomes to consider what freedom a person had to choose and achieve valued functionings" (Walker 2010, 161).

When relating this to the outcomes of the study, it becomes clear that quality education can enhance the opportunities which children with disabilities have in life. Their possibilities to find a job in the capital are better after having attended school. However, the quality of their education is essential for their future. Usually, children with disabilities have a background of poverty. Consequently, the schools which they attend are governmental schools which mostly have low quality regarding general education. This leads to the conclusion that their education might not lead to the same freedoms which other children gain by receiving quality education in private schools. Equity in education is not reached by the mere possibility of attending *any* school. Providing inclusive schooling for all, however, can lead towards educational equity and more social justice.

This last sentence finally guides us towards the meaning of inclusive schooling for an inclusive society. Having children with disabilities in school has effects on the whole family and therefore also on the community. This is the case because the children go to school like other children. They are given the possibilities to learn like other children. In a society in which education leads to better job opportunities and hence more participation, education clearly contributes to a more inclusive society (in contrast to rural communities, for instance). Once an Ethiopian friend told me that he was invited for an interview at a newspaper, but as soon as they saw that he was in a wheelchair, they said they would not be able to employ him.

Children who attend school together with children with disabilities can experience equity and equality and take this experience with them their whole life. Children are tomorrow's adults and will shape and form the daily lives of our societies. If they learn that inclusion is nothing special, it can become a reality also outside school as they might become future employers – with and without disabilities.

References

Ainscow, M. (2007). Taking an inclusive turn. *Journal of Research in Special Educational Needs, 7*(1), 3–7.

Barnes, C., & Sheldon, A. (2010). Disability, politics and poverty in a majority world context. *Disability & Society, 25*(7), 771–782.

Birks, M., & Mills, J. (2011). *Grounded theory. A practical guide*. Los Angeles/London/New Delhi/Singapore/Washington, DC: Sage.

Federal Democratic Republic of Ethiopia Ministry of Labour and Social Affairs. (2013). *Labour market dynamics in Ethiopia. Analysis of seven key indicators of the labour market (KILM)*. Addis Ababa: Federal Democratic Republic of Ethiopia. Ministry of Labour and Social Affairs.

Ingstad, B. (2001). Disability in the developing world. In G. L. Albrecht, K. D. Seelman, & M. Bury (Eds.), *Handbook of disability studies* (pp. 219–251). Thousand Oaks: Sage.

Miles, S. (1996). Engaging with the disability rights movement: The experience of community based rehabilitation in Southern Africa. *Disability and Society, 11*(4), 501–517.

Michailakis, D. (1997). When opportunity is the thing to be equalised. *Disability & Society, 12*(1), 17–30.

Schiemer, M. (2013). Zur Problematik der Interpretation von Daten aus fremden Kulturen. In E. O. Graf (Ed.), *Globale Perspektiven auf Behinderung* (pp. 129–146). Berlin: epubli GmbH.

Serneels, P. (2004). The nature of unemployment in urban Ethiopia. *Center for the study of African economies*. Oxford University. Retrieved November 23, 2016, from http://www.economics.ox.ac.uk/Centre-for-the-Study-of-African-Economies-Series/the-nature-of-unemployment-in-urban-Ethiopia

Tekeste, N. (1996). *Rethinking education in Ethiopia*. Uppsala: Reprocentralen HSC.

UNESCO. (1996). *International commission on education for the twenty-first century. Education: The necessary utopia, Report for UNESCO*. Paris: UNESCO.

UNESCO. (2000). *The Dakar framework for action. Education for all: Meeting our collective commitments*. Paris: UNESCO.

Walker, M. (2010). Capabilities and social justice in education. In H. U. Otto & H. Ziegler (Eds.), *Education, welfare and the capabilities approach a European perspective* (pp. 155–170). Opladen [u. a.]: Budrich.

Zehle, J. (2008). *Dropout im Schuleingangsbereich an staatlichen Primarschulen Äthiopiens als ein Indikator für Lernschwierigkeiten. Eine wissenschaftliche Untersuchung im Rahmen der interkulturell und international vergleichenden Sonderpädagogik in der qualitativen Eentwicklungszusammenarbeit*. Berlin: Logos.

Chapter 8
Concluding Remarks Related to the Study

Abstract This chapter presents a condensed view on the results and points at limitations, further possibilities and open questions in the analysis of the data collected. This includes an examination of terms like disability and their global applicability. The second part of the conclusion explores future possibilities of analysing the data and addresses questions that have not been answered yet. Regarding the vast body of data collected, there is still the need and the possibility to proceed in the analysis by referring to additional aspects that could not be considered so far. In addition, further comments are included in the last part of the conclusion, regarding topics that go beyond the research question and that were addressed earlier in the book.

Last but not least, this chapter involves current international discussions regarding disability/diversity and education as well as classification systems. This supports the aim of putting the research results into a broader global framework. By referring to studies from other countries, I elaborate links and differences and consequently implications for other cultural contexts. In doing so, the presented theory gets accessible to a broader scientific community.

At this point of the book, I would like to present a condensed view on the results and point out limitations, further possibilities and open questions in the analysis of the data collected. In addition, I include further comments regarding topics that go beyond the research question and that were addressed at the beginning of this book.

Overview of the Results

The outcome of this research is a rather complex concept of the effects that *feeling like a family* can have in school environments on the people involved. The major effect that could be observed was the "development of a sense of belonging", which had to be interpreted differently for children, parents and teachers.

The theory of "developing a sense of belonging" has to be seen as a result that reflects only one aspect of the field under study. Thereby, those participants who developed a *feeling like a family* are in the focus rather than those who didn't, even

© The Author(s) 2017

M. Schiemer, *Education for Children with Disabilities in Addis Ababa,*
Ethiopia, Inclusive Learning and Educational Equity 4,
DOI 10.1007/978-3-319-60768-9_8

though the latter were part of the whole analysis as well as the results. The different categories that emerged in relation to the interviews with the children, parents and teachers revealed processes taking place in each of these groups related to different conflicts that the participants had to deal with. From a macro-system perspective, negative societal and/or cultural attitudes towards disability and the low social reputation of the teaching profession formed basic conflicts for all of the participants. The teachers and parents seemed to solve these conflicts only on a micro-system and not on the macro-system level. By developing a *feeling like a family* mainly between parents and teachers, a "compensatory community" was established at school. This provided them with a feeling of belongingness which gave rise to positive aspects like respect, value and acceptance that might not always be given for them in the greater society. Yet, these processes could only unfold because the respective persons overcame their micro-system conflicts of changing negative attitudes and feeling ashamed of their child with a disability (parents) and taking on responsibility for quality education for the children with disabilities despite a lack of support, teacher training and material (teachers).

The children on the other hand could develop the necessary basis within school to solve their conflict of finding a place of belonging in the macrostructures of the greater society. This necessary basis was an improved or positive concept of self that was established through the highly valued access to school. The *feeling like a family* that was identified in relation to the children's interviews thus referred to their capability of supporting the family economically, which was expected to be reached by receiving education. The children's conflict, lying in the future, was not solved in any way. Realities in Addis Ababa predict a rather negative picture of the possibilities for people with disabilities on the labour market. However, expert interviews pointed at positive – although still slow – developments in Addis Ababa and beyond and an "atmosphere of departure" regarding changes in awareness and changes of negative attitudes towards disability in the society.

The theory of "developing a sense of belonging" describes the dependencies between micro- and macrostructures of the participants regarding their problem-solving strategies (*feeling like a family*). The model furthermore explains these strategies that were chosen by the different actors to deal with emotional stress related to disability and education on the school level. Last but not least, the consequences and results of choosing such a strategy are identified. "Developing a sense of belonging" can hence be understood as a model that makes processes in an educational environment visible that refer to different ways of constructing disability and dealing with the consequences in a majority world context. The advantage of this model is the inclusion of three different perspectives and the integration of micro- and macro-level structures. This makes it possible to compare and reflect on three different approaches towards – and effects of – dealing with disability in an educational environment in a country of the South.

When embedding these results in the cultural and societal environment that can be found in Addis Ababa, it became clear that the influence of a collectivist culture enforces the meaning of *feeling like a family* as well as "developing a sense of belonging". Furthermore, the aspects of religion and ethnicity received special attention, as these aspects added complexity to the process. Last but not least, the culturally valued aspects of family and community emphasise the importance of children with disabilities to develop a sense of belonging.

I want to conclude this overview with a quotation from Singal and Muthukrishna:

> […] [I]t is important to note here that in the South, the individual with disabilities cannot be simply disassociated from the family or other collective units. Rather, disability has a cascading impact on these units as a whole, to a greater or lesser extent. Thus, in order to understand a person with disability, we need to also take into account his or her familial positioning, role, and so on. (2014, 295)

Possibilities and Open Questions

This part of the conclusion explores future possibilities of analysing the data and addresses questions that have not been answered yet. Regarding the vast body of data collected, there is still the need and the possibility to proceed in the analysis by referring, e.g. to the single cases (child–parent–teacher) and compare the situations of children with different "kinds of disabilities" which were identified as such by the surrounding. Thereby, the geographical locations and hence special environmental circumstances of the schools can also receive more attention.

Another point that could not be elaborated further in the scope of this book is the question about the differences and the supporting systems that enable parents from poor backgrounds to organise school visits more often and to develop meaningful relationships compared to the parents from poor backgrounds who were not able or not willing to do so.

A further important aspect is the meaning of friends for children with disabilities and their social integration at school through building up friendships there.

Last but not least, one analytical step while working with the codes led towards the question about the children's responsibilities. There were certain aspects in the data that pointed into the direction that children actually took on a lot of responsibility for their own education (e.g. convincing their parents to come to school). The hypothesis in this context was that children from families who did not develop a *feeling like a family* had to take on comparably more responsibility for their education than others. It is clear that especially aspects related to the participants who were not involved in *feeling like a family* must be examined more closely in future analyses of the collected data.

Further Comments

Regarding the claim of this book to provide contributions that go beyond answering the research question – as addressed in the first part of the book – this last part is devoted to satisfying this claim involving four different topics:

- Future research (beyond the scope of the data collected)
- The aspect of culture
- Models of disability
- Patterns of orientation

First, by being basic research, this study can have implications for **future research** studies. The results indicate that the implementation of inclusive education is not happening satisfactorily for all parties involved in Ethiopia up to now. However, certain strategies are used to deal with problems that the people involved face on a daily basis at school. It would be interesting to find out how those already developed strategies (e.g. *feeling like a family*) could be used for supporting the development of making schools and the school climate inclusive. Additionally, knowledge about possibilities of community-based support regarding schools and an inclusive environment would be valuable, as it is often the communities and neighbourhoods that are very meaningful to the people. Furthermore, it became evident that strategies have to be developed that support people with disabilities on the labour market with the goal of making it accessible and inclusive. This includes first and foremost supporting institutions and potential employers by developing inclusive environments for people with disabilities. Research could be done also in this area to identify where support would be most effective. At the same time, research on the situation of the labour market itself regarding access for people with disabilities is an important issue.[1]

Second, the **aspect of culture** was included with special emphasis in the book. As became clear throughout the book, culture is a nonstatic term and difficult to grasp. However, it has major influences in a society especially on topics like disability. The problematic stigma that people with disabilities usually experience in many cultures could also be observed in Ethiopia and Addis Ababa. The construction of disability depends very much on religious beliefs. Additionally, important factors such as family and society and widespread attitudes as well as awareness play a special role.

Third, the question about the prevailing **model of disability** was posed. It was observed that very often a medical model of disability seems to exist especially regarding educational institutions. For instance, teachers in the study often learned about the causes of disabilities in their special needs course at the teacher training college rather than receiving tools and ideas about how to manage the classroom. In the greater society however, according to the experiences that the interviewees talked about, a charity model seems to constitute the dominant perspective on disability.

Fourth, the aspect of identifying **patterns of orientation** was raised in relation to Nieke's concept of culture (2008). The point there was that the lifeworld of a person or group is mainly constituted by the patterns of orientation which are used in the respective environment. With respect to the results of this research, the

---

[1] Research in this area can be found, e.g. in the project RESPOND-HER (http://respond-her.univie.ac.at/).

cultural patterns of orientation for the children with disabilities are first and foremost the importance and the value of family as such as well as the valued contributions to the community and society. In other words, these specific values serve as a pattern of orientation. They provide the children with a point of reference of what is valued in their society and hence what is expected from them as part of this society. This finally seems to give them the potential to deal with disability in their macro-system and become a part of the greater society. Therefore, it can be hypothesised that the *feeling like a family* also provided the parents and teachers with a pattern of orientation related to the cultural value of family which at the same time served as an anchor point that made it possible for them to deal with disability in a positive way within their micro-systems.

References

Nieke, W. (2008). *Interkulturelle Erziehung und Bildung. Wertorientierungen im Alltag.* Wiesbaden: VS Verlag für Sozialwissenschaften.

Singal, N., & Muthukrishna, N. (2014). Education, childhood and disability in countries of the South – Re-positioning the debates. *Childhood, 21*(3), 293–307.

Chapter 9
Critical Reflections on the Study

Abstract The critical reflections are kept relatively short compared to the high relevance and possible dimensions which the topics reflected on exhibit. This is the case because they are reflections and not elaborations of the relevant issues. On the one hand, as a constructivist approach towards the field was chosen, my role and background receives attention. On the other hand, the resulting model of "developing a sense of belonging" is discussed from a critical perspective and in the light of educational equity. This chapter provides the potential readers with critical input from myself. It shows that the work at hand has also been critically examined by me. Hence, it gives hints towards issues that could be elaborated more extensively and therefore would contribute to and continue my work.

The following critical reflections are kept relatively short compared to the high relevance and possible dimensions which the topics exhibit. This is the case because they are reflections and not elaborations of the relevant issues. On the one hand, as I chose a constructivist approach towards the field, my own role and background as a researcher receives attention. On the other hand, the resulting model of "developing a sense of belonging" is discussed from a critical perspective.

Reflections on the Role of the Researcher

Applying grounded theory from a constructivist point of view means that the researcher always influences the results; she is the one who constructs the data together with the research participants. Adams speaks of data as "situated knowledge", as they are "a product of the relationship between the researcher and her informants" (1999, 360). In other words, the concept of situated knowledge implies that data cannot be collected from the field as something that simply exists. Data are much rather constructed together with the interviewees. "Therefore, an honest presentation of our research requires that we include an explicit analysis of data as the product of a collaboration between ourselves and our informants" (Adams 1999,

© The Author(s) 2017
M. Schiemer, *Education for Children with Disabilities in Addis Ababa, Ethiopia*, Inclusive Learning and Educational Equity 4,
DOI 10.1007/978-3-319-60768-9_9

360). This collaboration is usually influenced by power relations that were already discussed in the chapter on ethical concerns. These power relations, however, are not always one-sided. In the field research, knowledge production is often team-work because inputs and outputs are controlled alternating between both parties (Ben-Ari and Enosh 2013, 424). "The final constructed products of knowledge are created from those same inputs and outputs of the ongoing process between researcher and participants" (Ben-Ari and Enosh 2013, 424). During the interview process, for example, it is the interviewee who decides what to say and what not to say. However, the researcher still decides how to work with the data and has a lot of influence on how the results will finally be interpreted.

> The participant will always own the construction of meaning she has ascribed to experi-ence, regardless of the interpretation placed upon this by the researcher within the publica-tion of his or her work. Secondly, the *researcher* is the one who has been motivated to explore the theoretical ideas before conducting research, and to try to construct knowledge from experience: it is a practical necessity that some individuals should do so, if we are ever to have any knowledge at all. (Millen 1997)

This conclusion certainly has its validity. However, results should be discussed with participating parties if possible, not to get their consent but to unveil misunder-standings, include their views and be able to identify bias or aspects that have been overseen. This is especially important when conducting research in a country of the majority world with a minority world background. All of these points have ethical implications, which is why researchers are always in the duty of reflecting their actions and learning from their experience (Dennis 2010, 123). It was my intention to identify misunderstandings and understand aspects that seemed to be unclear. This was possible especially during the second phase of interviews, during which the same participants were interviewed for the second time. The beginning of these interviews was used for clarifying points from the last interview and for helping the interviewees to remember what was the content of the interview conducted 1 year before. The results of the analysis were discussed in a workshop in Vienna in a group in which also three members from the staff of the Department for Special Needs Education at the Addis Ababa University participated. It was not possible to directly discuss the results with the participants in Ethiopia. This was only feasible regarding preliminary results from the first phase of field research. These were com-municated to the schools during the second phase, and a summary in written form was given to participants who were interested. The children also received a leaflet with information about the results and about what children in the other countries of the larger project had answered. However, unfortunately, discussions about the final results did not take place.

Additionally, it is essential to reflect on the background of the researcher. This can have meaningful influences on the results of a research study. I have an educa-tional background of special needs education as well as of global history. Thus, historical aspects were part of the study from the very beginning, as I give a lot of importance to historical aspects. Furthermore, I grew up in a Western culture in a so-called developed country with good social security and public health systems. Not having lived in poverty nor having a disability as defined in this book, it requires a considerable amount of reflection processes to be able to approach the field that was studied openly. This is important because essential points raised by the participants might get lost if the researcher is not fully aware of possible bias. Also, being a foreigner to the culture under research yields challenges into the research process. In her second edition of "Constructing Grounded Theory" (2014), Charmaz integrates a chapter on data and cultural contexts. Although this chapter is not very extensive, she writes about the complexities of societies in different cultures that have realities which have historically grown and might not always be accessible for the researcher (Charmaz 2014, 330). I am aware of the fact that many aspects of the field of research might not have been accessible for me. However, there was access to certain data and these were interpreted. Yet, it has to be taken into account that an Ethiopian researcher who grew up in Addis Ababa might have had access to the participants in a different way and hence might have obtained results that could have offered an emic perspective on the realities of the participants' lifeworlds but would also exhibit certain bias.

Critical Discussion of the Concept "Developing a Sense of Belonging"

Having finished the analysis and interpretation of the data, the part "school access of children with disabilities" of the refined research question could be exchanged with the core category *feeling like a family*. Consequently, the question would be: *In which ways does "feeling like a family" at school support or hinder children, parents and teachers in dealing with emotional stress situations that are created through negative cultural and societal attitudes towards disability?*

From such a perspective, it becomes clear that eventually not barriers and facilitators for the education of children with disabilities were in the focus but barriers and facilitators for developing a sense of belonging, as this was the most important process that could be identified from the emerging categories of the participants' interviews. The children told us stories about where and how they could help and how other people helped them. These were clear indicators of the importance of community and the support which can be given and received there. Belonging to such a community and a society in general became very meaningful.

The stories which the parents told us had a greater focus on exclusionary aspects grounded in the disabilities of their children. For instance, neighbours and other community members started confrontations or insulted them. On the other hand, positive developments within the communities could also be observed. One teacher supported parents who had children with disabilities in her community. She told them where they could send their children to school and convinced them that they were able to learn etc. Such incidents highlight the influence which a community can have on its members. Therefore, developing a sense of belonging and finding one's place is very important to anyone living in a community in order to be able to lead a quality life.

Feeling like a family thus played a major role. Education, however, assumed the role of a facilitator. As a capability which finally might become a functioning, it helps children to find their place in society.

At this point, it has to be repeated that the majority of the families from the sample were from a poor economic background. Hence, poverty was mostly a fact with which parents and children had to deal. In my discussions about the results with the Ethiopian team from Addis Ababa University, it was highlighted that this also explains the great significance of children supporting their families. According to the Ethiopian colleagues, such expectations cannot be found to this extent in families from more stable economic backgrounds (personal conversation July 3, 2014). A large part of the Ethiopian population – even though it has declined during the last years – still lives in poverty. According to the World Bank (2014), 29.6 % of the Ethiopian people lived below the poverty line[1] in 2011.

Quality education for children with disabilities might decrease poverty if children are enabled to make use of their education and become economically independent. Inclusive education is one aspect that could support such developments. Regarding the result of this book, it is not suggested that *feeling like a family* is *the* solution for making inclusion successful in Addis Ababa. However, "developing a sense of belonging" to the school in the case of children, parents and teachers is a very strong argument for positive developments regarding quality education for children with disabilities. The aspect of *feeling like a family* is a very peculiar one in this context. It can have positive as well as negative influences on the children. What stood out in this book was that the results seemed to implicate rather positive notions regarding disability and education in certain educational environments. Therefore, it has to be emphasised, first, that many negative aspects were also addressed in the interviews and, second, that family is not only about positive aspects like receiving support but also about duties and responsibilities which might be challenging. Supposing that children would have family duties and relations with their teachers at school, this could have far-reaching consequences for the children. Hence, there are reasons why school is not family for them: schools can be changed; families usually cannot. This means that relationships have different qualities at school, and dependencies have different meanings in the different environments. Children might depend greatly on the support of their families in all of their major life areas. Hence, it is not surprising that the children's *feeling like a family* gave them a lot of motivation because it provided them with a future perspective of being meaningful to the family as well as independent. However, the *feeling like a family* did not exist in the children towards their teachers. Therefore, they usually "only" depended on teachers regarding education. Yet, also at school, social integration

---

[1] A poverty line specifies a society's minimum standard of living to which everybody in that society should be entitled. This concept is very country-specific. Every society has its own views on what constitutes a minimum standard of living, which is why most countries develop a national methodology to measure poverty accurately and do not solely rely on internationally known poverty lines. However, for international comparisons, the World Bank has developed the well-known '$1 per person per day' poverty line using purchasing power parities (PPP) and estimating from decile data. (Braithwaite and Mont 2008, 4)

takes place amongst friends and the school community, which indicates that school is not only there for education. The fact that there seemed to be no family feeling in children towards teachers ensures and maintains a certain distance that might be necessary for the children also regarding the teaching learning process. However, even though they were not mentioned by children in this way, relations to friends at school might have similarities to "feeling like a family", as friendship and supporting peers played an important role for the children with disabilities. This is another aspect yet to be explored in another paper, as mentioned earlier.

Moving from the micro- to the macro-system of the children, the following quotation becomes especially interesting in the light of the discussed collectivist and individualist cultures. Peters argues that in the majority world "personhood depends more on social identity and the fulfilment of family obligations than on individual ability" (2007, 122). This is yet another supporting aspect for the meaning that finding a place in society – and hence developing a social identity – has for children with disabilities in Addis Ababa. Fulfilling family obligations enables children with disabilities to fulfil their social role.

> A *social role* is a combination of behaviors, functions, relationships, privileges, duties, and responsibilities that are socially defined, widely understood, and recognized within a society. People who fill roles that are positively valued by others will generally be treated well, whereas persons who occupy devalued roles will typically be treated badly. (Lustig and Strauser 2007, 196)

Being poor and having a disability are conditions that lead towards a devaluation of people in the society. According to Lustig and Strauser (2007), people who exhibit these features usually experience a "variety of harmful life experiences". A further negative experience for children with disabilities might be a disappointment of the high expectations placed on education. This does not mean that education is useless or not necessary. The problem is the high expectations that are often placed on education only. The feeling of belonging that children were striving for related to community and society is an aspect lying in the future that can still be disappointed. In other words, there is uncertainty about this issue, and the result of their efforts in education is not visible until they leave school. This is an essential aspect; education is perceived as very positive as long as children are at school. It is expected to support children in fulfilling their social role and consequently, according to Lustig and Strauser (2007), be treated well – in other words, be accepted and included in society.

The fact that none of the defined conflicts of children, parents and teachers was finally solved and only preliminary solutions were identified in the school settings is essential. Looking at the whole issue from this perspective, it becomes clear that there might be certain aspects that were not revealed because the *feeling like a family* relieved the participants from addressing them and empowered them temporarily. In this way, *feeling like a family* could also just serve as a strategy for briefly overcoming emotional stress in the particular situation of parents having a child with a disability, teachers not being content with their job and children finding themselves with the conflict of the question of belonging. Yet, the importance of family, community and social life cannot be ignored in the cultural context of this book. This is also what makes the theory of "developing a sense of belonging" so significant and important.

References

Adams, L. L. (1999). The mascot researcher: Identity, power, and knowledge in fieldwork. *Journal of Contemporary Ethnography, 28*(4), 331–363.
Ben-Ari, A., & Enosh, G. (2013). Power relations and reciprocity: Dialectics of knowledge construction. *Qualitative Health Research, 23*(3), 422–429.
Braithwaite, J., & Mont, D. (2008). *Disability and poverty: A survey of World Bank poverty assessments and implications.* (Discussion Paper No. 0805).
Charmaz, K. (2014). *Constructing grounded theory* (2nd ed.). Los Angeles: Sage.
Dennis, B. (2010). Ethical dilemmas in the field: The complex nature of doing education ethnography. *Ethnography and Education, 5*(2), 123–127.
Lustig, D. C., & Strauser, D. R. (2007). Causal relationships between poverty and disability. *Rehabilitation Counseling Bulletin, 50*(4), 194–202.
Millen, D. (1997). Some methodological and epistemological issues raised by doing feminist research on non-feminist women. In *Sociological research online*.
Peters, S. (2007). Inclusion as a strategy for achieving education for all. In L. Florian (Ed.), *The sage handbook of special education* (pp. 117–130). London/Thousand Oaks/New Delhi: Sage.
World Bank. (2014). *Ethiopia. World development indicators.* Retrieved May 29, 2014, from http://data.worldbank.org/country/Ethiopia

Chapter 10
Integrating the Perspective of the Capability Approach

Abstract In this chapter, the capability approach is discussed more in depth. Different studies are referred to, to be able to contextualise the meaning of the capability approach in relation with the presented research. The meaning of different cultures is elaborated in detail. Last but not least, education is related to the capability approach as a capability itself.

In describing the results of the interviews with the children, parents and teachers, I chose the capability approach as a contextualizing perspective and the idea of inclusive education as a basis; the focus was placed on educational equity and social justice. However, this does not seem to illustrate sufficiently how the different parts are interlinked. I want to give a clearer idea of the reality which I explored and also open the discussion on how the insights which I have offered for the specific case of Addis Ababa, Ethiopia, could be useful for other countries.

"[...] [T]he kind of education that best articulates the concept of Sen's capability approach seems to be the one that makes people autonomous and, at the same time, develops people's judgement about capabilities and their exercise" (Saito 2003, 29). In the context of this book, autonomy would finally lead towards possibilities of supporting one's family.

The capability approach looks at capabilities which exist in human beings and which can lead to certain functionings, provided that the circumstances, the environment, society, etc. enable individual persons (or a group) to use those capabilities and turn them into functionings. "In contrasting capabilities with functionings, we should bear in mind that capability means opportunity to select. The notion of freedom to choose is thus built into the notion of capability" (Nussbaum 2011, 25).

Biggeri's (2007) studies identified education as a capability of the children of his sample. This seems to be equally true for what I found in Ethiopia. What does this mean?

In the capability approach, one of the most important goals is to reach well-being and quality of life as well as equity and equal opportunities for all people. The quality of life and the values are identified and specified by the people themselves.

[...] [W]hen dealing with children, it is the freedom they will have in the future rather than the present that should be considered. Therefore, as long as we consider a person's capabilities in terms of their life-span, the capability approach seems to be applicable to children. (Saito 2003, 26)[1]

In the context of my research, education seemed to be a valued capability, in the lives of almost all the interviewees. In order for the children to reach this capability, it must be directed and insisted upon in order to become a functioning. If implemented successfully, education can thus contribute to reaching well-being and quality of life. However, this can only happen if the environment can offer the necessary framework conditions (conversion factors), which are educational equity, equality of possibilities, and social justice amongst others.

Once the necessary framework conditions are granted, it is necessary to locate and position inclusion and inclusive education within this process, which is strongly dependent on transformation (and development): society has to become inclusive. Schools have to develop to become inclusive. Systems will have to change in order to be able to become inclusive.

Inclusive means that diversity is seen as something given and something which benefits us all. It is about change: a change in attitudes and a change away from capitalistically guided focusses of economic growth through achievement. My approach to inclusion is thus broadened from (dis-)ability to all kinds of diversity that lie within the human race.

Looking at other countries from this angle, the research at hand teaches us that it is very valuable to look at the deeper structures of a society. The insights we gain can be of great help for introducing equity in education, for working towards inclusion and inclusive education. As there is no global concept for how to introduce inclusive education, it is necessary to focus on the values in diverse societies, the logic of their living together and the functioning of communities, as this is important for the success of such an endeavour. Without including these aspects in the process of transforming societies to become more inclusive, it will not be possible.

To make it even clearer why cultural issues are of major importance when speaking about inclusive societies (not only inclusive education), I want to refer briefly to the example of rural Kenya:

"Because rural parents did not conceptualize their children's worth as predicated on their ability to compete in a [W]esternized educational system, their children were included in age-appropriate culturally normative activities. The contributions those children made to their families and communities' well-being were valued" (Mutua and Swadener 2011, 215). This also included children with mild and moderate intellectual disabilities. The authors of the Kenyan study emphasise that there is a "colonial impulse to minimize and devalue the inclusive activities of rural

---

[1] This quotation continues: "The fact that children need to have support from parents, society or others in terms of choosing which capabilities to exercise will lead us to consider what role education can play in the capability approach" (Saito 2003, 26). This is a very interesting way of approaching the capability approach and education. Two further interesting questions to discuss would be to what extent children can choose for themselves and when they need support and if education could or should support or guide these choices. Unfortunately, it would go too far at this point to discuss the topic from this angle.

communities in Kenya" (Mutua and Swadener 2011, 215). Furthermore, they state that usually international commitments like *Education for All* "are colonial interventions that fail to capitalize on conceptions of inclusiveness that are already embedded in the daily practices of rural communities." (Mutua and Swadener 2011, 215) In quoting these arguments, I want to put special emphasis on the meaning and the importance of (at least) trying to understand and valuing different cultures.

> Community conceptions of disabilities do not always align with [W]estern formulations of disability or inclusiveness. Pursuing equity in access and participation in the future may require starting with a sound understanding of ways in which local communities understand and make available inclusive spaces for all, including persons with disabilities. (Mutua and Swadener 2011, 220)

In the case of the study at hand, one of the most important aspects in working towards educational equity and inclusive education in Ethiopia was undoubtedly the involvement of the families and surrounding communities. This approach clearly supports children with disabilities in using the capability of education for achieving the functioning of being a valued and contributing member of their society – not least by being able to support their own family. In other words, experiencing educational equity and being granted the opportunity to participate equally in social life leads to more quality of life. This is a goal which was valued by all the children in the research.

Simplified view on turning the children's capability of education into functionings (Fig. 10.1):

This explains how from the perspective of the capability approach children can be empowered through inclusive education and educational equity to lead the lives they have reason to value.

If we look at the functionings, we can see that some of them lie in the future, as argued by Saito (see quotation earlier in this chapter). In other words, the freedoms which children gain through the capability of education are partly only realised in their future. When speaking about freedoms, it is also necessary to speak about the term "values". "Feeling like a family" is the core category and exhibits certain

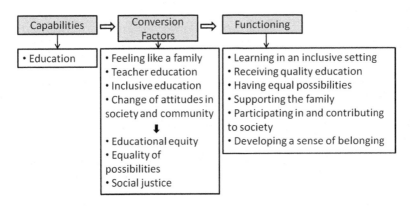

Fig. 10.1 Education as a capability

values. "The exercise of freedom is mediated by values, but the values in turn are influenced by public discussions and social interactions, which are themselves influenced by participatory freedoms" (Sen 1999, 9). Hence, the value that family has in Ethiopia (or parts of it) determines some of the freedoms which are granted through education (e.g. supporting the family). In other words, education can lead to the possibility of doing justice to the value of family by being able to support the latter. The last part of Sen's quotation clearly shows the importance of aiming at an inclusive society, as only inclusion can ensure participatory freedoms for people with disabilities. These freedoms lead to the possibility to participate in the mentioned discussions and interactions which influence values in a society. Consequently, it is of great importance not only to have the possibility to participate in society and to enjoy or live with the given values but also to participate in discussions and thus in shaping the values of this society and finally the society itself by *really* being part of it.

References

Biggeri, M. (2007). Children's valued capabilities. In M. Walker (Ed.), *Amartya Sen's capability approach and social justice in education*. Basingstoke: Palgrave MacMillan.

Mutua, K., & Swadener, B. (2011). Challenges to inclusive education in Kenya: Postcolonial perspectives and family narratives. In A. Artiles, E. Kozleski, & F. Waitoller (Eds.), *Inclusive education. Examining equity in five continents* (pp. 201–222). Cambridge, MA: Harvard Education Press.

Nussbaum, M. C. (2011). *Creating capabilities. The human development approach*. Cambridge, MA/London: Harvard University Press.

Sen, A. (1999). *Development as freedom*. New York: Oxford University Press.

Saito, M. (2003). Amartya Sen's capability approach to education: A critical exploration. *Journal of Philosophy of Education*, 37(1), 17–34.

Chapter 11
Inclusive Education and the UN Convention on the Rights of Persons with Disabilities (UNCRPD)

Abstract The UNCRPD has already been mentioned in the former chapters. However, there is need of discussing global discourses and questions about the convention and its implementation as it has become a topic of high relevance not only in Ethiopia. Especially article 24 on education of the convention is of major importance for the research at hand. Religion and belief as well as poverty are issues that have already been addressed throughout the study. Hence, it became visible that more factors than disability have to be considered when talking about education and the UNCRPD. Putting these facts in the centre of this chapter allows a critical approach towards questions about the implementation of the UNCRPD.

The main focus is put on questions about how education and inclusion in Ethiopia need to be broadened beyond "disability" and related to other issues of disadvantage. These include aspects of poverty, ethnicity (minorities) and other challenging conditions. Discussing such issues brings forward aspects that are meaningful also on a global level and enriches debates about disability/diversity and culture on the background of the implementation of the UNCRPD.

Having brought inclusion and inclusive education into the focus, I want to dedicate the final chapter of this book to one of the most important documents which has guided discussions on disability in the last 10 years: the UN Convention on the Rights of Persons with Disabilities.

> It can be argued that the UNCRPD constituted the biggest victory for the disability movement in the three decades of its existence. The Convention has been heralded as a major step forward for disabled people and as representing a paradigm shift on how we think and act about disability. (Meekosha 2011, 1384)

Inequity in education as a global phenomenon is one of the issues which are addressed in the UN Convention on the Rights of Persons with Disabilities (UNCRPD).

The UN (2006) has already been mentioned in previous chapters. There is a need for an in-depth discussion on global discourses and questions about the Convention and its implementation, as it has become a topic of high relevance, not only in

© The Author(s) 2017
M. Schiemer, *Education for Children with Disabilities in Addis Ababa,*
Ethiopia, Inclusive Learning and Educational Equity 4,
DOI 10.1007/978-3-319-60768-9_11

Ethiopia. Especially Article 24 on education is of major importance for the topic at hand. Point 1 of 5 says:

1. States Parties recognize the right of persons with disabilities to education. With a view to realizing this right without discrimination and on the basis of equal opportunity, States Parties shall ensure an inclusive education system at all levels and lifelong learning directed to:

     (a)   The full development of human potential and sense of dignity and self-worth, and the strengthening of respect for human rights, fundamental freedoms and human diversity;
     (b)   The development by persons with disabilities of their personality, talents and creativity, as well as their mental and physical abilities, to their fullest potential;
     (c)   Enabling persons with disabilities to participate effectively in a free society. (UN 2006, Art. 24, 16)

In short, the Convention aims at a person's "development to the fullest potential to participate effectively" by introducing an inclusive education system. This goal is also based on the human rights discourse and pursues equal opportunities in life. In other words, the ultimate goal is to reach educational equity and equality. This sounds very much like the capability approach, where people's capabilities ("fullest potential") should be converted ("full development") into functionings that are valued by the individual ("participate effectively"). In regard to participating effectively, however, the UNCRPD fails to address the importance for the individual (and the community) to value his/her own achievements and goals. "Participate effectively" sounds like a demand-driven and economically relevant participation in a society rather than reaching a life which the people themselves have reason to value.

In an article comparing Germany, Iceland and Sweden, Biermann and Powell (2014, 680) highlight the fact that Article 24 is the one that has been discussed as the most controversial. Referring to Degener (2009), they explicate that the discussions about the choice between inclusive and special schools or an abolishment of special schools resulted in a compromise. Hence, no specific ideas were articulated, but a general human right for inclusive education was declared. The thus created vagueness led to multiple interpretations of inclusive education. Other authors also discuss the problems that persisted after the finalisation of the UNCRPD, in particular regarding inclusive education.

> This Convention (UNCRPD) is the outcome of five years of work by a UN Committee on which people with disabilities played a leading role on an equal basis with representatives of national governments. The outcome has been welcomed by the disability movement but many issues proved contentious, not least that of inclusive education. (Mittler 2008, 3)

Regarding the implementation of the UNCRPD, three different dimensions have been identified which challenge traditional perspectives on disability and education in all signing states (Biermann and Powell 2014, 680). Referring to Scott (2008), the authors define them as follows: **paradigms of disability and ideals of education** as the first dimension (cultural–cognitive), **special education as a profession and school as an organisational form** as the second dimension (normative), and **educational politics and jurisdiction** as the third dimension (regulatory) (Biermann and Powell 2014, 684). These three dimensions pose major challenges for nation states regarding the implementation of Article 24.

Considering this concept with Ethiopia in mind, it is not easy to fill the three dimensions with content. The knowledge which we have gained from the study, however, provides us with possibilities to think about certain issues regarding cultural–cognitive, normative and regulatory aspects that have to be considered. For instance, we might have gotten an idea of the challenges in the area of education and the history, culture, language and traditions, everyday challenges that form the disability paradigm in this society and are responsible for it; in other words, studies on the situation of children with disabilities like the one at hand are able to provide us with information that helps analyse the challenges and barriers with which a state might be confronted while trying to implement the UNCRPD. But this does not mean that traditional perspectives on disability and education which are challenged by the three dimensions should automatically be changed. In this regard, we also have to be careful about what we define as traditional. When looking at the normative and regulatory dimensions in Ethiopia, we may find that Western standards prevail in the capital. It can therefore sometimes be difficult to identify traditional cultural perspectives. Certain aspects like the influence of religion and belief were easy to identify, whereas more subtle aspects, like the meaning of receiving and providing help, needed a deeper analysis.

This clearly shows that the results of the study provide a basis for identifying important points and elaborating the relevance and extent of the mentioned dimensions – and therefore challenging traditional perspectives – from an Ethiopian point of view. Further studies focusing on complementary aspects would complete the picture of challenges when thinking about the implementation of Article 24 in Ethiopia. Identifying special aspects of a society regarding inclusive education is a relevant tool that must be used if inclusion is to become a reality.

Next to people with disabilities, there are other groups who do not receive education and who are discriminated and left behind. Therefore, we have to broaden our perspective when speaking about inclusion and exclusionary aspects, especially when looking at poverty as an important dimension. We have to address all those people who are disabled, discriminated or/and excluded by society or certain environments or conditions and prevented from active participation if we want to speak about inclusive education and, beyond that, an inclusive society.

Religion and belief as well as poverty were relevant aspects throughout the study, which has shown that these, having a great impact on the life situations of people, are also disabling factors and have to be considered when talking about education and the UNCRPD. Referring to Ingstad (2001), Grech describes:

> how the inability to take care of a disabled family member is often bound to the inability to cope with extreme poverty, and not necessarily to negative attitudes and/or lack of concern. At the most basic level, the exclusive focus on negative attitudes and oppression strips disabled people and their households of any form of agency and the ability/possibility to resist and control/change their circumstances, and influence other people's attitudes and behaviours. After all, poor people continue to survive and ensure their own reproduction despite

> the hardships imposed by their physical, social, economic and natural environments, and in the almost regular absence of formal safety nets. (2011, 90)

This statement demonstrates how important it is to include poverty amongst other risk factors when looking at the situation of people with disabilities. Consequently, difference and diversity are terms that can enrich debates in the context of inclusive education and disability. "An inclusive education system promotes an ethos in which difference is respected and valued, but also actively combats discrimination and prejudice through its policies and actions" (Kaplan et al. 2007, 23). Placing these facts at the centre of this chapter allows a critical approach towards questions about the implementation of the UNCRPD.

Critical Voices Regarding the UNCRPD and Human Rights in General

> One of the most heated human rights debates is indeed whether human rights are a universal or rather a Western concept and, concomitantly, whether they are universally valid or not. (de Sousa Santos 2008, 12)

An evaluation of the UNCRPD must involve the aspect of human rights, since they provide a solid background and information regarding the historical developments. The UNCRPD is based on the original human rights as declared in 1948. Many would agree that human rights should be recognised and implemented on a global level. De Sousa Santos on the other hand argues: "As long as human rights are conceived of as universal, they will operate as a globalized localism, a form of globalization from above" (2002, 44). In other words, human rights have been developed by and for mainly Western countries. Looking more closely at the issue especially during the post-war period, it can be found that human rights served the "economic and geopolitical interests of the hegemonic capitalist states" (de Sousa Santos 2002, 45). Consequently, the human rights chapters do not include many aspects from perspectives of majority world countries. Meekosha and Soldatic state that de Sousa Santos positions the human rights discourse in the row of colonial heritage, meaning that the constitution of the human rights is mainly in the hands of a hegemonic North which disregards important "global power imbalances" which play an essential role (2011, 1388). In this respect, it is striking that Odysseos and Selmeczi argue that Third World countries (sic) were actually fighting for human rights while trying to be released from the colonial powers. Furthermore, these struggles "were crucial in establishing universal human rights as a paradigm through the emergence of such struggles in the United Nations" (Odysseos and Selmeczi 1034).

It is interesting to observe that these struggles, which also had influences on the development of human rights, did not lead to the Northern countries involving the struggling parties (colonised countries) to a greater extent regarding the concept of human rights. Therefore, human rights cannot be seen as universally applicable without considering certain cultural circumstances. One of the main aspects mentioned by de Sousa Santos in this context is human dignity, which may be defined and interpreted differently in different cultures. "As they are now predominantly understood, human rights are a kind of Esperanto which can hardly become the everyday language of human dignity across the globe" (de Sousa Santos 2002, 57). The author sees more incompatible aspects "in the exclusive recognition of individual rights, with the sole exception of the collective right to self-determination [...] in the priority given to civil and political rights over economic, social, and cultural rights; and in the recognition of the right to property as the first and, for many years, the sole economic right" (2008, 14).

It is not surprising that here, too – like in the study at hand – the critical point of bringing "Northern" concepts to "Southern" parts of the world receives attention. Turning again to the UNCRPD, Meekosha and Soldatic point their critical voices towards "potential limitations when adopting Northern conceptualisations of disability rights" (2011, 1384). In their article, they place the UNCRPD in a cultural, historical and political context in order to be able to approach it in a meaningful way.

Bearing in mind what was discussed earlier about individualist and collectivist cultures, as well as referring to the arguments of de Sousa Santos, the following statement becomes especially interesting:

> Individual rights are not a universal concept, but rather reflect the dynamics of an industrialised society. Many countries in the global South are predominantly based on agriculture and subsistence farming, which reflects more traditional community structures. Human rights originated in the Western liberal political tradition, whereas non-metropole cultures have different traditions of emancipatory struggle. (Meekosha and Soldatic 2011, 1388)

In the light of the capability approach, this raises the question to what extent it is related to the individual and how much attention should be paid to groups and communities in this context. There has been some criticism stating that the capability approach is designed only for the individual, although it would also be important to highlight capabilities and functionings, for instance, on the part of communities. From my point of view, this is an essential aspect and cannot be forgotten in the discussion about equal possibilities, living a quality life and reaching functionings that are valued – by the whole community.

Considering rights for people with disabilities on such a background makes it more challenging to think of individual rights in global terms. It is essential to not only point out such differences but also include the meaning of certain power relations between North and South from a Southern perspective (Meekosha and Soldatic 2011, 1389). The striking conclusion that Meekosha and Soldatic draw from that is: "Given the close connection between poverty and disability, it could be argued that a redistribution of power and wealth both between rich and poor countries and within poor countries could have more impact on the lived experience of disabled people in the global South than would human rights legislation" (Meekosha and Soldatic 2011, 1389).

Reflecting on this argument makes it clear that not only the implementation of rights for people with disabilities is at issue but also a much greater change of relations on a global level.

However, referring to the UNCRPD, again dimensions such as history, tradition, culture, current situation and challenges of a society are essential and have to be regarded in the South when trying to implement a convention that has been mainly developed by countries of the North. Even though there is justifiable criticism of the Northern influence in the context of international conventions and other documents (see, e.g. the chapter on the ICF in this book), the importance of approaching issues like rights for people with disabilities cannot be ignored. However, what has to be highlighted is the significance of the participation and involvement of the majority world in all contexts. In his book "The idea of justice", Amartya Sen argues that human rights are ethical confirmations that the freedoms at which those rights point are of major importance. Therefore, those freedoms should be the starting points for discussing the relevance of human rights.

> The importance of freedoms provides a foundational reason not only for affirming our own rights and liberties, but also for taking an interest in the freedoms and rights of others – going well beyond the pleasures and desire-fulfilment on which utilitarians concentrate. (Sen 2009, 367)

Consequently, Sen concludes that agreement is needed for the social framework of human rights, meaning the importance which certain freedoms have in a society.

In Ethiopia it seems that certain aspects of the human rights declaration and/or the UNCRPD have gained more or less importance. The Ethiopian government signed the UNCRPD in 2007 and ratified it in 2010. However, it did not sign and ratify the optional protocol (UN Enable, online; FDRE 2012). The optional protocol is important because international complaints are possible only by ratifying this document. This means that people who feel that one of those rights has been violated can report to the international authority in Geneva (Bürli 2015, 63).

In spite of this, the Federal Democratic Republic of Ethiopia stated that, within the implementation process of the UNCRPD, a program of human rights training across the country has taken place. Amongst the people involved were law enforcement officers and other professionals of jurisdiction. These trainings were supported financially by the Norwegian government. Additionally, ethical education – including ideals of human rights – is being taught in primary, secondary and tertiary level schools (FDRE 2012, 32). Having education as a human right, Ethiopia is also trying to reach goals of education for all. "A national Council on inclusive education and training has been set up to promote inclusive policy and the special needs education strategy throughout the country" (FDRE 2012, part 2: 39). What becomes apparent here is that human rights seem to play a major role in the ongoing political discussions about education in Ethiopia.[1]

---

[1] However, there are many critical voices regarding human rights in Ethiopia.

Accentuating the power relations between North and South, it is easy to draw a line to issues of the rights of people with disabilities by looking at the dynamics which they provoke: "It is important to contextualise violations of the rights of disabled people not only in terms of the struggles in the global North, but also in terms of power relations between North and South and within the global South" (Meekosha and Soldatic 2011, 1389). Grech also points at the first part of this statement when saying that "relationships of power" are often left out in discussions about transferring knowledge from West to South. Furthermore, he highlights the problematic aspect of adopting a Western "language of 'rights'" (Grech 2011, 88). Another challenging point identified by the author is the fact that disability studies focus on disability in the West. This presents a very Eurocentric or Western view on disability in the academic field. "[…] Western disability studies and its tenets, notably the social model of disability and the language of 'rights', are transferred indiscriminately from North to South and absorbed almost unquestionably by development agencies, southern organisations and other intermediaries" (Grech 2011, 88). He goes on to criticise the process of knowledge from the West being generalised and transferred to the South, "where critical issues related to context, culture, economy, history, community and relationships of power among others are often bypassed or reframed to accommodate a minority world view" (2009, 88). Similar arguments can be made when speaking about human rights. This is why de Sousa Santos concludes that human rights are "only universal when they are viewed from a Western standpoint" (2008, 12).

In the context of the capability approach – which according to Nussbaum is one species of a human rights movement – she argues against de Sousa Santos. She states: "It has frequently been said that the human rights movement […] is Western in origin, and that the endorsement of international human rights norms as major human goals thus reinforces the subordination of non-Western cultures to a Western ideology" (2011, 102). Next, she raises the point that lots of the values included in the human rights catalogue had existed long before in Indian and Chinese cultures. She therefore concludes that the argument of another kind of "imperialism" does not have enough substance (2011, 103). However, it is not surprising that lots of the values to be found in the human rights can be found in different cultures. It might thus be important to look not only at values but also at the importance and the power of those values and how they are lived and implemented in a society and in different contexts. Religion and/or God, for example, may play a role as a value (system) in lots of different cultures. However, the implications, the meaning, the power and the influence which it may or may not have are completely different (the same is true when looking at disability). I would like to conclude this discussion with Sen's statement:

> The possibility of disagreement always exists in pronouncements about human rights, and critical examination is part of what can be called the discipline of human rights. Indeed, even the viability of claims about human rights […] is closely linked with impartial scrutiny. (Sen 2009, 370)

Additionally to the challenges that are provoked through power relations between and within states, one question is still open: how a convention that is not mainly based on Southern norms and beliefs can be implemented in countries of the majority world.

The Implementation of the UNCRPD and Its Challenges

Despite all the critical arguments laid out in the last chapter, it can be said that disability has become a very important human rights issue over the last decades also in countries of the global South. This change of visibility can be seen on a global level, although mainstreaming of disability happens more or less effectively in different parts of the world. McEwan and Butler state that the positive developments that took place, for instance, in Uganda regarding rights and participation of people with disabilities were only possible because the visibility of the topic had increased (2007). However, there are more possibilities to approach the topic which could be successful in improving the situation for people with disabilities. "Yet, while disability has become a quintessential human rights issue, other discourses and solutions, such as collective rather than individual approaches, have tended to become marginalised" (Meekosha and Soldatic, 2011, 1387).

As already stated, giving preference to collective over individual approaches under certain circumstances is especially meaningful when looking at the study at hand. There, I highlighted the meaning of community, family and other collective structures as most meaningful for people involved in the education of children with disabilities in Ethiopia.

Taking these results as a starting point for implementing Article 24 of the Convention, a sustainable basis could be developed for developing specific and effective steps towards an appropriate inclusive education system. By saying "appropriate inclusive", I want to emphasise the fact that inclusion and inclusive education as a concept also have to be defined including the realities of a particular society, culture and a country as such. In other words, a universally applicable concept of inclusion does not exist.

At this point, it is interesting to look at the agenda for the Sustainable Development Goals (SDG) as adopted in September 2015. In the SDGs that will be relevant for all countries until 2030, goal number 4 clearly speaks about inclusive education: "Ensure inclusive and equitable quality education and promote lifelong learning opportunities for all" (UNDP 2015a). The SDGs are innovative in terms of being relevant for all countries, not only countries of the majority world. Additionally, goal number 4 is not only about primary education but about life-long learning. Next to pre-primary and primary education, this includes technical, vocational and tertiary education. Furthermore, skills for decent work, literacy and numeracy are targeted at. Another goal is education for sustainable development and global citizenship. Last but not least, it is aimed to substantially increase the supply of qualified teachers (UNESCO online). To be able to reach such goals, we need to know what can and cannot work and what the people involved need. Working towards the implementation of the UNCRPD only makes sense if it happens on a sustainable basis. This means first and foremost that it has to make sense for teachers, children and parents. Starting with these arguments, it clearly makes sense to look at practices that have proven successful for teachers and families who are already sending their children with disabilities to school (whether it be inclusive or special education).

In many countries, the implementation of Article 24 of the Convention signifies a change from a special education system to an inclusive system. Richardson and Powell (2011), for example, compare different systems of special education. At the end of their book, they find that:

> [i]n research on special education, macro-level comparisons have been relatively neglected, especially the explicit comparison of the development of education systems over time. As noted at the outset, the considerable variability has, more often than not, been displayed with the chief intention to affirm cultural variation itself. [...] Lacking are systematic analyses of similarities and differences, especially the principles and the relationships to general education and other neighbouring institutions. (Richardson and Powell 2011, 259)

As mentioned before, the abolishment of special schools and special education in general was much discussed during the development of the UNCRPD. In Ethiopia, education appears to be one of the rights that can be achieved in agreement with other goals of the government.

At this point, according to Richardson and Powell, it would be necessary to go deeper into the educational history of Ethiopia, which was already done at the beginning of this book. In a next step, it would be important to obtain answers to the questions: "What is inclusive education?" Or more precisely: "What does inclusive education mean in the Ethiopian context compared to other contexts?" We would have to think about what kind of inclusive education can be successful in a certain environment and why other kinds cannot.

The establishment of special education – as we understand it in Western contexts – has only just begun in Ethiopia. This means that developments that have taken place in Western countries and led to a very strong system of special education (like in Germany) have not taken place to the same extent in Ethiopia. This could be seen as an opportunity and as a head start when it comes to inclusive education. In other words, Ethiopia is not confronted with having to change excluding structures of institutions that have grown for more than 100 years (e.g. special needs trainings for teachers, special schools, etc.). Some experts who were interviewed during my study argued that Ethiopia could use the non-existence of a strongly grown system of separation for the development of an inclusive system. In this context, Zehle (2015) argues that in Ethiopia it is not the idea to change from an existing system of special education to an inclusive system; instead, the idea is to allow children and young people who have been excluded from national education institutions for more than 100 years to access quality education according to their individual skills and needs. The real challenge for the Ethiopian society hence lies more in changing societal attitudes such as "children with disabilities cannot learn" or "cannot contribute to society" towards more inclusive attitudes where children and people with disabilities are seen as valued members of society who can improve the community's well-being. Seeing this from the perspective of the capability approach supports the assumption that well-being in this context cannot be understood only in terms of the individual, since we know that family and community play essential roles when it comes to developing equity and equality in education. Furthermore, the capabilities and functionings which are developed in this way continuously contribute to the individual's as well as the community's (and family's) well-being. The implementation of inclusive education in Ethiopia seems therefore to visualise much more clearly the benefits for individuals and for the community as such.

In Ethiopia, the lack of options to send children with disabilities to school has to be seen in the context of the extremely challenging problem of poverty which most families experience. For people with disabilities, this intersectionality between poverty and disability can have devastating consequences.[2] Hence, the implementation of the UNCRPD could be one way of offering equal possibilities for people with and without disabilities and people living and not living in poverty.

> At the international level, the UN Convention on the Rights of Persons with Disabilities provides a clear framework for disabled people to attain the human rights that previously have been denied to them. The overarching goal in both cases is to ensure that disabled people of all ages have access to at least the same opportunities and life chances as are available to their fellow citizens. Whether or not these opportunities are realised depends in large part on the interest and commitment of civil society, particularly national and local voluntary and professional organisations. (Mittler 2008, 8)

As a conclusion of the discussion, the key question that must be asked is how education and inclusion in Ethiopia need to be broadened beyond "disability" to consider other kinds of disadvantage as well. These include aspects of poverty, ethnicity (minorities) and other challenging conditions. Discussing such issues reveals aspects that are meaningful also on a global level. For example, poverty cannot be ignored as a factor that influences families in handling their day-to-day problems while also having a family member with a disability, as already stated earlier. Inclusive education hence has to be seen on the background of the realities of the people and societies. Ethnical conflicts cannot be neglected either when talking about making a society more inclusive. These are interdependent factors that play important roles. Such discussions enrich debates about disability/diversity and culture on the background of the implementation of the UNCRPD – especially inclusive education. The aspect of culture receives additional attention as the UNCRPD is approached from a critical perspective on the grounds of cultural diversity. I am now referring to a quotation which I already cited earlier in this book:

---

[2] For more detail on intersectionality in the context of disability, see, for example, Grech, S. and Soldatic, K. (Eds.) (2016). *Disability in the global South. The critical handbook* (International Publishing Switzerland, Springer).

In many countries, inclusive education is still thought of as an approach to serving children with disabilities within general education settings. However, internationally, it is increasingly seen more broadly as a reform that supports and welcomes diversity amongst all learners (United Nations Educational, Scientific and Cultural Organization (UNESCO 2001). (Ainscow 2007, 3)

And this may be the key issue in realising inclusive education: to recognise the meaning and importance of diversity amongst all learners in educational environments. This leads to placing disability at the same level as other aspects of individual diversity and backgrounds that influence people on their way to reaching functionings which they have reason to value in the society in which they live.

References

Ainscow, M. (2007). Taking an inclusive turn. *Journal of Research in Special Educational Needs, 7*(1), 3–7.
Biermann, J., & Powell, J. J. W. (2014). Institutional dimensions of inclusive schooling: Comparing the challenge of the UN Convention on the Rights of Persons with Disabilities in Germany, Iceland and Sweden. *Zeitschrift für Erziehungswissenschaft, 2014, 17*(4), 679–700. 679.
Bürli, A. (2015). Zur Umsetzung der UN-Behindertenrechtskonvention. In A. Leonhardt et al. (Eds.), *Die UN- Behindertenrechtskonvention und ihre Umsetzung. Beiträge zur Interkulturellen und International vergleichenden Heil- und Sonderpädagogik* (pp. 55–66). Bad Heilbrunn: Klinkhardt.
de Sousa Santos, B. (2002). Toward a multi-cultural conception of human rights. In B. Hernández-Truyol (Ed.), *Moral imperialism. A critical anthology* (pp. 39–60). New York: University Press.
de Sousa Santos, B. (2008). Human rights as an emancipatory script? Cultural and political conditions. In B. de Sousa Santos (Ed.), *Another knowledge is possible: Beyond northern epistemologies* (pp. 3–40). London: Verso.
Degener, T. (2009). Die UN-Behindertenrechtskonvention als Inklusionsmotor. *Recht der Jugend und des Bildungswesens, 57*, 200–219.
Federal Democratic Republic of Ethiopia (FDRE) (2012). Implementation of the UN convention on the rights of persons with disabilities (CRPD). (Addis Ababa, FDRE) Retrieved November 23, 2016, from http://www.molsa.gov.et/English/SWD/Documents/ETHIOPIA%20 Implementation%20of%20the%20UN%20Convention%20on%20the%20Rights%20of%20 Persons%20with%20Desabilities%20Initial%20Report.pdf
Grech, S. (2011). Recolonising debates or perpetuated coloniality? Decentring the spaces of disability, development and community in the global South. *International Journal of Inclusive Education, 15*(1), 87–100.
Ingstad, B. (2001). Disability in the developing world. In G. L. Albrecht, K. D. Seelman, & M. Bury (Eds.), *Handbook of disability studies* (pp. 219–251). Thousand Oaks: Sage.
Kaplan, I., Lewis, I., & Mumba, P. (2007). Picturing global educational inclusion? Looking and thinking across students' photographs from the UK, Zambia and Indonesia. *Journal of Special Education, 7*(1), 23–35.
McEwan, C., & Butler, R. (2007). Disability and development: Different models, different places. *Geography Compass, 1*(3), 448–466.
Meekosha, H. (2011). Decolonising disability: Thinking and acting globally. *Disability & Society, 26*(6), 667–682.

Mittler, P. (2008). Planning for the 2040s: everybody's business. *British Journal of Special Education, 35*(1), 4–10.

Nussbaum, M. C. (2011). *Creating capabilities. The human development approach.* Cambridge, MA/London: Harvard University Press.

Richardson, J. G., & Powell, J. J. W. (2011). *Comparing special education: Origins to contemporary paradoxes.* Stanford: Stanford University Press.

Scott, W. R. (2008). *Institutions and organizations.* Thousand Oaks: Sage.

Sen, A. (2009). *The idea of justice.* Cambridge: The Belknap Press of Harvard University Press.

UN. (2006). *Convention on the rights of persons with disabilities and optional protocol.* New York: United Nations.

UNDP. (2015a). *The millennium development goals report 2015.* Retrieved November 23, 2016, from: http://www.undp.org/content/undp/en/home/librarypage/mdg/the-millennium-development-goals-report-2015.html

UNDP. (2015b). *Sustainable development goals. Goal 4: Quality education.* Retrieved November 23, 2016, from: http://www.undp.org/content/undp/en/home/sustainable-development-goals/goal-4-quality-education.html

UNESCO. (2001). International Bureau of Education. The Development of Education. National Report of Ethiopia by Ethiopian National Agency for UNESCO (Final Version) March 2001. Retrieved on June, 2017, from http://www.ibe.unesco.org/International/ICE/natrap/Ethiopia.pdf

Zehle, J. (2015). Inklusion im äthiopischen Schul- und Bildungskontext. In A. Leonhardt et al. (Eds.), *Die UN- Behindertenrechtskonvention und ihre Umsetzung. Beiträge zur Interkulturellen und International vergleichenden Heil- und Sonderpädagogik* (pp. 206–214). Bad Heilbrunn: Klinkhardt.

Chapter 12
Appendix: All About Working with the Data

Abstract The appendix provides the reader with detailed information about the sample, on how data have been collected and which challenges could be identified. The sample is described in terms of selection of the sample, selection of the research sites, the participants and their socio-economic backgrounds.

Methods Used in the Research Process

The situations of the children participating in the research were looked at from different perspectives by using interviews, observations and other methods. Hence, the following participants were addressed:

– Children with disabilities as subjects who speak about their own experiences
– Parents, legal guardians or other educators (professional as well as non-professional)
– Experts of the education system and disability in general (government, NGOs, colleges, university, etc.)

The empirical design of the study included:

– Guided interviews (with parents, children (using cue cards/pictures and other supportive material), teachers and further[1] experts)
– Narrative interviews (with parents and teachers)
– Focus group discussions (with parents and children)
– Observations of classrooms during class and schoolyards in the breaktime
– Appraisals of the environment of the school
– Writing a research diary

Narrative and guided interviews were analysed in depth in the literature. Their potentials as well as the problems that arise while applying these methods have been pointed out by several authors (Clandinin 2007; Denzin and Lincoln 2005; Friebertshäuser and Prengel 1997; Glinka 2009). Guided interviews are especially useful for those phases of research where content fields have already been

---

[1] The "further" in "further experts" indicates that children and parents are also perceived as experts.

© The Author(s) 2017
M. Schiemer, *Education for Children with Disabilities in Addis Ababa,*
Ethiopia, Inclusive Learning and Educational Equity 4,
DOI 10.1007/978-3-319-60768-9_12

prestructured. Narrative interviews on the other hand enable the researcher to make use of the biographical perspective. Therefore, it makes sense to use this method at the beginning of the empirical research as it can help to capture unexpected features. The observations and appraisals as well as the research diary influenced the research process, as they were incorporated in the researcher's reflections on the ongoing research process as well as in the analysis.

Collection of Data

I had the possibility to visit the field of the investigation four times. The first visit served for preparatory purposes, during the second visit (first phase of field research) I started interviews and observations in the field, and the third and fourth visit (second and third phase of field research) served for more intense consultation of the same and additional sources and participants, after having identified topics that emerged through interview analyses from the first phase of the field research.

In preparation for the first phase of field research (first guided interviews), questions had been developed on the basis of the environmental factors of the ICF-CY to initiate the narration. Certain topics were brought up to support the interviewees in general and particularly those who were not used to speaking freely about their experiences. In addition, questions that arose during the flow of speech were added accordingly to deepen the understanding of backgrounds and coherences.

In the second phase of field research, interview guidelines were developed in the form of a "pool of questions". This pool included questions that were identified to be of possible interest based on the data from the first phase. Moreover, before each interview, the previous interviews that had been conducted in the first phase with the same person were examined in regard to any existing links and emerging topics and to clarify unclear statements. Additionally, narrative methods were used where possible.

Furthermore, focus group discussions were considered as very fruitful. As mentioned earlier, questionnaires that had been used for the larger project led to adding this new method to the research process. During the first phase of the field research, illiterate parents discussed questions which the research team had to read out to them from the questionnaires. In this way, focus group discussions emerged without my intention. Realising that these discussions contained interesting aspects for the research at hand, an additional informed consent was produced, and discussions were taped with the parents' permissions. These questionnaires had initially been developed only for the comparative larger project and were not intended to be used for the book at hand. They had been used by me during the field research for collecting quantitative data in order to compare the three countries in another paper. However, the unforeseen discussions provided me with valuable data. Consequently, the focus group discussions were implemented as a fixed part of the qualitative research instruments in the second phase of the field research, not only for parents but also for children.

As to the interviews with children, different materials were used. Next to cue cards, cards with different topics, cameras for the children to take pictures of their favourite locations, people, etc. in the school, games (throwing a dice with pictures/topics, a miniature of a classroom with children, teachers, desks, etc.) and hand puppets were used in case children found it difficult to feel free or interact with the research team. The materials were also adapted for their use for blind children. Experience showed that the hand puppet was one of the best items for getting access to the children. Additionally, the focus group discussions with children worked very well.

Regarding the observations, I and my Ethiopian assistant Yeshitla visited the classrooms during the lessons. Yeshitla and me developed guidelines for observation in advance, and both of us made our observations independently. The same procedure was followed in the appraisal of the school compounds where aspects like accessibility, traffic in front of the school, toilets, condition of the schoolyard, classrooms, etc. were examined. In this way, new impressions and information could be obtained that otherwise might not have been gathered with such quality. Having this information from an etic (me) as well as from an emic (Yeshitla) perspective added to the possibility to be critical towards possible cultural bias.

Having the option to visit the field on several occasions opened lots of new possibilities. One positive aspect was certainly that the participants' level of confidence increased and relationships could be established. This was particularly significant for the interviews with children.

Besides, regarding the theoretical level of grounded theory and by referring to the early publications of Glaser and Strauss, Charmaz highlights the "[s]imultaneous involvement in data collection and analysis" as one of the essential elements when using grounded theory in practice (2006, 5). Therefore, analysis of data was an ongoing process throughout the data collection. Data was constantly being compared, while next steps of interviewing were decided on. The construction of analytic codes and categories by working with the data took place throughout the field research. Charmaz – in reference to Glaser and Strauss – speaks of this process as one of the pillars when "doing" grounded theory, as it is important that these codes and categories are drawn from the data directly as opposed to deriving them from earlier formulated hypotheses by following a deductive way of inquiry (Charmaz 2006). These aspects are more related to the chapter of analysing the data; nevertheless they are also relevant at this point because they illustrate how interconnected the steps of data collection and data analysis were throughout the research process. This is important because "[...] data form the foundation of our theory and our analysis of these data generates the concepts we construct. Grounded theorists collect data to develop theoretical analyses from the beginning of a project" (Charmaz 2006, 2).

The Sample

The proposal for the larger project had clear indications regarding the sample to start with into the field. The target group of the investigation included children who had different structural and functional disabilities in the areas of hearing, sight, intellectual abilities and motor activities (OECD 2005; Terzi 2008; WHO 2001, 2007). The minimum size of the sample was $n = 8$ (cases). This number resulted from the goal of including two children of each "group of disabilities" (hearing, visual, intellectual and physical disability), one male and one female child. In order to reach the number of eight cases by the end of the project, the initial sample was aspired to contain 16 cases. Specific information about the collected data can be found in the subchapter on "participants".

The age range of the sample was to reach from 8 to 12. This age range was chosen based on the fact that school attendance is free and compulsory in Ethiopia for children aged 7–14 (Ethiopian Ministry of Education 2011a). Furthermore, the individual development of the child had to be considered. Hence, the phase of childhood ought to be at the centre of the research rather than adolescence. Additionally, the children of the sample should be assignable according to the cross-national OECD category A, "disabilities" that include children with somatic impairments (OECD 2005). Such a research outline sounds inappropriate indeed after having read the introductory parts of this study. Classifications, age ranges, different "types" of disabilities do not comply with the overall goal of stepping aside from such categorisations and seeing disability from an environmental and social perspective. Therefore, apart from the project proposal, realities had to be faced during the investigation and categorisations had to be overlooked for the independent research project at a certain point of the research process. The predefined sample served pragmatic purposes; however, in-depth classifications were criticised and avoided where possible after having entered the field. This was done by analysing the data focusing on environmental, societal and cultural factors rather than on biomedical aspects related to disability. Additionally, the age range indicated above could not be complied with, as children with disabilities in Addis Ababa often do not start school at 7 years of age. In many cases, they only have the possibility to enter school at a later age. This happens because schools refuse to take them or because parents do not know about the possibility or do not want to send their child to school. Additionally, the age is in general not regarded as important, and births are not always reported officially. Hence, birth certificates often simply did not exist, and the year of birth was not known. This led to indications of the age of the children differing up to 5 years when asking teachers, parents and children. Therefore, the aspect of age was given less relevance in the research.

Theoretical Sampling

> Theoretical sampling is the process of data collection for generating theory whereby the analyst jointly collects, codes, and analyzes his data and decides what data to collect next and where to find them, in order to develop his theory as it emerges. This process of data collection is controlled by the emerging[2] theory, whether substantive or formal. [...] The

---

[2] In their first publications, Glaser and Strauss spoke of emergence, as they stressed that categories emerged directly from the data. However, they state: "Of course, the researcher does not approach reality as a tabula rasa. He must have a perspective that will help him see relevant data and abstract

initial decisions [for a theoretical collection of data] are not based on a preconceived theoretical framework. (Glaser and Strauss 1967/2008, 45)

The process of deciding what data to collect next took place simultaneously with
the data collection and analyses of the interviews from the predefined sample. In other
words, theoretical sampling was used by adding cases and experts if more information
was expected to be gained regarding certain topics that had come up during earlier
interviews. Glaser and Strauss formulate the basic question regarding decisions in
theoretical sampling as follows: "[W]hat groups or subgroups does one turn to next in
data collection? And for what theoretical purpose? In short, how does the sociologist
select multiple comparison groups?" (Glaser and Strauss 1967/2008, 47). Therefore,
the decisions concerning the gathering of further information depended on theoretical
considerations. Throughout this process, the way towards a theory was paved, as decisions to include certain topics and not to include others defined the phenomenon that
was going to be investigated in depth. However, the researcher has to stay alert also in
this situation in order to be able to keep his/her theoretical sensitivity and not become
doctrinaire (Glaser and Strauss 1967/2008, 46).

> The sociologist should also be sufficiently *theoretically sensitive* so that he can conceptual-
> ize and formulate a theory as it emerges from the data. [...] Theoretical sensitivity of a
> sociologist has two other characteristics [next to a continual development]. First, it involves
> his personal and temperamental bent. Second, it involves the sociologist's ability to have
> theoretical insight into his area of research, combined with an ability to make something of
> his insights. (Glaser and Strauss 1967/2008)

Hence, it is essential to reflect on the personal affinities as a researcher as well as
having the talent to identify meaningful aspects that come up during the research.
Lamnek (2005) describes theoretical sampling as a constantly developing process
where comparison groups that have been chosen based on certain theoretical considerations from the first phase of research are analysed. This analysis takes place
by focusing on selected considerations that have been identified as crucial for the
further development of the emerging theory. It is thus not the goal to capture *all*
features of all data of the comparison groups. The main criteria for the theoretical
decisions follow theoretical goals and are of theoretical relevance (Lamnek 2005,
106). This comparative analysis enriches the diversity and intensity of the whole
analysis (Lamnek 2005, 107).

To give a short insight into the theoretical sampling of the book at hand, some
examples are given here. During the research process, it was decided to include
interviews with religious representatives, as it became clear that religion plays an
important role regarding perceptions of disability. Furthermore, different NGOs and
other organisations in Addis Ababa were consulted as they were mentioned in the
interviews as points of reference. Additionally, at one point, it became apparent that
teacher education was an important issue amongst some of the participants. Hence,
a teacher training college was visited for interviews as well as the university, where

---

significant categories from his scrutiny of the data" (Glaser and Strauss 1967/2008, 3). In the book
at hand, when talking about emerging categories, subcategories, etc., it has to be understood
always from a constructivist point of view. Hence, emerging categories were always also constructed by the researcher herself.

teachers studying special needs education were interviewed. Moreover, the Ministry of Education was consulted several times in order to conduct interviews with the Minister, special needs experts and consultants in order to get more information about political developments regarding special needs education. More information about the participants of the research project will be given in detail below.

Site Selection

The goal was to include schools from as many different areas of the city as possible in order to obtain a broader picture of the situation of the schools also regarding geographical circumstances within Addis Ababa. The 16 cases that were aimed at provided us with the possibility of choosing eight schools, as in each school one girl and one boy was to be interviewed ($8 \times 2 = 16$). Additionally, this provided the possibility to include more schools. Theoretically, the sample would be drawn from two schools of each "disability group" (two schools teaching children with hearing, visual, physical and intellectual disabilities respectively). In each school, one boy and one girl would be included in the sample.

The selection of locations for conducting interviews included several challenges. Naturally, it was a problem to find children with disabilities in the schools visited that matched the ideas regarding the kind of disability, age and gender. However, in some cases, people in the streets of the districts chosen could tell the research team where to find schools that accepted children with disabilities. Nevertheless, the main problem was to find children who matched the defined age group of 8–12.

Seven schools were eventually included in the field research. Two of these accepted children with physical or multiple disabilities (e.g. a combination of speech problems and the need to use a crutch), two had special units for children with intellectual disabilities, one was a special school for the deaf, one had a special unit for children with hearing disabilities, and one was an integrative school specialised in children with visual problems. All of the schools were free of charge (no tuition fees had to be paid). Five schools were governmental schools. This indicates that they should be accessible for all children. Usually, those schools are frequented by children from poor families. Children from wealthier families attend public or private schools which collect tuition fees and in most cases offer a better quality of education. The last two schools were supported by different churches. It was by intention that schools accessible to the majority of the (poor) population were chosen. The following graph illustrates the characteristics of the schools and the cases interviewed. The numbers reflect the situation of the school year 2010/2011 (Table 12.1).

It was interesting to observe that in all schools there were about 10% more female students than male students. The same was true regarding the numbers of teachers. Nevertheless, the higher the grades, the fewer female students could be found.

Table 12.1 Description of sample schools

School	School type and location	No. of students	No. of teachers	Disability related information	N° of SwD[a]	Interviewed SwD
A	Governmental Grades 1–8 *Poor area, not central, in the hills*	2365	74	Accepted children with physical and visual disabilities, integrative setting	13	3 cases (2f/1 m) 4 SwD in a FGD[b]
B	Governmental Grades 1–8 *Poor area in the outskirts*	1810	85	Accepted children with physical disabilities, integrative setting	8	2 cases (2f) 4 SwD in a FGD
C	Governmental Grades 1–8 *Relatively central area, on a hill*	1752	81	Accepted children with physical and intellectual disabilities, special units for children with intellectual disabilities: special setting	32 integrated 38 special unit	3 cases (1f/2 m) 4 students in a FGD (1 SwD)
D	Governmental Grades 1–8 *Relatively poor area, not central, on a hill*	1899	85	Accepted children with physical and intellectual disabilities, special units for children with intellectual disabilities: special setting	24	2 cases (1f/1 m) 4 SwD in a FGD
E	Supported by the church Grades 1–8 *Central area*	541	23	Accepted children with visual and physical disabilities, integrative setting	?	4 cases (1f/2 m)

(continued)

Table 12.1 (continued)

School	School type and location	No. of students	No. of teachers	Disability related information	N° of SwD[a]	Interviewed SwD
F	Supported by the church Grades 1–6 *Not very central area*	98	14	Special school for children with visual disabilities: special setting	98	4 cases (2f/2 m) 4 SwD in a FGD
G	Governmental Grades 1–8 *Central area*	1614	91	Accepted children with hearing disabilities, special units for children with hearing disabilities; special setting	92	2 cases (1f/1 m)
Total						20 cases

[a]Students with disabilities
[b]Focus group discussion

Participants

Having followed theoretical sampling throughout the different phases of the field research, the sample that resulted for the research project in the first phase of the field research consisted of[3]:

– Twenty cases (child–parent–teacher)
– Ten experts from within the schools (principals, special needs experts)
– Two experts from outside schools (general special needs education expert, teaching staff from the Department of Special Needs Education of Addis Ababa University)
– Two focus group discussions (parents), resulting in 74 interviews

Additionally the following data was collected in order to obtain more information also on a level other than face-to-face discussions:

– Twenty class observations
– Seven appraisals of school compounds
– Writing of a research diary

---

[3] In the preparatory phase, first interviews had already been conducted in the Ministry of Education and the associations for the blind, for the deaf and for the "intellectually disabled" about the general situation of persons with disabilities. This took place in the framework of getting information for a new project (RESPOND-HER; for more information see http://respond-her.univie.ac.at/). However, it also provided the researcher with some information on the general situation of persons with disabilities in Ethiopia.

Before the second phase of the field research started, 8 of the 20 cases were chosen for deeper analysis after having analysed the first set of interviews. This decision was made with the aim of achieving the greatest diversity of participants – and not beyond – within the sample. Too many data are not considered to make sense, as could be deduced from the abundance of data from the first phase. However, during the first analysis of the cases and the expert interviews of the first phase, open questions as well as first categories and emerging topics were identified.

In the second phase of the field research, the mentioned eight cases were reinterviewed (in cases where children had left the school, or opted out etc. another case out of the 20 was chosen to replace the student). This research phase resulted in:

- Eight cases (child–parent–teacher)
- Six experts from within the schools (principals, special needs experts)
- Seven focus group discussions with parents
- Five focus group discussions with children
- Five experts from outside schools (Minister of Education, special needs expert from the Ministry of Education, Finnish advisor to the Minister of Education, expert from the Ethiopian Centre for Disability and Development, administrative head of the Ethiopian Orthodox Tewahedo church), resulting in 47 interviews

The third phase of the field research followed similar guidelines. Analyses of interviews had been conducted as far as possible (the dates for the field research were predefined and were hence not very flexible). According to the results, the last opportunity to conduct interviews resulted in interviews with:

- ENDAN (Ethiopian National Disability Action Network)
- LIGHT FOR THE WORLD Austria (Expert for Ethiopia)
- Teacher Training College Ethiopia (head of the Department of Special Needs Education)
- Dean of the College of Education at Addis Ababa University
- RSDA (Rehabilitation Service for the Deaf Association)
- Expert for teacher education
- Focus group discussion with students of the Department of Special Needs Education, Addis Ababa University
- [Observation of an "inclusive" class (integration of children with hearing disabilities)], resulting in seven interviews

The amount of data collected was still considered extensive. Hence, focused coding was used to be able to manage bigger amounts of data, as will be explained later.

The following table gives an overview of data of the 20 children and parents who were interviewed. They are the original data as collected in autumn 2010.

Table 12.2 Overview of 20 cases

CASE	Semret	Semenesh	Bezanesh	Tsyeon	Negest	Yilma	Zenebu
Child	Female	Female	Female	Female	Female	Male	Female
Age[a]	16	13	14	13	10	14	10
Disability	PI	PI + VI			II	II	II
First language	Amharic	Amharic	Amharic	Amharic	Amharic	Amharic	Amharic
Grade[b]	7	5	2	?	C[c]	C	SN class
Parent/Caregiver	Meseret, Grandmother Widowed	Tensay Grandmother Widowed	Kefeyalew Father Married	Berehe Mother Widowed	Abraham Father Married	Fatuma Mother Widowed	Mamite Mother Married
Age[d]	65	60	50	40	55	52	40
Education	Basic	None	10th grade	Basic	Illiterate	Illiterate	8th grade
Mother tongue	Amharic	Amharic	Amharic	Amharic	Gurage	Oromo	Amharic
Religion	Orthodox Christian	Orthodox Christian	Orthodox Christian	Orthodox Christian	Islam	Orthodox Christian	Orthodox Christian
Occupation	Housewife	Daily labourer	Constructor	Daily labourer	None	Housewife	Housewife
Household income[e] (monthly)	500–1000 ETB[f]	Below 300 ETB	500–1000 ETB	Below 300 ETB	Below 300 ETB	Below 300 ETB	300–500 ETB
No. of births	6	2	3	2	5	4	4
No. of members in household	7	2	5	4	7	7	6

CASE	Nadi	Mubarek	Melat	Fantahun	Dawit	Herut	Serawit
Child							
Age	Male	Male	Female	Male	Male	Female	Male
	9	8	9	10	10	12	10
Disability	II	VI	VI	VI	PI	HI	HI
First language	Amharic	Amharic	Amharic	Amharic	Amharic	Amharic + SL^g	Amharic
Grade	SN class	1	2	3	4	3	3
Parent/Caregiver	Rahel Mother Widowed	Fatima Mother Married	Almaz Mother Married	Mulualem Caregiver Single	Mulukene Mother –	Rahima Mother Single	Wongel Mother Single
Age	35	53	30	30	30	25	25
Education	10th grade	6th grade	Diploma	Bachelor (BA)	None	7th grade	None
Mother tongue	Amharic	Amharic	Amharic	Amharic	Amharic	Amharic	Gurage
Religion	Islam	Orthodox Christian	Orthodox Christian	Orthodox Christian	Orthodox Christian	Orthodox Christian	Islam
Occupation	House-wife	None	None	Volunteer	Daily labourer	Housewife	Small scale trading
Household income	Below 300 ETB	300–500 ETB	300–500 ETB	1000–5000 ETB	Below 300 ETB	Below 300 ETB	300–500 ETB
No. of births	1	4	1	0	1	1	3
No. of members in household	5	6	3	7	2	2	5

(continued)

Table 12.2 (continued)

CASE	Kefeyalew	Michael	Embaye	Yirgashew	Lilly	Berhanu
Child	Male	Female	Male	Male	Female	Male
Age	10	9	12	13	10	11
Disability	HI	HI		II	HI	HI
First language	Amharic	Amharic	Amharic	Amharic	Amharic	Amharic
Grade	3	3	4	2	2	4
Parent/Caregiver	Beyene	Eskedar	Semira	Bamlak	–	Mersha
	Brother	Caregiver	Mother	Mother		Father
	Single	Divorced	Married	Divorced	–	Married
Age	18	48	33	40	–	36
Education	10th grade	12th grade	None	3rd grade	–	9th grade
Mother tongue	Amharic	Oromo	Amharic	Tigrinya	–	Amharic
Religion	Orthodox Christian	Orthodox Christian	Orthodox Christian	Orthodox Christian	–	Orthodox Christian
Occupation	Student	Head of home for orphans	Daily labourer	Janitor	–	Weaver
Household income	300–500 ETB	–	500–1000 ETB	Around 300 ETB	–	Up to 400 ETB
No. of births	4	–	2	5	–	2
No. of members in household	7	841	4	6	–	4

[a] In most cases an estimation
[b] In the first phase of the field research (2010)
[c] In the special unit of school C children start in class C and change to B and A. After being successful in class A they can start in the regular grade 1
[d] Sometimes parents also had to guess their own age
[e] This was sometimes difficult for parents to estimate
[f] At the time of the research approximately 23 ETB (Ethiopian Birr) equaled 1€. This is an approximation, as between 2009 and 2012 the development of the ETB went from 1€ being 17 ETB to 25 ETB
[g] Sign language

Socio-economic Background

More than 80% of the families (parents[4] and children) involved in the research originated from a poor or very poor background. In other words, they had a daily income
below 2€. Many of the parents were daily labourers with no fixed income. As indicated above, this was the case because of the intention to only include governmental
schools, which were free from tuition fees and therefore affordable for poor families. As far as ethnical backgrounds are concerned, most of the participants were
Amhara of descent. However, a small percentage also originated from Oromo,
Guraghe, Tigrinya or other ethnic groups. Despite the different descents, all of the
children were raised speaking the Amharic language. The number of family members was, unexpectedly, usually not high and between (in most cases) two and four
and (in few cases) up to seven persons. Sometimes the reason for avoiding having
more children was the disability of the child itself or the fact that the mother and
child/children lived in the city while the father stayed somewhere else to work.
Additionally, almost half of the children did not live with both parents or with neither parent. Some parents were widowed or children had been given to relatives
(aunts, grandmothers, etc.) and child care institutions.

References

Charmaz, K. (2006). *Constructing grounded theory: A practical guide through qualitative analy-
sis*. London/Thousand Oaks/New Delhi: Sage.
Clandinin, D. J. (Ed.). (2007). *Handbook of narrative inquiry. Mapping a methodology*. Thousand
Oaks: Sage.
Denzin, N. K., & Lincoln, Y. S. (Eds.). (2005). *The sage handbook of qualitative research*.
Thousand Oaks/London/New Delhi: Sage.
Ethiopian Ministry of Education. (2011). *Education sector development program IV (ESDP IV).
2010/2011–2014/2015*. Addis Ababa: Ethiopian Ministry of Education.
Friebertshäuser, B., & Prengel, A. (1997). *Handbuch qualitative Forschungsmethoden in der
Erziehungswissenschaft*. Weinheim: Juventa.
Glaser, B. G., & Strauss, A. L. (1967/2008). *The discovery of grounded theory: Strategies for
qualitative research*. New Brunswick: Aldine Transaction.
Glinka, H.-J. (2009). *Das narrative interview*. Weinheim/München: Juventa Verlag.
Lamnek, S. (2005). *Qualitative Sozialforschung. Lehrbuch*. Weinheim: Beltz.

---

[4] Including caregivers.

OECD. (2005). *Center for educational research and innovation: Students with disabilities, learning difficulties and disadvantages. Statistics and indicators.* Paris: OECD.

Terzi, L. (2008). Beyond the dilemma of difference. The capability approach in disability and special educational needs. In L. Florian & M. J. McLaughlin (Eds.), *Disability classification in education. Issues and perspectives* (pp. 244–262). Thousand Oaks/London/New Delhi/Singapore: Corwin Press.

WHO. (2001). *International classification of functioning, disability and health.* Geneva: World Health Organization.

WHO. (2007). *International classification of functioning, disability and health. Children & youth version.* Geneva: World Health Organization.

Printed by Printforce, the Netherlands